PRAISE FOR

Another Eve

Shame and Desire on the Oregon Coast

"In this gorgeous eco-memoir about purity culture, motherhood, and queer awakening, Minor maps out how shame settles into the body, and how the natural world can loosen its grip. Written with salt water and fire, *Another Eve* offers us a wilder, truer gospel."

—GREG WRENN, author of *Mothership: A Memoir of Wonder and Crisis*

"The literary traditions of the American West have long been built on acts of mapping meant to exert dominion over the land and the people who live there. But what happens when topography becomes about mutual freedom rather than control? Lyrical and humble, Elissa Minor's *Another Eve* presents an against-all-odds love story—both a queer romance and the redemptive love the author finds for herself—where the high deserts and wet coasts of the West are sites of ongoing transformation and hope. Told with the confidence of a writer who doesn't feel the need to move linearly through life or on the page, Minor's memoir is a sweeping examination of family secrets, religious fear, carnal desire, and one woman's searing search for the self-knowing grace and forgiveness we all deserve."

—KEETJE KUIPERS, editor of *Poetry Northwest*

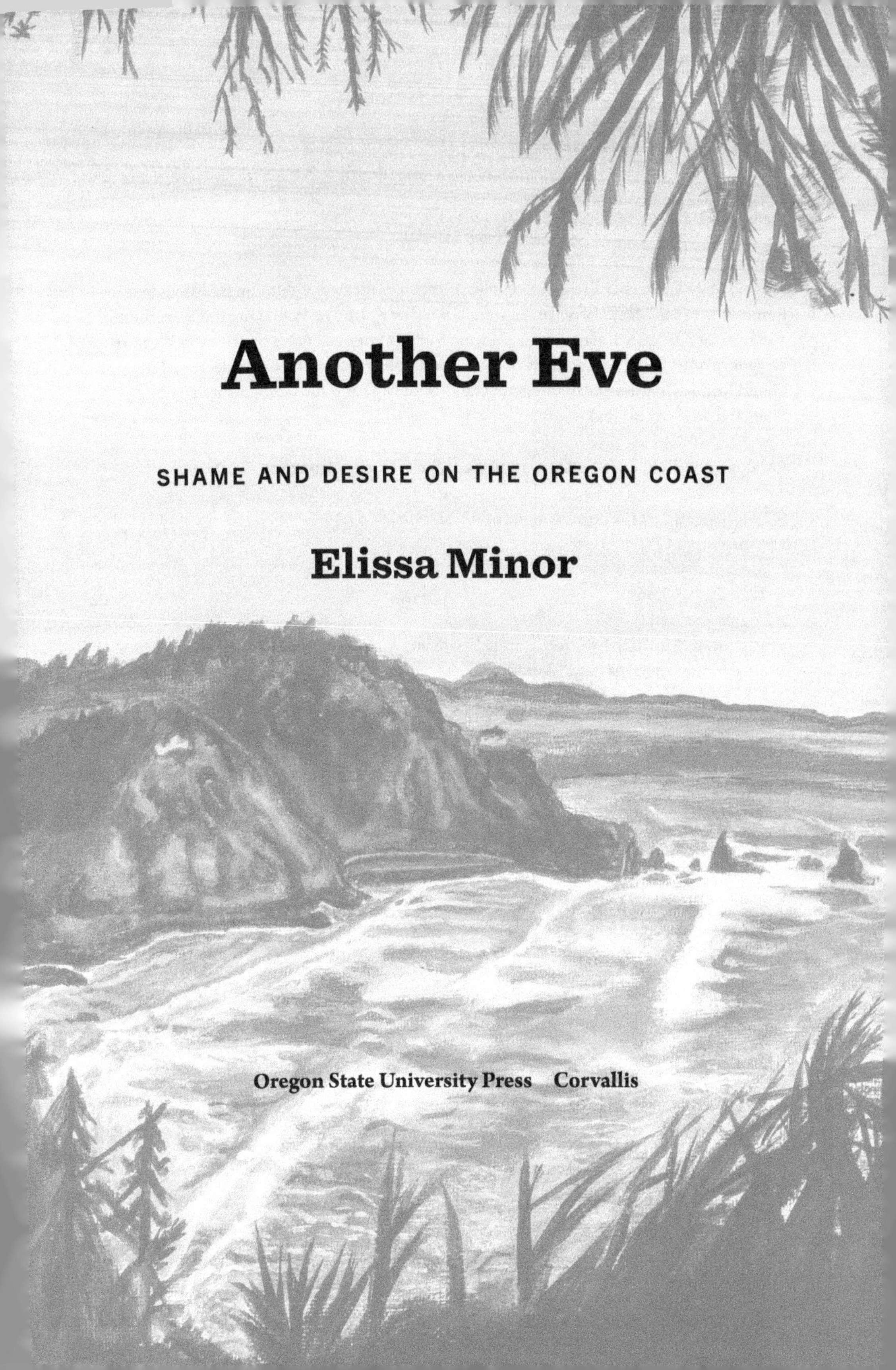

Another Eve

SHAME AND DESIRE ON THE OREGON COAST

Elissa Minor

Oregon State University Press Corvallis

Oregon State University Press in Corvallis, Oregon, is located within the traditional homelands of the Marys River or Ampinefu Band of Kalapuya. Following the Willamette Valley Treaty of 1855, Kalapuya people were forcibly removed to reservations in Western Oregon. Today, living descendants of these people are a part of the Confederated Tribes of Grand Ronde Community of Oregon (grandronde.org) and the Confederated Tribes of Siletz Indians (ctsi.nsn.us).

Cataloging-in-Publication Data is available at the Library of Congress.

∞ This paper meets the requirements of ANSI/NISO Z39.48-1992 (Permanence of Paper).

First published in 2026 by Oregon State University Press
Printed in the United States of America

Oregon State University
OSU Press

Oregon State University Press
121 The Valley Library
Corvallis OR 97331-4501
541-737-3166 • fax 541-737-3170
www.osupress.oregonstate.edu

For Katie, of course.

Remember the first night of crabbing season?
Do you see them on the horizon? The masthead lights.

"When we call a place by its name it is transformed from wilderness to homeland." —TERRY TEMPEST WILLIAMS

"If there is poetry in my book about the sea, it is not because I deliberately put it there, but because no one could write truthfully about the sea and leave out the poetry." —RACHEL CARSON

"There is a Quichua riddle: *El que me nombra, me rompe.* Whatever names me, breaks me. The solution, your course, is 'silence.' But the truth is, anyone who knows your name can break you in two."

—CARMEN MARIA MACHADO

CONTENTS

PROLOGUE

Just after my twentieth birthday, my mom took me into her cedar-lined closet and pulled a worn, soft-sided suitcase from one of the shelves.

"No one told me what to expect when I went through the temple," she said. "You should know this stuff is pretty weird." I was a week away from my first temple ceremony, the last and most vital step in my wedding prep. I don't remember what I replied, if anything. I was busy worrying about eternal consequences. The church had expressly forbidden its members from talking about what happens inside the white marble walls. The penalties for such a misstep were costly.

But it didn't seem to faze my mom. She unzipped the suitcase and pulled out a green embroidered apron, a white pleated shawl and veil, and white slippers. I'd given my whole life to this religion, but this was the first I'd learned about ceremonial clothing. I traced my fingers over the apron. My mom told me that my grandmother had stitched it by hand, and that she'd made one for me as well. My fingers were mesmerized by the feel of the stitches, my eyes by the emerald green satin.

I smiled, because I didn't want my mom to worry. Inside, though, it felt as if someone had tightened a fist around the welt that had been growing in my stomach for months.

After returning the clothing to her suitcase, my mom asked me, "Do you have any questions about what it's going to be like?"

I sat and thought. I knew what I needed to ask her, but I was embarrassed to say it out loud. I sat on my heels and shifted my weight back and forth.

"Do I have to get naked?" I whispered.

Mom got cagey. Visibly uncomfortable. "No, no," she said quickly, then added, "I mean not *really*. Sort of? You'll be covered *almost* the whole time."

☾

During a Wednesday night "combined activity" with the Young Men eight years earlier, I watched in rapt silence as Brother Jenkins poured water from a pitcher into a clear plastic cup. He handed it to his wife, who carried it to a table where eight twelve-year-old boys were seated.

"Darren," he instructed the first boy, "take a sip of that water, swish it around your mouth, and spit it back into the cup." Peals of laughter erupted around the room. Darren shrugged his shoulders and did as he was told. He passed the cup to the boy next to him, who followed the same instructions. Once every boy around that table had taken—and returned—a sip of the water, Sister Jenkins carried the cup back to her husband, who placed it on the table in front of him and asked us to take a long, hard look. The water was cloudy now, almost viscous, and filled with floaters (mainly pieces of the granola bar one of the boys had been eating).

Next to me, my friend Meta made a faux gagging sound.

"Meta, would you please come up here?" Brother Jenkins asked. She flopped in her seat and then reluctantly walked to the front of the room. He handed her an empty cup, identical to the first one, and asked her to pour fresh water into it from the pitcher. She did as she was told and handed it back to him.

He held both cups aloft—clear water in his right hand, disgusting spit slime in his left. "So, which cup do you want to drink from?" he asked the room, then turned to Meta specifically, who pointed at the fresh cup. He handed it to her, and she not only took a sip but drank the whole thing down to multiple snickers from each corner of the room.

Brother Jenkins laughed, too. "That cup of water was delicious because it was pure. Meta, still thirsty? Do you want to drink this one?" He held the spit-water close to her face. She clapped a palm over her mouth and shook her head. It was hard to hear over the laughter now.

"Think of the human body as a pure vessel, like that gorgeous cup of water that Meta just emptied." Brother Jenkins motioned with his hand for us to settle down, then continued, "Now imagine how your body gets sullied every single time you let someone use it for pleasure before you are married, like *this* cup that every boy at that table spat into."

Ah. Yes. I saw it finally, the point to this whole strange fiasco.

Of course it was about sex. It was always about sex.

"Darren, which of these girls would you want to marry? The clear, pure one, or the one filled with gross bits of other men?"

☾

A week after my mom showed me her temple clothes, I knelt at a white altar in the Celestial Room of the Portland temple and promised to be forever obedient to the boy who, three years earlier, had taken me to junior prom. The ritual was meant to "seal" us (Mormon-speak for getting married) as Eternal Companions for time and all eternity. I'd promised in the same temple the day before to never reveal what I saw there, at the (I hoped metaphorical) penalty of death. I'd seen the risk my mom took in her closet for what it was: an act of love, an act of defiance.

Across the altar, Matt held my shaking hand in the sacred Patriarchal Grip: our pinkies interlocked, our index fingers stretched and pressed against the inside of the other's wrist. My grandmother's satin apron circled my waist, its embroidered leaves a symbol that I was Eve, the serpent's best friend.

Under that, though, I wasn't wearing my ivory wedding gown. It had been deemed *not white enough* a week before; the last-minute dress I wore in its stead was so white I thought it might blind me. I spent the ceremony awash with shame. I wasn't pure enough to choose the correct dress, I wasn't worthy enough not to be tempted by all the things that tempted me.

I was just Eve, the one who screwed things up for all of us with her little apple trick.

My legs trembled at the altar's base. My sole comfort was a faint sense of the Douglas fir trees towering over the marble temple where we knelt. They rose taller than the spires, dwarfing even the golden statue of Moroni that stood on a stone ball at the center steeple. Unlike the other Mormon women I knew, I could never conjure an image of God holding me the way I could those old-growth trees.

Even then, deep down, I knew the wild would save me.

☾

My life so far had been awash with ceremonial white. As a newborn, my mom dressed me in a gown of snow-white lace before she placed me in my father's outstretched arms. A dozen men, all in suits and ties, closed in a circle around us, and I was "given a name and a blessing" that foretold my work as a faithful sister in Zion. When I turned eight, I zipped a white cotton jumpsuit up to my chin and met my father where he stood beaming with pride, waist-deep in the baptismal font. He lowered me into the water and when I came up for air, I was a member of the church, completely free of sin. I rode home in the back of my family's Volkswagen Dasher, panicked that I could be seconds away from committing any sin that would ruin my newly unblemished record.

But good girls don't fixate on their next wrong move. So I fixated instead on the bare aspen trees that lined the snowy highway, their bark as white as the wet jumpsuit I'd just peeled off my body. By this moment in my young life, my parents had dragged me through miles of forest throughout the American west, and I already knew the unique way the wild could simultaneously ground me and help me transcend the problem of my body and its desires.

I met Matt when I was thirteen. Together we attended church dances and early morning seminary; we went to concerts and movies and kissed chastely on the couch in his parents' basement. After high school, I left for BYU, one of the only colleges to which my father allowed me to apply, and Matt left on a two-year mission. While he knocked on doors in Queens looking for souls to save, I secretly fell in love with the girl across the hall in my dorm. These shame-filled years boiled down to one supposed truth: everything I desired was bad.

I spent sleepless nights in that dorm room knowing only one thing for certain: the blue spruce trees, Utah junipers, and Bighorn sheep that blanketed the canyons surrounding the university held their soft palms to my back. Not all a woman's desires could be bad, I learned, in a landscape like the eastern edge of the Great Basin. When I knew nothing else, I knew this.

It turned out that wearing white keeps you just a razor's breath away from ruin. At forty-three and with three kids in tow, my desire became too loud to ignore. I set fire to my life because of the lure of the frank bows of the female body—the arch of the back, the soft skin at the nape of the neck.

☾

God, it turned out Eve was stunning. It turned out I wanted her.

THE CASTLE

This story begins the way so many fairy tales end: I walked up the stairs of the Castle and fell into the arms of the woman who would become my wife. It was a humble geometric house with weathered cedar siding in a town of three hundred people. No turrets, no crenelated walls. A fortress of domesticity on a hill two hundred and fifty feet above the pristine northern Oregon coastline. The only royal thing about it was that it stood on the corner of Drawbridge Drive and Knight's Armor Road, which is why the woman who would become my wife had named it such.

Below the deck where we stood, the ocean swirled and broke against tall sea stacks, the tide at that exact minute was neap; a low of just under two feet. But I wasn't thinking about the tides, about the sea, about anything but her Uranian blue eyes. They reflected the chambray button-up she wore tucked into her jeans, which she'd cinched with a thick brown leather belt. We'd been corresponding through text messages and emails, but this was the first time I'd seen her in the flesh. How would I have known that when she pulled me in to smell my hair, her hand on the back of my neck, the sea below us was just finishing its ebb? Or that the beaches I now know intimately would have been moderately exposed, the waning gibbous moon having pulled the sea back from the sandy intertidal as if it were a too-warm bedspread?

I leaned against the railing to look out over the expanse. The woman who would become my wife put her arms around my waist and nuzzled her nose into the back of my neck. I'd expected her to be taller, somehow; I was pleased by the way our bodies fit together. The ends of her soil-brown bob grazed my shoulders, and an electric, unnamable jolt pierced my skin. In front of us, a sparrow chased a red-tailed hawk along the thermals between hemlock trees, and from the road, a retiree called to his off-leash springer spaniel, Honeybadger.

The three rocky sea stacks stood like imposing sentries in the ocean's raucous waves while behind it all, the sky was fissured with white-edged clouds.

"What are those rocks called?" I asked, pointing to the colossal stacks rising from the sea.

I felt her shrug. Her breath was quick and timid on my neck. "I don't know that they have names."

The guttural barking of sea lions resounded off the stacks. The sparrow had stepped up its attack, this time dive bombing directly onto the hawk's back feathers mid-flight. A familiar impulse stirred: name the birds, name the Boomer wrangling Honeybadger, name the rocks. It was a compulsion that drove my loved ones crazy, to learn the names of places and objects, or, in the absence of a known name, to choose one myself.

"What would *you* name them?" I asked her, a nervous tremor in my voice, acutely aware that the woman who would become my wife was caressing both my bare arms with the tips of her fingers. The August breeze came in over the water, and I wished I'd worn a sweater.

I pivoted away from the railing until I was facing her instead of the sea. She pursed her lips and furrowed her brow, an unconscious gesture that I would later come to know meant she was deep in thought.

"Stay long enough and maybe you can name them yourself," she finally said. Our faces were inches apart. Her skin was as pale as mine but a completely different color, her undertones pink instead of my yellow, and it had the suppleness of a woman at least ten years her junior. Where her sunglasses perched on the top of her head and along her temples, though, small white strands of hair curled outward at their ends, the only indication that she had just crested forty.

She had handed me a gift: three glorious sea stacks, standing sentinel in the ocean over which her house loomed, mine to christen. I knew, of course, that just two minutes with a search engine would give me an established name for these rocks. But I wasn't interested in the known world. I was interested in the new, the unmapped, the untamed. In this woman's invitation to stay.

I had a different name the day I met the woman who would be my wife. My divorce wasn't final yet, and until it was, I wore Matt's last name like a heavy piece of costume jewelry I couldn't wait to take off at the end of an event. I'd spent the entire twenty-three years of my marriage feeling like an imposter when I heard or saw his last name attached to my first.

Naming is an imperative human impulse. To name is to make the strange familiar, even intimate. We name our pets. We name our children. We name our homes. We name hurricanes. We name full moons. We name minerals, elements, nail polish colors, and cannabis strains. But I couldn't name the sensation behind my breastbone when the woman who would become my wife met my eyes. I could only put my hand there, the area above the neckline of my goldenrod dress, breathe deep, and pause.

She hadn't kissed me yet. Below us, the water had gone slack—that almost imperceptible cessation at the turn of the tide when for a sacred few minutes, the water is completely unstressed, without any discernible flow pushing seaward or landward. Those who live by the sea know the importance of slack water: it's the best time to set out by boat, to dive into the waves. Even Bram Stoker's Dracula could only pass running water when the tide was slack. It's a moment when change is imminent, when what seemed impossible one moment seems possible the next.

Kathryn Schulz writes, "All of falling in love is a kind of hiatus, a pause in the normal order of things." Could we feel it? The water gone slack? A pause in the fabric of time itself. A shift in possibility. A suspension of psychic energy. The stillness that precedes a great change. *Hold still. Kiss her gently. Sink into each other until the clock starts again.*

The woman who would become my wife took my hand and led me into her living room, her feisty miniature labradoodle, Marco, at our heels. From the couch where we fell into each other, we could still see the rocks looming out the window, watching as if they had eyes.

I named each of her body parts in my mind as I touched them.

Shoulder, collar bone, earlobe, décolletage. Breast.

Katie. The woman who would become my wife was named Katie.

☾

Katie and I came together in a place where so many other things meet.

The north Oregon coast is a region of mass convergence. Take the gaping maw of the Columbia River, where it flows into the Pacific near Astoria, a convergence of forceful currents and shallow turbulent channels with such propensity for tossing ships it is known as the Graveyard of the Pacific. Or the convergence that has residents of the Pacific Northwest bolting furniture to walls: the Oregon coast lies in the Cascadia subduction zone, where the continental plate moves westward and causes the oceanic plate to subduct beneath it. The resulting convergent plate boundary sits like a ticking clock, waiting for just the right slip in the earth to fracture the landscape into something unrecognizable.

Coastal Oregon is not just a convergence of geography; it is also a convergence of history, of past and present. I am only the latest in a ten-thousand-year march of people seeking sustenance and solace along the craggy shoreline where the Pacific meets our little slice of Cascadia. Before there were city folk and rural folk, before there was even a highway linking the urban with the coastal, there were Indigenous peoples. Among them: Yacona, Tillamook, Chinook, Nehalem, Nestucca, Siletz, Yaquina, Alsea. Millenia before I showed up with my obsession to name the sea stacks and other geographic marvels I encountered on adventures with my new love, each had surely already been christened, many times over. The original names that still survive in memory do so because of the fierce efforts of the descendants of Oregon's Indigenous people. As often as makes sense, I have tried to include the Indigenous place names in these pages.

In turns, the explorers Lieutenant John Meares, Captain Meriwether Lewis, and Lieutenant William Clark ushered in a much starker cultural convergence: White European settlers and Indigenous tribes, a convergence that would bifurcate the land, its people, and their cultures into *before* and *after*.

☾

Before and after. Just before I hopped in the car to meet Katie in Oceanside that first time, she texted me a photo of Marco from their early morning beach walk. He held a parkour pose on top of a tall, twisty piece of driftwood just above the wrack line, a tuft of beach grass stuck in the fur behind his ear as if a feather in his cap. The caption simply read "Before." That first date lasted two full days and one even fuller night, and the demarcation was clear: before, after.

When I pulled into my Portland driveway after our time together, vibrating with sex and limerence, she texted me another photo from the beach. Six American golden plovers, in miniature against a vast sky and an even vaster ocean, perched in the intertidal, the clouds reflected in the wet sand under their feet. Their black and white bodies stood in stark contrast to gleaming golden-flecked wings, while the rays of sun hit the surf behind them, a kind of magic future-telling. The caption: "After."

Convergence.

That night, I dreamt that the Pacific rose high enough to encroach on my house in the city. The wetlands that abutted the house filled with seawater, waves crashing at thirty feet high. The waves swallowed the blackberry thicket along the fence and lapped at the pathway next to the cherry tree in the backyard. Sea stars hung in the brambles, kelp from the branches of the pines that lined the fence.

I woke not in fear but with awe: finally, finally, something had found me. Too enamored to stay away, the ocean had followed me home.

My life until then had been marked by decades that left me disassociated from my own self, my own sexuality. It would take time and effort—and Katie's patience—for me to fully inhabit my body. To be comfortable around my lover naked. To use the word *fuck* in relation to sex and feel passionate instead of dirty.

Ultimately, it was the untamed wild that reacquainted me to my body. I used muscle and sinew to run from sneaker waves and scamper down steep dunes, to traverse the side of mountains where the ghostly stumps of gargantuan trees have given rise to other life: ferns, red huckleberry, alder saplings. Here, in the nexus of so many things (past and present, land and sea, fishermen and conservationists, storm and calm) stood a castle that was not a castle, a woman who would become my wife, and a westward view—the ocean for miles—that would help me see my way forward.

THREE ARCH ROCKS

When I told my mom how hard it was proving to name the rocks, she laughed. She'd been birding up and down that part of the Oregon coast for decades and she knew it better than I did.

"They *have* a name," she said over the speakerphone. Katie sat beside me, plugging away at a spreadsheet, half-listening.

"What is it?" I hoped the name was as unique as the natural bulwarks that I couldn't take my eyes from. They were the first things I saw in the morning when I raised the blinds next to Katie's bed—or, in their absence, my first clue that the town was foggy and socked-in—and the last things I saw bathed in moonlight before I closed the same blinds at night.

"The Three Arch Capes, I think?" my mom said, a shrug in her voice.

"Why three arches?"

Katie jumped in on this one. "Each of the rocks has an arch in the middle. You can only see them from certain angles." I'd seen the arch through the middle rock, but I hadn't noticed it on the others. I felt deflated. Sea stacks of this magnitude deserved a much more creative name.

Later that day, we stared at the rocks from a state scenic viewpoint. Katie had a beanie slouched low over her sunglasses. "That doesn't seem right," she said. Marco sat in her arms, sniffing at the view as if tasting a fine wine, his salt-and-pepper fur blowing in the breeze.

I scratched behind Marco's ear. "What do you mean?"

"Well, we are standing on Cape Meares, right here. A cape is a long stretch that juts out over the ocean. But those sea stacks are just rocks. More like islands than capes."

We were startled by giggling behind us; a group of teenage girls in fleece jackets bounced past us on the path, too intent on their laughter and their phones to notice either the sunset or the eagles' overhead orbit. A stout woman in a BYU sweatshirt followed after them at a clipped pace, barking orders. Without thinking, I shrugged Katie's arm away. How many times by the end of this weekend will those girls be warned about their fate should they have sex before marriage? They would be akin to a chewed stick of gum, hardening in the air. A strip of tape so besmirched by human hands it has lost all stickiness.

A cup of water dirtied with spit and food debris.

A thing no one in their right mind would ever, ever want.

☾

That night, I cozied up next to Katie in front of the fireplace, a computer in my lap. I was gathering facts. For one, I learned that a cape is indeed by definition a large headland that extends sometimes miles into the ocean. While a bay is characterized by having land on three sides, a cape is characterized by having three sides of water. Katie had been right. These rocks, by their very nature, were not capes.

And then, through a series of rabbit holes, I found it: our rocks were collectively called Three Arch Rocks, and during his presidency, Teddy Roosevelt established them as Three Arch Rocks National Wildlife Refuge to assure that the roughly quarter million seabirds that nest there each year would continue to thrive. It was the oldest wildlife refuge west of the Mississippi. The massive basalt stacks were the protected home of nesting common murres and hundreds of tufted puffins. The fifteen acres of rock that form the refuge are also the only pupping sites on the north Oregon coast for the federally threatened Steller sea lion.

Katie gestured for me to put my feet in her lap. As I told her what I'd read, she rubbed my feet with the herbal salve she'd developed for her acupuncture practice.

"Apparently the refuge is so protected, it's been closed to all public access for almost a hundred years. Boats have to stay at least five hundred feet away, and planes are restricted to a clearance of . . ." I searched the article, "two thousand feet." Katie returned my socks to my feet. The rocks were to be enjoyed only from the capes that surround them, and from the houses that sit between those capes, where people like me and Katie used scopes to pick out the orange beaks of oystercatchers, fork-tailed storm petrels, guillemots, and sea lions sunbathing in large piles.

Katie leaned forward. "Did Matt ever rub your feet?"

"No. You're the first."

"Do you like it?

"It's amazing. Only thing that stops the pain."

"Did you ever ask him to rub them?" We'd been together a few months, but she still didn't see the extent to which I had been taught my entire life that a good woman only wants one thing: a good man. And I'd had that. I wasn't supposed to want anything else. Not even a foot rub.

When I didn't answer, she nodded at my computer, urging me to keep reading. I read out loud about the formation of the stacks in the refuge. Once part of Maxwell Point, the basalt cape that sits on the north side of Oceanside Beach, erosion and time had left them fending for themselves in the middle of the sea. The arches in all three rocks were formed by the incessant pounding of breakers over hundreds of thousands of years.

I would come to know what that was like, to have the ocean lap at you until you are changed, an imperfectly chiseled version of who you once were.

☾

Three Arch Rocks Wildlife Refuge stared at us through the bedroom window. Moonwashed, the rocks were uncanny, voyeuristic outlines of their daytime selves. Katie lay next to me on her queen-sized bed and asked me what I wanted.

The rocks didn't move, listening.

"I don't know how to answer that," I said. We'd had this conversation many times—Katie hoped I'd state my desires, but I was unable to pinpoint or name them. I wanted those rocks, and that water, and I wanted to know their history, their particulars, their names. But that's not what she was asking.

What did I want?

I'd spent my life trying to want what I was told to, at least on paper. A man. A temple sealing. Prayers as a couple at bedtime, scripture study in the morning. But I had never really wanted them.

She put her lips against my ear. "Just tell me," she whispered, "what you *want*."

I wanted her hands on my skin. I wanted this moment, and this bed, and the roiling ocean entire. But when I opened my mouth to tell her, only silence.

The full moon shed a thick billow of cumulus clouds and cast a glowing halo above Katie's head. The rocks glowed even brighter. I thought of the part of the stacks we couldn't see: the sixty feet of vertical extension below the ocean's surface. Chances were the hidden, submarine portion of the rocks boasted sides thick with bluish-black bay mussels and rock scallops, around which lingcod and sea bass circled.

The secret part. The part of the rocks that held desire, if a rock could want. And on the seafloor surrounding the rocks, the bottom was craggy and undulating. Desire lived there, too, fiercely guarded by underwater spires that stood thirty or more feet high.

A castle under the water with wanting in its keep.

"For now," I pleaded with Katie, "I just need you to tell me what *you* want."

She whispered instructions against my neck, where she'd buried her face.

I was practiced in obedience.

And then.

Katie gave me what I didn't know I wanted, the desire I could not name. I was stacks, spires, and spindrift all in one. The fire in the stove popped and crackled. I knew that when we woke, the fire would have put itself out, but in this moment, it felt impossible that there would ever be anything but flame.

NETARTS BAY

(Tillamook: *Nataats*)

The tide was rising—a flooding tide—and it forced Katie, my mom, and me back through the tunnel to Oceanside Beach. When we emerged on the other side, Mom pointed at the sky just above the shoreline.

Katie and I looked at the brown pelicans, riding the offshore wind in single-file lines above the water. Mom raised her field glasses, but the pelicans moved too quickly to study. They were birds on a mission. Line after line of the giant-beaked birds appeared from the north as if they were being called to something. Katie suggested we jump in the car and drive south to the bay in the hopes of catching them when they landed.

Netarts Bay is only a mile from Oceanside, but the tides differ by over an hour. A forested but sandy spit separates the salt bay from the Pacific. It was there, on Netarts Spit, that the Tillamook people first settled, and it was there that the pelicans were landing in droves. This time they were so close we didn't need the field glasses. At least five hundred of the four-foot-tall birds were gathered on the spit, patiently waiting as if for instruction.

The instruction came from the tide. The water spilled into the bay, and with it a shoal of small silvery fish. One after another the pelicans took wing and hovered above the swirling water; they dove and twisted and disappeared head-first, only to bob back up, long beaks pointed skyward. In one quick motion, they expelled the excess water from their throat pouches and swallowed the fish whole before returning to the sky to repeat the process. What pull inside the pelicans knew the tides, brought them to this exact bay, at this exact time, in this exact month?

I'd felt it, too. That pull. Like an internal clock telling me to get up and move, to follow the tide, to find the thing that will sustain me. To leave a religion, to leave a marriage. It brought me here, to this coastal town, to the bed where I found Katie waiting, night after night.

☾

My first memories of the shoreline come not from lived experience, but they *are* embedded in my DNA.

It is 1966. My sixteen-year-old father drives a yellow Volkswagen bug around his hometown of El Cajon with a surfboard strapped to the roof. He is tall and lithe, dark hair, eyes the color of coffee grounds. "Don't Worry Baby" blares over the car stereo, but his strict Mormon upbringing steers him away from making love not war, from mind altering substances. His rebellion is simple, is all physics, the rebellion of sliding down the white caps of waves, of staying upright while a tunnel of water curves over his head. Life in El Cajon is a performance against the backdrop of the tides and the sun. Summers here mean bathtub-temperature water, bodies clamoring on bodies as they splash in the surf to cool down. Sand, always, in his wheel wells. Later he will surf in college in Hawaii, serve a mission for his church up and down the coasts of Honshu and Okinawa, but today he measures time by the tides at LaJolla beach and the 4/4 beat of "Surfin' USA."

My mother, on the other hand, is up north in the high desert. While Dad drives the 101 and dives headfirst into oncoming breakers, she milks cows and hoes sugar beets in a tiny eastern Oregon farm town. Where my dad's childhood is punctuated by the tacky feeling of salt on the skin, hers is coated in a constant film of dust from the arid stretch of land that barely keeps her family afloat. And then, the sea: when she is seventeen, her parents abandon farming and move to a run-down, mildew-laced house in Coos Bay, a hilly community battered by the offshore breeze and unpredictable currents of the southern Oregon coast. Here the Coos River enters the bay of the same name, a confluence of fresh and salt water that in turn opens into the Pacific. A far cry from the flat, parched parcels of farmlands that dotted her earlier childhood, the city takes up roughly fifteen square miles, over five of which are water. Another good chunk is sea cliffs, and then long stretches of cold sand so dangerous she feels a malicious tide always at her back.

This is not my father's beach. There are no boys in sunglasses with boards tethered to their ankles, no bikini-clad girls with suntan lotion smeared on their backs. This beach bites your skin. The water feels a moment away from ice. This kind of shoreline comes with rules in the form of *never*: never turn your back to the ocean, never touch a wet log on the sand, never swim against a rip tide. To make money for college, my mother works eight-hour shifts at the shrimp factory, where she stands in knee-deep muck and rhythmically rips the heads and tails off cocktail shrimp. At night, sleepless, she can still smell them.

Months into their courtship, my father brings my mother home to Southern California to meet his parents. When he takes her to the beach, she pulls a down parka and beanie from the trunk of the car. My dad looks at her, confused. It's eighty degrees on that beach, full sun, not even a hint of a breeze. But she hasn't known a beach without an arctic wind. She's never let the ocean lap at her feet, let alone trust it to hold her while she swims. My mother knows the ocean wants one thing: to pull you into its arms, to claim you for its own.

☾

Pause. Elissa, go further.

If epigenetics holds—if the experiences of our ancestors are written in our genes alongside eye color and asthma risk—then my genes hold memories of another body of salt water.

1847. My ancestors left Nauvoo, Illinois, to follow Brigham Young in the Mormon exodus and eventually landed in Salt Lake City. Mormon lore holds that only months before, Brigham—delirious with Rocky Mountain fever—crested the mountains in the back of a wagon and upon seeing the Salt Lake Valley and its accompanying lake proclaimed: "This is the place. Drive on." The Mormons had found their promised land, a valley so remote and wild that nobody else in their right mind want to tame it. Here they could be left alone to practice their faith, free from the persecution that led to the murder of their founder and first prophet, Joseph Smith. According to historians, 330 births were recorded during the Mormon migration. One of them was my great-great-grandmother Sarah. Family genealogical records tell me that Sarah and her mother lived to ride on, though many other mothers and infants were lost to the trail.

A hundred and fifty years later, at her sewing machine in the tiny ranch-style house where we lived, my mom sewed me a dress and bonnet that reminded me of *Little House on the Prairie* to celebrate Pioneer Day. Each July, all the families gathered at the church for a pancake breakfast in our costumes. I sang with the other children: "Pioneer children sang as they walked, and walked, and walked, and walked." This was the most important thing we learned about pioneer children: they never complained. They happily collected cow patties for fuel and ate a few bites of cornmeal mush a day. They walked miles upon miles with only the clothes on their back, no toys, and (unlike us) they did it all with a smile.

At church, my brothers and I were expected to be quiet and reverent as we heard stories of the traumas our ancestors endured: long skirts fatally caught in wagon wheels, snake bites, the constant threat of unfriendly encounters. Over four thousand pioneers were estimated to have died on the trek, deaths that are romanticized in children's songs and stories. All for the end goal of a lake so salty that few species can survive in its waters aside from algae, bacteria, and brine shrimp. Terry Tempest Williams says Great Salt Lake is made of "water in the desert that no one can drink. It is the liquid lie of the West."

The church taught us the lake and its briny flats were our inheritance. So, too, were the blood and toil of our pioneer ancestors. The greatest sin would be to dishonor their sacrifice by turning away from the gospel. Another song from my childhood: "True to the faith that my parents have cherished, true to the faith for which martyrs have perished . . . faithful and true we will ever stand."

The salt was our religion, and it was in our blood, our bones, our souls, the very nuclei of our cells.

Or was it?

Epigenetic theory teaches that trauma can be passed down from generation to generation and change our DNA, affecting the way we respond in daily situations.

Eight-year-old me in my pioneer bonnet had been taught that Brigham Young was a hero, that he helped his followers flee from the scourge of violence and persecution against them. I knew about Joseph Smith being tarred and feathered, jailed and shot. I did not yet know that Joseph Smith and Brigham Young forced young girls to marry them and stole the wives of other men to add to their polygamous harems. I didn't know, complaining about my long pioneer dress in the summer heat, that vigilante violence was de rigueur in the nineteenth century, and the early Mormons were the instigators of violence as often as they were the victims.

What if the trauma in my DNA is not *only* that of giving birth in a covered wagon, or losing a young child to dysentery somewhere in the mountains between Illinois and Utah? What if, instead, it is the trauma of my female ancestors wanting to protect their barely teenage girls from the hands of church elders insistent on taking them as second, third, and thirteenth wives? What if my inheritance includes the ever-present threat of violence both sexual and physical?

And so my inheritance is both a fear of salt water and a reverence for it. A brackish Utah lake. An ocean churning with dangerous tides. But I've inherited an even bigger fear. My queer self still carries the fear that I won't get into heaven without a husband, that my only role in life is the childbearing predetermined by my biology.

Somewhere sequenced onto my genetic code is the protective impulse to please everyone but myself. To "bear the souls of men" as per Mormon scripture. To not consider my own pleasure, the way I do night after night in bed with Katie.

I have been bred to want nothing.

☾

Brigham Young has been referred to as the "American Moses." Moses led the Israelites through the desert on a mass exodus. So, too, did Young lead his seventy thousand followers through parched earth to their own version of a promised land: the salt flats that make up the miniature, almost imperceptible intertidal zone of the Great Salt Lake. Brigham claimed revelation directly from God about the westward migration; Moses claimed revelation when, miracle of miracles, he thrust his staff into the Red Sea, parting the waters to allow his people safe passage.

And yet.

There was no miracle. Just a night sky. A ripe, rotund moon. Syzygy.

Moses's great feat was simply an understanding of the tides. Dr. Bruce Parker, former chief scientist of the National Oceanic and Atmospheric Administration, contends that since Moses had spent his early years in the wilderness at the Suez region of the Red Sea, he would have known ancient moon-based tide prediction methods. He would have been well aware that every so often, if timed just right, the tide would drop low enough that a sandbar would appear in the middle of the Red Sea, passable only for a few hours. He would have seen large trade caravans read the moon to pass right through the sea without getting wet. Pharaoh, on the other hand, was a child of the Nile and the Mediterranean, both tideless bodies of water. That chump and his troops followed Moses right along the sandbar just in time to be swallowed by the tide, with the Israelites safely triumphant on the other side.

I've seen the sea work this way. Just below our coastal house lies Lost Boy Cave, an underwater grotto that is only accessible about four times a year at a drastic minus tide. The cave belongs solely to multi-colored starfish, sea urchins the size of Cinderella pumpkins, and wall-clinging gooseneck barnacles. But for a few brief hours a year, if you time it like Moses did, you can walk into Lost Boy Cave on foot and gape at the rock formations worn away by years of violent tides. Katie and I took my daughter there and I am here to tell you: it really is a miracle.

Be careful. Touch the rock walls dripping with brine, regard the crabs and oyster catchers. Listen to the barnacles crackle and pop as they dry. Watch the clock. If you stay too long, your passage back will be blocked, and the ocean will swallow you the way the Red Sea did Pharaoh and his hapless men.

☾

Pause again. Further.

Four billion years ago. Today life on earth will start. It's possible that it happens in the tenuous intertidal zone, when the distance between the earth and the moon is much smaller than it will be when you read this. The result is hundreds of miles of briny flats repeatedly wetting and drying according to the moon's whims. Surface conditions are too harsh for life, but today, inexplicably, magic will happen in that intertidal space marked by the back and fill of the tide. Carbon-based molecules brought here from asteroids, liquid water, and the sun's scorching energy together ignite the very first spark of life, probably a single cell with the first double helix on our planet. It sits in the surf and waits.

As Jonathan White posits, "What if we are born in a tidepool and our attraction to the sea is a coming home?" That first living cell knows nothing of Moses, of Brigham Young, of my dad's surfboard or my mom's shrimping job, of purity culture and the shame that will decimate my relationship to my own body, a body for which that cell will be the first building block. Brave cell, spark of life, lodestone for what is to come: you carry already within you the pull to reinvent, to ebb and flow, to become something other than what you have been.

It's you I have come home to: here, where the saltwater meets the land, where Katie's hands above the sea stacks make me cry out with a guttural primacy that can only have come from you.

OCEANSIDE BEACH

Months after I told Matt I was gay, Oregon experienced one of the worst wildfire seasons on record. It was 2020, and if the world was burning, so was I. As we divided up our lives and tried to make the transition as smooth as possible for the kids, the hills to the south of our house started burning. We saw the fire over a distant ridge, the sky a viscous, irradiated orange, and felt everything but the crackling heat itself. Normally, Mount Hood's silhouette stood sentry on the far side of Portland, but in her place was only smoke that crept in through the windowpanes and doorjambs. I checked the air quality index obsessively as it slunk up and down—mostly up—depending on the wind and how the embers carried. When I went to bed on Wednesday night, the AQI registered 450, deemed "extremely hazardous."

It was the year of collective breath-holding—the Covid-19 pandemic had already been raging for six months. We were already wearing masks, but now I layered mask on mask and instructed my kids to hold their breath as we ran between the car and the house. It felt as though we were moving through sludge that tried to work its way through the layers of fabric hammocked over my mouth. I'd spent months falling asleep each night thinking about what it would feel like to be on a ventilator, the plastic tube snaked down my throat, the mechanical buzz on each draw of air. Now here was a new, more imminent, threat to my family's lungs.

There was nothing safe left to breathe.

Thursday morning, the Forest Service placed our neighborhood in a level one evacuation zone, the prelude to actual flight. It was time to take assessments, to decide what to pack, what we had time and room to take with us into this potential new life where behind us was only ash. On the news, we watched as the agglomerated fires razed entire towns, as people in neighboring cities fled outward to places filled with so much peripheral smoke that they looked to be burning themselves. So much loss. So much left to the impulse of the winds, the capriciousness of flames.

☾

I'd already lit a match, months earlier—the sky still blue, the air still clear. *I'm a lesbian,* I'd finally said aloud to my husband of twenty-three years and my three teenaged children. We waited to see where the sparks would land. Sparks became embers; soon Matt and I were entrenched in the painstaking work of uncoupling, and the whole family took stock of what to carry with us into the next chapter—what to save from the gulping flames I'd lit, and what to leave smoldering. Matt started dating, and the kids struggled to adjust to life with parents who were baby-stepping apart (different bedrooms now, different houses soon), all of us painfully aware that the traditional version of the five of us around a dinner table each night had been shattered.

We'd started holding our breath long before the actual wildfire smoke skulked in through the doorjambs.

And this was all enunciated by a global pandemic, by lockdowns and rising death numbers and the rush to a vaccine. By Black men and women dying at the hands of police officers in horrific numbers, by my children as they took part in protests in downtown Portland, where President Trump had sent National Guard troops with tear gas and flash bombs. By an aggressive campaign for a contentious and crucial presidential election.

Which is to say: flames, flames, everywhere.

(Flames have the curves of a woman, soft and fluid around their edges.)

As I packed the house for a potential evacuation, I frantically texted a chestnut-haired woman with whom I shared a mutual flirtation. After leaving my marriage for the hypothetical *idea* of a woman, here was a real one, flesh and blood. She was headed to the coast to escape the smoke. Did I want to meet her there?

(I wanted to meet her there. Holy shit I wanted to meet her there.)

I filled the living room with suitcases and bags. The fires now razed eight hundred thousand acres of the state; outside, the sky glowed the uncanny orange of pumpkins left to rot on the stoop.

The apocalypse. We'd been joking about it for months—2020 being what it was—the apocalypse. Now it was actually coming.

☾

The evacuation orders in our neighborhood were lifted when the winds turned the next day. Nothing immediate had changed: the skies still blazed orange, the air still carried the acrid smell of charred timber. It took almost a week for me to feel safe enough to put away the suitcases and hang the pictures back on the walls.

Then the rain came. A thunderstorm so resplendent it felt like there might be a god.

Smoke persisted through the rain, but not for long. Within two days the ache in my throat cleared and I could blink without the feeling of grit on my eyeballs. The AQI dropped into the three hundreds, then the one hundreds, then into solidly double digits. We worshipped each spit of rain. How it felt to breathe again.

It wasn't a win. All told, the climate-fueled inferno razed a million acres of land, taking in its wake four thousand homes, five entire towns, and nine human lives. And although we were in the clear, our house was still sweltering. Matt would be moving out soon, the kids would have to adjust. He had a new lover I would have to accept as part of the loss that came with coming out. When that first spark is fanned by a wayward wind and converts to flame, there is no predicting what direction it will go, what it will take down. I had started the process intentionally, but there was nothing intentional about it now; it felt like I was completely at the fancy of the elements around me, a queer woman in this not-so-brave new world. I could move forward through the smoke, or I could capitulate to the flames.

Fire kindles more fire.

Desire kindles more desire.

I first admitted to myself that I liked women ten years before, on a lone night in Washington, DC, at a writer's conference. The Poet lay down on the crisp white hotel bedspread holding an almost-drained glass of whiskey and kicked off her boots. I did not so much as touch her wrist, but my body responded in her presence the way it had never responded to another bone-and-sinew human. Standing five feet from her, wanting to kiss her, wanting to trace her collar bone with the tip of my index finger, I learned the difference between being desired and desiring. My whole life, I'd thought love and sex meant being desirable to a man, meant giving yourself in to the lust of another. But here was real desire—the lust my own, a pull both corporeal and primal. *Move closer to her,* desire said*, and you will burn. Breathe her in,* it said*, and the world will blaze.*

Which is to say: flames, flames, everywhere.

The week I came out to Matt, I'd dreamed about cats. It was the kind of dream where I was trying to walk but I couldn't, not because my feet were cement (I'd had that dream, certainly), but because I was carrying too much. I had all three cats in my arms, a bag of chips, stray laundry, my blue light glasses, magazines. Every time I took a step forward, something fell from my grip. I'd lose a shirt, or a cat, or a book. I'd bend down to pick it up just as something else fell out of my arms.

Listen: to move forward, you have to let some things go.

Some things have to burn.

☾

"The heart is an organ of fire," wrote Michael Ondaatje. Traditional Chinese medicine agrees. The part of the body most associated with fire is the heart. My acupuncturist wife has explained to me that the body's energy (*Qi)* is divided up into the same five elements as the earth (because the earth *is* a body). The goal of treating a patient is to keep all five elements in balance, otherwise symptoms will arise. Inside the body, fire is not just associated with burning and heat; it is also all about urgency and speed. A person with imbalanced fire will present with manifestations linked to the heart and circulatory system: high or low blood pressure, palpitations, racing heart, flushed complexion. Too little or too much fire in your body will cause a chronic need to bustle, struck with too much haste and the inability to slow down. Exposure to the fire element in the human body has much the same effect as fire on the earth: dryness and damage to systems that are fragile and vulnerable to heat.

The cure for too much fire in the body is another of the five elements: water.

I had set my life on fire, burned it unrecognizable by my own hand. To help quench the flames, I needed moisture, sustenance, balance, and restoration. So

I found water. I found it in the form of Oceanside. I found it in the form of the whole goddamn ocean.

The night of our wedding, Katie and I asked the guests to change from their formal wear into warm beach gear and meet us at Oceanside Beach. And there, with the Pacific at our backs and the new moon directly overhead, we lit a bonfire. The spring tide was so low we could hear the waves but could not see them. Forty of us drank and laughed as the raging fire kept us warm. They had all come to celebrate the life Katie and I were embarking on together, to bear witness to the way I'd balanced my life of fire with an equally vital life of water. My brothers fed the bonfire for hours, tossing new logs on each time it seemed to be burning down. Matt sat on a log, laughing and chatting with some of our oldest friends. Our kids played volleyball in the dark and struck up conversations with strangers. My old dormmate from BYU, now also out and proud, held an energetic conversation with Katie's best college friend. Their laughter merged with the swath of waves striking wet sand and the popping of the fire. Cans of beer appeared as if in unlimited quantities from a large cooler and were passed hand-to-hand around the fire.

I held Katie's palm, not paying attention to the conversation she was having with the chestnut-haired woman beside her, the same woman I'd flirted with all those years before. The sea stacks at Three Arch Rocks were barely visible in the moonlight. I could just make out the curvature of each rock as if it were painted in relief against the night sky. Then the rocks morphed into something else entirely: I saw the image of a giant stone woman floating, weightless, on her back in the ocean. And although I couldn't see them, I knew tufted puffins had burrowed into the crevices of her body, their yellow breeding plumage recently exchanged for the dressed-down boredom of parenthood.

I thought of Rumi, in all his mystic wisdom: "Set your life on fire," he wrote. And then: "Seek those who fan your flames."

FAWN GULCH

But before the wedding and the bonfire that would usher us into our new life together, there was the Castle and its respite.

On a Saturday morning, I woke as the sun made a slow arc across the east side of the Castle. I stumbled to the kitchen in my boxers and San Francisco Giants tank, bleary-eyed and ready for caffeine. Through the sliding glass door, the sea stacks were completely obscured by a scrim of fog: the Castle was socked in. A flicker of movement took my eyes to the glass patio door, and beyond it to the lawn, where a doe and a fawn chewed Katie's shrubs. The baby's legs wobbled as it walked toward its mother in the fog, who nibbled red huckleberries in our side yard. Two lateral lines of spots ran from the fawn's ears to its tail, and other spots cascaded outward in a sort of zigzag pattern. Next to the fawn's foot, a torn plastic bag tumbled lightly in the breeze, a remnant of the chaos the raccoons unleashed on the trash the night before.

I had been taught at sixth grade outdoor school that if a fawn had spots in a straight line, it was a male, and if the spots were patterned in a zigzag, it was a female. It's an old myth that has been proven untrue time and time again, yet it was the first thing I thought of looking at the fawn on the grass: *welcome to the world, little girl.* I was being silly. There were only two foolproof ways to know the sex of this deer: wait to see if it grows antlers or look between its legs.

Name it: shame. Purity culture had left me an intelligent middle-aged woman who couldn't seriously think about or talk about sex and genitals without abject shame. It crept in at the thought of sexing this baby deer in my yard. I noticed it and tried to shrug it aside. The fawn (*my fawn,* I thought) faltered and dropped to the lawn when its legs buckled, its hind end barely missing the plastic bag that had come to a standstill on the grass. It seemed content to sit there, waiting for its mom to finish. It was not looking around to see if anyone saw it fall. As far as I knew, deer didn't feel shame the same way we do. When it was time for this fawn to find a mate and reproduce, it would do so without feeling dirty for how powerfully its body *wants*.

I'd been indoctrinated that gender was predisposed by God before birth, that your sex declared at birth would guide the nature of your life. Before we were all born into human bodies on this earth, Mormons teach, we lived as spirits in the aptly named Spirit World.

Even there, even before *bodies*, we had gender—and gender determined what kind of body we were each born into. And then, having those bodies, we were sorted into gender buckets: women were destined to marry churchgoing men, bear children, and keep house. Men were responsible for holding the Lord's priesthood, marrying a woman to bear multiple children, and providing for their families. I was twenty-three and pregnant with my first child when General Relief Society President Julie Beck said that women in the Spirit World "wished to work side by side with righteous men to accomplish eternal goals that neither can attain independently. Female roles did not begin on earth, and they do not end here. A woman who treasures motherhood on earth will treasure motherhood in the world to come."

Here I was, no longer side by side with a man, and with my kids only half of the time. The guilt was sometimes visceral, fixed somewhere between my rib cage and heart.

The fawn was still seated on the grass. Its mother had moved incrementally farther away to nibble on our pampas grass. A small break in the fog let the biggest sea stack sneak its head out. I turned when I heard Katie's slippers shuffling across the kitchen. She slipped her hand into mine.

"What are you doing, Babe?"

I pointed to the pair on the lawn, then raised a finger to my lips to remind her not to alert the dogs.

"Oh wow," she whispered. I wove my left arm around her waist, noting the warmth of her robe. "Have you named them yet?

I nodded. "That one," I said, pointing to the doe, "Is Maude. And the little one on the grass is Logan."

She pursed her lips together and nodded. "I like it."

"And I am afraid to tell you that your lawn is now called Fawn Gulch."

She laughed. "Do you even know what a gulch is?"

"Of course. It's a really pretty natural area and a word that sounds cool with *fawn*," I smirked.

"Okay. Sure. Pretty sure it's a narrow ravine with steep sides. I think usually there is a creek there, too."

"Eh," I waved it off. "I like my definition better. Welcome to Fawn Gulch. Stay awhile." She pulled me to her just after the doe and its offspring dipped out of sight. I rested my chin on her right shoulder and could feel the definition of her arms where they held me, her biceps forged from a winter spent chopping firewood. Being held by strong arms felt familiar, but it was the breath of a woman skimming my cheek.

Katie didn't seem clearly like *either* gender. She was as manly as she was womanly. Like so many of the cisgendered men I knew, she could tell you which engine ran any given model of car and could likely *fix* that engine if anything happened to it, even though she had deliciously soft hands that she hated to dirty. She danced ballet as a girl but played rugby in college. The tool spread on her workbench rivaled that of my late grandfather, and her commitment to pristine kitchen towels, perfectly roasted vegetables, and neatly folded underwear rivaled that of any Mormon homemaker I'd ever known.

Her chest was square and broad for her small frame, her pectorals as chiseled as her biceps. Yet attached to them, her breasts were high and round, the bust of a woman somehow untouched by gravity or time. When Katie stood still, she often crossed her arms in front of her chest and planted her feet in a wide, steady stance; she walked with a manly swagger that seemingly conveyed confidence but was really the result of an Achilles tendon injury in her early twenties. And that same swagger was just as titillating when she pulled on a tight pink Diane von Furstenberg sheath with knee-high black boots as it was when she wore a custom men's suit. Her face, though, was an unabashed illustration of classical feminine beauty: her jawline soft and barely-there, her nose and ears adorably tiny, her chin ending at a perfect point.

Katie didn't fall outside the prescribed gender binary as much as she encapsulated it fully: she was a man, she was a woman.

She was *both*.

She was *and*.

A conjunction, a connector of disparate things.

WAIOHULI BEACH

Katie and I didn't fall in love in Oceanside. It happened a week before we met in person, on another beach over two thousand miles away. I had taken Clementine to vacation in Maui, our first big foray back into the world since the pandemic had upended our lives. We rented a condo directly across from Waiohuli Beach on Maui's southwestern shore, where we spent hours on a white sand beach. I sat with my book and looked up to see her crashing headfirst into the waves. It was our first solo trip since I'd left her father eighteen months earlier.

I'd matched with Katie on a dating app a few weeks earlier and struck up a correspondence, but we didn't get the chance to meet in person before Clem and I boarded our flight. And yet I still mark Maui as the place we fell in love, the place I knew I'd found my person. I texted Katie throughout the day, regaling her with tales of our travels. We sent selfies from our respective beaches: in hers she was bundled in a winter jacket and a hat because of the biting Oceanside wind, and in mine, I was in a modest bikini top, white streaks of sunscreen visible on my shoulders. Clementine and I surfed and rode horses and walked long stretches of shoreline nature preserves to spot Hawaiian stilts and black-crowned night herons.

And late at night, Katie sent me the first nude photos meant for my eyes alone.

The heat between us—across almost three thousand miles, across a whole ocean—kept me up most nights. I'd fix Clementine fresh mangoes and pasta for dinner, then once she went to bed, I'd retreat to my room to talk to this woman who had captured the fullness of my desire.

Maui oozed sensuality. The air sticky, the fruit plump and honeyed. The foliage lush, the flowers fleshy and pungent. I could feel the rhythm of the place as if the island were breathing, filling me on each long, languid exhale.

On the fourth night of the vacation, Katie sent me an audio clip via text: quick successive breaths, percussive in their quietude. She was touching herself.

☾

I'd been taught my whole life that touching yourself was a sin. Nude photos, too. Only a Jezebel would show her naked body to someone who was not her husband. God wanted me to be married to a man before I was ever seen or touched—even by myself.

My body was a temple, they told me each week in Sunday School, each Wednesday youth night. What I knew about temples was that they were secretive and mysterious, too sacred to be spoken about out loud. Only the righteous were granted access, and only God decided who made the cut. So if my body was also a temple, it stood to reason that it, too, was meant to be kept hidden, was not to be spoken of. It meant I should be selective about who was allowed in.

Wait, no: it meant only God could make that decision.

When I married Matt in the temple, it felt as if the entire building was going to swallow me up. I learned why my mom's answer about nudity was cryptic when I was asked to strip nude and draped with a white sheet. . The temple matron anointed my flesh with small dots of olive oil consecrated by the Melchizedek priesthood (this body of mine, this temple). I learned the secret handshakes and changed into the undergarments I was to wear from that day forward. They were all white, knee-length, with large cap sleeves to cover each shoulder, a reminder to keep my body pure.

My brothers weren't allowed at my wedding. One was too young, and the other had stopped attending church after high school, so he wasn't worthy. I kneeled across from Matt in the altar of the sealing room, both of us wearing the leafy green overlay aprons meant to represent Adam and Eve, surrounded by our parents, grandparents, and dozens of adults who had known me most of my life. But instead of feeling connected to tradition, I had never felt more alone.

☾

Confession: I was an early and creative masturbator (I'd grind on my favorite stuffed animal or wrap my legs around the post of my footboard so I could push my vulva against it through my underwear). These were the blissful years before I turned eight, when the purity culture messages would start in subtle but earnest ways. This was before I knew to associate the potent buzz between my thighs with abject shame. At five, six, seven, I thought religion just meant not lying to my parents about stealing my mom's perfume and not fighting with my brothers; it meant folding my arms across my chest as I walked from the Sunday school classroom back to the chapel to show reverence for God's house. It meant not drinking the iced tea that my best friend across the street drank every day during the summer.

I discovered when I was nine that if I took a throw pillow from the couch and put it underneath me on the open-riser staircase, I could rub my hips against it to get a warm electrical feeling through my pelvis. I didn't connect this to sex, to boys, to anything other than what it was: the pillow felt good against the area I knew was private, the area I wasn't supposed to talk about or show anyone. I could get lost this way, moving quickly back and forth, all sensation in the dark behind my eyelids. Between the stair risers, I could see the television blazing the nightly news, the sound a backdrop to what was happening to my body. And then: my mom, behind me.

"Elissa, we don't do that." She said it gently, almost timidly, like she wasn't sure if she was doing the right thing.

Shame. It trickled from my hairline down into my smallest toenail. I stood quickly and abandoned the orange pillow on the stairs for the solace of my bedroom, where I sat on my quilt and wondered if I'd ever be able to look my mom in the eyes.

We didn't speak of it again. It was enough that I knew I had done something shameful. Without broader context for my young self, though, the shame lived not in the act of grinding against the pillow, but instead in having a body with lightning-pulse urges that could not be quenched.

The shame was the hunger, not the stimulation.

The shame was the wanting.

But I didn't stop. More accurate: I *couldn't* stop. By the time I was an early teen, I'd been masturbating so long and so often that shame was the constant soundtrack of my daily life, always lilting in the background of everything I did. It always built the same way: I'd be sitting in the pews at church (fielding warnings against the evils of sex and self-pleasure), acutely aware of how many days it had been since I last touched myself. When the bread and water came around for the sacrament, I popped it in my mouth and chewed, promising God the same thing I promised him the week before—that I would never, ever, masturbate again. I now had complete control of my body. I gave it up to Jesus, confident he could give me the strength I needed to stop committing this sin that had most of my life felt out of my own control.

After church, we'd have a family dinner—roast beef that had simmered in the oven for six hours, potatoes, gravy, and corn. The meal that to this day tastes like Sunday. We would watch what my dad called "stupid movies" (a scandalous thing—my Mormon friends weren't allowed television on Sunday), play a game of Monopoly or Taboo in the dining room, and then we'd retreat to our respective spaces for homework and sleep.

There, lying in the dark, the thirst would start. It came from deep inside my body and seemed to infiltrate the nucleus of every cell: *quench me.*

Shame came too. *You are a horrible sinner. You must be a slut. Why can't you stop thinking about this? You are going to touch yourself. You are going to touch yourself. You are dirty. Do it. Do it. Do it. Not worth trying to resist. This is who you are.* It was a possession of my body. There was an actual physical ache in my pelvis, and suddenly the only important thing was making it go away. I didn't want to climax as much as I *needed* to climax. *This is Satan doing this and I don't even care.*

Orgasm wasn't the only or most intense culmination of these moments. Shame was the second wave, and it crashed the hardest. The electrical aftershocks from coming were inconsequential compared to the self-hatred that I pulled over me like a cloak.

I usually ended these nights with my knees on the ivory carpet of my childhood bedroom, begging for God's forgiveness, promising him I would change, that I would never do it again, that I would prove to him and to myself that I could learn not to want.

I wanted so badly not to want.

☾

While on Maui, I decided to take Clementine snorkeling at La Perouse, an embayment along the southernmost point of the island. According to the internet, La Perouse seemed to be everything I wanted: wild, rugged, not highly trafficked. I was ready to feel lava rocks under my sandals, to dive in and reach the inlets in the bay where we could gawk at creatures as they shimmied underwater.

I woke at 7:30 and left Clementine asleep in the hide-a-bed. My destination: the water sports rental store a block away from the condo. There, a man in his fifties with leathered skin fitted me for a snorkel mask. He wore a blue floral Hawaiian shirt with his company logo on the front. When he asked me to put the mask over my face, I breathed in to check the seal right when he asked me where I was snorkeling.

"My daughter and I are going to La Perouse Bay," I told him, the words echoing against the inside of my mask. I pulled it back over my head and rubbed the sore spot it left on my chin.

"So you guys are like hardcore snorkelers." His shoulder length hair hung in stringy hanks down each side of his face.

I didn't understand his assessment. "I mean, we've been a few times and we like it. Definitely wouldn't consider us hardcore."

"Good swimmers, though, yeah?"

"We can get from here to there, most of the time." I felt my phone vibrate in my hand and leapt at the thought that it was probably a text from Katie.

I was looking down at my phone when I heard him laugh. "You definitely do not want to go to La Perouse, at least not to snorkel. I don't even snorkel there and I've been snorkeling for years." His warning alarmed me, afraid as I already was of the ocean. He added, "Plus it's almost a full moon. Conditions are ripe for the Night Marchers and that bay is like *their spot*."

My hand burned where it held Katie's text. *Getting to know you has felt like a thunderclap in my life,* she had written.

I thanked the man and left without snorkel gear. When I got back to the condo, I googled "Night Marchers." Island lore held that the Night Marchers, or *Hukai'po,* were ancient Hawaiian warriors—men and women—whose spirits emerge from the sea on specific nights when the moon is nearing fullness and parade towards the sites of old battles. Dressed for combat in elaborate helmets and cloaks, the Night Marchers carry clubs, spears, and torches, and they don't march so much as float a few inches above both water and land. To announce their advancement, these spectral warriors beat on war drums and blow tones with conch shells. They only march in darkness, setting out on their journey just after sunset and not returning to the sea until just before sunrise on the following day. Witnesses have said a foul, musky odor often precedes the sound of drums and the sight of torches. Though not many people live to tell stories about the *Hukai'po;* it's said that anyone who looks directly into the eyes of the apparitions will die a violent death.

A drumbeat, a stench, a spattering of torchlight. Losing my religion meant losing the part of me that believed in things unseen, in ancient stories. But I felt this one almost viscerally; it was hard not to believe in this otherworldly place that there were forces at work outside of scientific reasoning.

I could hear Clementine's steady breathing from where she still slept on the pull-out sofa. Around us, tortured spirits were preparing for a night journey to right past wrongs. And across the ocean, a woman I had yet to meet was experiencing the very idea of *me* as a thunderclap.

☾

Mormonism is clear in its stance on masturbation. The church holds the Law of Chastity as one of its central tenets. Spencer W. Kimball, among the most revered of the church's former prophets, famously said from the pulpit at Tabernacle Square that "when the sun grows cold and the stars no longer shine, the law of chastity will still be basic in God's world and in the Lord's church. Old values are upheld by the church not because they are old, but rather because they are right. Total chastity before marriage and total fidelity after are still the standard from which there can be no deviation without sin, misery, and unhappiness." He further clarified that the Law of Chastity includes "all sexual relations outside marriage—petting, sex perversion, masturbation, and preoccupation with sex in one's thoughts and talking. Included are every hidden and secret sin and all unholy and impure thoughts and practices."

The problem, then, wasn't actually my inability to stop touching myself. The problem was my very *thoughts*. The problem was *desire*. The problem was *me*.

So at sixteen, I decided the only way I could overcome my compulsion to touch myself was to confess to the bishop. There were sins, we had been told multiple times a week, that could only be forgiven by confessing to a priesthood authority. Maybe the reason I wasn't able to stop was that I had never properly repented.

Mormon clergy are unpaid members of the congregation with other, real-world vocations who serve for a handful of years at a time. And there was no picking and choosing: your ward was determined by your address, and the church chose the bishop for each ward. Our bishop at the time was Bishop Highland, a lawyer in his mid-forties who also happened to be my friend's father. I saw him regularly in the grocery store, at sleepovers, at youth events, and—of course—every Sunday looming over the congregation from on high where he sat with his counselors on the pulpit. I made an appointment with him, knowing it would be the scariest thing I'd ever had to do: sit across the desk from a man whose pool I often swam in and tell him my worst and darkest secret. That in the dark, alone, the urges in my body superseded the urges of my spirit.

"Bishop," I told him, my voice and hands shaking, "I need to repent for something."

He smiled and nodded his head, urging me on. When he noticed me trembling, he said, "Take your time." His voice was soft and kind. A painting of Jesus ministering to adoring children hung above his head. Bishop Highland's already-gray hair tufted out from behind his ears.

I cleared my throat. "I've been committing the same sin over and over." My eyes didn't leave the blue Berber carpet beneath my feet.

"What is it?" he asked. When I wouldn't meet his eyes, he reached a hand across the desk and tapped his finger to get my attention. "Sister Minor, there's nothing you could have done that you can't be forgiven for."

I twisted the hemline of my skirt between my fingers, just above my knees. I'd never said the disgusting word out loud, and I certainly wasn't going to say it to him. Instead, I said, almost under my breath, "I touch myself."

Then I looked up. I had never seen a grown man more uncomfortable. Bishop Highland looked away from me, removed his elbows from the desk, straightened his maroon paisley tie, and cleared his throat. Now he was the one avoiding eye contact.

"Are you sorry? And have you prayed about it?"

I nodded an enthusiastic yes, looking directly at him, willing him to meet my gaze.

He didn't look up or wait for an answer. "Do you want to save yourself for your husband?"

Of course I did. Did I look like someone eager to miss out on the highest level of heaven? He must have been able to perceive my nodding while actively avoiding my eyes, because he followed with: "Don't do it again and you will be forgiven."

I left his office and closed the door behind me. Alone in the church hallway, I stared at the stainless steel drinking fountain and held back tears of mortification. I wondered if he'd ever be able to make eye contact with me again. I certainly knew I would never again jump from his diving board.

Thirty years later, I'd look back on this moment and know that Bishop Highland was poorly trained, and perhaps it made him uncomfortable to be counseling a teenage girl about her sexuality. Or more: maybe my confession brought his own shame to the surface, something he'd done in the past, something he, too, was trying not to want.

But I interpreted his reaction differently at sixteen.

I thought he was disgusted. That there was something inherently wrong, inherently *sexual,* about me. And if I didn't try harder, it would be my downfall.

☾

My days on Maui felt like a series of mornings and nights in bed. I played Katie's audio message in my room as the ocean lapped against the sand of Waiohuli Beach outside my open window. Those breaking waves were the backdrop against which I heard her breathing: sharp, quick, almost imperceptible. This was the first time I realized that masturbation is not necessarily a solo act. It taps us into the broader universe of living things, of water, of land, of ebbing and flowing. Of the tides.

Katie was thinking about *me*. She was touching herself *for me*. On her side of the Pacific, all those miles away, the same ocean was also breaking and slapping against the sea stacks beneath her house. We were together in this intensity, connected by an ocean. And we wanted each other. This time, I let the wanting fill me, I let it be the most important thing in the world. I surrendered to it.

Before I went to sleep, Katie sent another picture of her wearing her signature blue dress shirt, unbuttoned and skimming down the side of each erect nipple. Her eyes were the same blue as the ocean water outside my window before the sun went down (the ocean, the sky, her eyes: blue to me but actually a scattering of light, a reflection, a trick of this earth), her nipples the brownish-pink of the coral beds underneath.

The next morning, I was determined to send her a photo that would make her want me as much as I wanted her. I contorted my body into various positions on the bed and on the rug. I held my lips in a pseudo pout. I stood against a wall with my top off. I took pictures in just a bra. I took pictures fully nude just before stepping into the shower. In the end, though, I could only send her a picture of me lying back on the bed in my full coverage bikini top and jean shorts.

As much as I believed otherwise, the old voice in my head grew louder and louder. *Only a slut would take pictures like that. No good woman thinks this much about sex. Get your mind out of the gutter.*

Want nothing. Want nothing. Want nothing.

I was afraid if I actually sent one of the photos, I'd end up back on my knees in an act of self-flagellation, there on the sand-covered rug of an Airbnb, begging for forgiveness from a God I hadn't believed in for over fifteen years.

Clementine and I spent a full day playing on the beach, and when I lay in bed that night, warm and sticky under a white cotton sheet, I could hear coqui frogs chirping out my open window. If I listened hard enough, would I catch the quick percussive beating of the Night Marcher's ancient war drums, just beyond the warbling frogs and light patter of rain? And if I did, would I survive? I'd been thinking about those drum beats all week. They echoed in my head alongside Katie's thunderclap.

Hawaiians believe, I learned as I continued my online reading, that there are only two ways to survive an encounter with the phantom warriors. The first is sheer luck: if one of the ranks happens to be your ancestor, and they recognize you as they pass, they'll point at you and yell "*Na'u*!" ("mine" in Hawaiian). Once claimed by an ancestor this way, nobody in the procession will harm you. And if you aren't lucky enough to spot an ancestor among the marchers, the most important thing you can do is avoid looking at all costs. Take to the ground, play dead, eyes closed. One glance and you'll be struck down.

I thought of my ancestors then, in that room where I could *feel* more than *hear* the drumbeats growing closer. They were the beats of the women in my lineage who birthed babies on the wagon train to Utah, of every man and woman on that trail who believed in Joseph Smith's words so much they were willing to risk their lives for him. Apparitions in their own right, they still march somewhere in their pioneer bonnets and overalls, to the cadence of their own distant drums.

None of them would be quick to claim me as theirs, when it came to it. I had thrown everything they worked and sacrificed for away.

But I could claim myself for myself.

Mine. This body was mine.

The beating cadence grew steadily louder, and my wanting swelled to a fever pitch. Desire became its own syncopated rhythm against the steadiness of my marching pioneer ancestors. There in that generic bedroom, I came without even touching myself. And in place of shame, I felt only more desire.

☾

Bishop Highland had likely read an internal publication that had been circulating since the late 1980s from prophet Spencer W. Kimball's office. Released to all ward clergy, it warned bishops of a direct link between masturbation and homosexuality, insisting that to keep youth chaste, pure, *straight,* they needed to reinforce the dangers of self-pleasure.

Misogyny being what it is, the authorities in Salt Lake City were almost assuredly thinking about boys when they preached about both masturbation and homosexuality. Bishop Highland must not have known what to do with me. Did he *know,* though? Did he know who I was before I did?

I was on the masturbation to lesbian pipeline.

Well over a decade into my marriage to Matt, a few years after leaving the church, we sought the advice of a sex therapist. All we knew was that sex *wasn't working.* Neither of us drew much pleasure from our sexual relationship, and sex became the elephant in every room. When a sex scene came on the television or in a movie we were watching together, I held my breath, hoping he wasn't thinking what I was: *Why isn't it like that for us?* By the time we walked into the therapist's office, our sex life had all but dried up. During the first session, the two of us met with her together, then we each had an hour-long session alone with her.

During my private session, she read me a number of questions from a form on a clipboard and jotted notes as I talked. When she came to the question, "How old were you when you first started masturbating?" I froze. Could I admit to a stranger that I was practically born with desire? And how on earth could that be relevant? Afterward, she told me she suspected I was a "more sexual person" than my husband, because research showed the earlier a woman masturbates, the more sexually driven she is overall. But how could that be possible when I was the one who never wanted to have sex, who couldn't enjoy it?

When we were teenagers, there was a wall on the west side of our high school that dipped low enough to hoist ourselves up on it, and from there the lowest point on the roof was accessible. Matt and I once climbed the wall just before our midnight curfews. We hadn't thought in advance, so we had no blanket to spread on the flat stretch of roof before us, but that didn't stop us from lying down and making out under the stars. As we kissed fully clothed, he started to move above me, pressing the full weight of his body against mine, an act that usually ended with him having to sneak into his house to change his pants before his parents noticed the stain. This time, though, I felt an electric build ignite in my pelvis, familiar to me from my solo sessions. And then I was surprised with an orgasm of my own. I thought he might find it sexy or exciting.

"An *orgasm*," he said, dumbfounded. "That's for later. We shouldn't have done that. That's for later." He adjusted the wet splotch on his pants. Why wasn't his orgasm for later, I thought? This was my first orgasm with a partner, and there it was, same as always: shame. Welcome, old friend. Settle in. Make yourself at home.

Years later, Matt would apologize for what he said on the roof, and I would reassure him how unnecessary an apology was. He was a product of purity culture, too. The Law of Chastity had shaped everything we knew about ourselves as sexual beings, and it was a law that prioritized the pleasure of men over the pleasure of women.

The sex therapist sat us down together after our individual meetings. "I have to be honest," she said, tapping her fountain pen against her yellow legal pad, "You two have me stumped."

"What do you mean?" I asked her. Matt was silent.

She cleared her throat and took a long swig of chamomile tea. "You are great communicators. You clearly love each other. I honestly can't say I have any idea why sex is such a problem for you." She told us there wasn't much point in making another appointment with her. Nowhere on her form of questions had been anything about sexual orientation.

Eight years later, in the painful final throes of our marriage, we went to see another therapist—a couples counselor we'd seen off and on for years. This time the problem wasn't sex but its absence.

Some things loom larger in their absence. When Katie and I hike in our coastal forest, we pass the remnants of ancient Sitka spruce, stumps the size of cargo vans left behind from the nineteenth-century logging boom. That's how sex felt for most of my first marriage: it was gone, but the wreckage was too big to sidestep, painful vestiges of the life we were trying so hard to make work together. And now we wanted our therapist to tell us how to incorporate sex *back* into our relationship after so many years without.

She was quick to answer. "You could try masturbating in front of each other. Don't even touch each other. Just watch, learn what the other likes."

I pulled my hand from Matt's and shook my head. "I will never be able to do that." The therapist tucked a piece of gray hair where it had fallen from the bun on top of her head and tilted her head as if to ask why.

A chewed stick of gum. Tape robbed of its stickiness. A cup full of spit.

I left the room.

☾

My lived experience makes it hard to see the crusade of the Night Marchers as anything other than a people stuck in a loop of trauma, replaying it in the hopes of finally being free. Rising from the past, haunted by lost battles and wrongful deaths, the warriors raise their torches to the night and set out to reprise it once again, hoping for a different outcome.

Or is it the opposite? Are they trying to fix their own battle mistakes, to come forth from the water when the moon is just right not to *replay* the past but to *change* it? Perhaps the warriors' chanting cadence is driven by little more than shame. A shame so vast that to look them in the eyes means certain death.

☾

I wouldn't have believed anyone who told me that just months after getting home from Maui, Katie would paint me nude on a white canvas and hang it above the bed where we slept. It still hangs there, a talisman inside a house buffered by coastal winds: a promise that I can, just maybe, reclaim my body for my own. That my body doesn't have to be a temple. It just gets to be flesh and blood. It just gets to be mine.

By the sea, my body has a different way of worshiping; it is less a temple and more an altar where I get to sacrifice only what I please. And I wish to sacrifice nothing of myself, of my pleasure. I bring to this altar an offering: brightly colored sea glass, yellow carnelian agates, sometimes a completely unbroken sand dollar, a dark gull's feather. Abraham slaughtered a ram on his altar of unwrought stone; on mine, I destroy the version of myself that doesn't believe she is allowed to want.

I let Katie worship here. I worship here, too.

THUNDERCLAP CASTLE

A thunderclap. A bellow that shakes the trees and sends creatures into their dens. A growl of a shockwave formed from lightning's electricity. A sky so profoundly changed that it feels the need to announce itself: *I'm here,* it says. *Take me seriously.*

Getting to know you has felt like a thunderclap in my life.

I understood what Katie meant. She has arrived in my life and pulled up a chair so quickly it sometimes sent me reeling. What other term for what was happening between us but a thunderclap? Maybe a thunderclap was simply the announcement of a great change in the weather system that was my life.

Katie was everything I didn't know I needed. While I came of age as an obedient Mormon girl in the Portland suburbs, she spent the nineties as a queer kid in a rural Eastern Washington college town, relentlessly bullied by the farm kids who didn't understand why a girl would act so much like a boy. As the only child of an esteemed marketing professor and a pharmacist, hers was a childhood of high expectations. And she met them all. She won admission to Carleton College, where she was both an English literature and a pre-med major, then on to Chinese medical school. There were years when she worked in labs performing surgery on mice hearts, and years she taught human anatomy at her old graduate school. When we met, Katie was simultaneously running a successful acupuncture practice and a manufacturing company. It seemed like she'd lived five lifetimes in the amount of time it had taken me to live only one.

But those lucky enough to know Katie well, to scratch beneath the surface of all the shine and success, know a woman with a soft, vulnerable underbelly that she hides from the world. This Katie sat in front of a Minnesota doctor at twenty-one years old, her intestines actively bleeding, who informed her she had such a raging case of Crohn's Disease that she shouldn't expect to live past fifty. Some weeks, I could only watch while her body accepted nothing but bone broth, her fat stores dwindling to almost nothing. And then, like the moon, I'd watch her grow bigger again, healthy and able, until the next time she wasn't.

The day she compared our meeting to a thunderclap via text, I asked her to elaborate. *I register important events in my life that way, as a thunderclap*, she told me. I often wished I had been there for her earlier thunderclap moments: the day she got the keys to the building that would house her acupuncture practice, say, or the day she brought Marco home from the breeder, small and fluffy and impish. Mostly, I wish I could have been there the day of her Crohn's diagnosis, when she sat alone, scared, and small in a paper gown on the exam table.

It hits me like a thunderclap, the way one can love so fully in retrospect.

☾

What Katie didn't know when she told me about her thunderclap was that I am irrationally afraid of thunderstorms. She found out during our first winter together, when a south-south-westerly squall arrived just after the sun went down. It whipped up enough lightning to illuminate the house; enough thunder that the picture windows in the living room of the Castle shook and bent as if made of liquid. The skies churned.

Katie rubbed my back each time the thunder made me jump, the way I'd seen her do with Marco on the Fourth of July when fireworks exploded outside. "You're safe," she said. "The thunder is really far away." And she'd count the beats after each bolt of lightning, before the clap--*one Mississippi, two Mississippi, three Mississippi*--to prove it. When the power went out, we stoked the fire in the woodstove until the thunderclaps and lightning strikes came one after the other, the space between them razor thin.

I felt validated in my fear when I saw that each sonorous shake of the Castle had started to rattle Katie, too. She grabbed my waist and steered me toward the bedroom, away from the picture windows overlooking the bluff where the storm danced. Marco jumped up onto the foot of the bed, quaking, while my dog, Cricket, shook in her bed on the floor. With the covers pulled to our chins, Katie and I huddled together, noses touching, arms around each other. "It can't last too much longer," Katie reassured me. Rain from the cumulonimbus clouds pelted the bedroom window sideways. Katie's body was all warmth and harbor.

Under the duvet, I ran my fingers over her chiffon-soft skin. As the storm raged, I touched her lip with my thumb and then kissed her. Her body pulled even closer to mine as if I were magnet and she metal. Wordlessly, we undressed under the duvet; the warmth of skin-on-skin muted the sound of the gale-force winds outside. Against her body, my own came alive, and I ran my hands along the curvature of her spine, the silken luster of her thorax, until I had traced her lines to where they converged at the bottom of her pelvis. It felt as if I could channel the electrical properties of the storm outside and use them for my beloved's pleasure. Short bursts of sound from her lips punctuated the air, whispers against the tempest outside. Underneath me, Katie rose against my weight. I could control the quickness of her breath, the movement of her hips, with my fingers.

As she came, her teeth sunk into the soft flesh of my shoulder.

A thunderclap.

COLUMBIA RIVER BAR
(Chinook: *Wimahl*)

The squall lasted three days, and then a calm settled over the little horseshoe-shaped bowl that is Oceanside. For the next twenty-four hours, we watched as the masthead lights from ship after ship passed behind Three Arch Rocks, a veritable parade of recreational and commercial vessels. I sipped my tea and stared seaward at the tiny lights as they moved south, imagining each of the ships anchored for the last several days near the mouth of the Columbia River, that old graveyard of the Pacific, waiting out the storm and hoping for safe passage.

The Columbia River Bar is a torrent of roiling water where the mouth of the Columbia River sits like a three-mile-wide gaping maw between Oregon and Washington, and it is considered one of the most dangerous bar crossings on the planet. The river's current pushes more than one hundred and fifty billion gallons of fresh water a day into the brackish Pacific to create massive standing waves. With the Clatsop Spit to the south and Peacock Spit on the north (named so after the USS *Peacock* wrecked at the bar in 1841), vessels of all sizes need to exercise extreme caution at each crossing. The undertow, winds, and swells want only one thing, and that's to capsize your ship. The water under the bar is home to the corpses of thousands of such vessels, dismembered and covered in algae at the water's bottom.

Almost twenty years before this parade of ships made its way past the Castle windows, I had stood out on the south jetty of the bar with my close friend, Eileen. She had come to visit from Idaho, and it was our first time meeting in person. A mutual friend had introduced us a few years earlier via email, and since then, we'd exchanged almost daily long missives, sharing every intimate aspect of our lives with each other. We had so much in common: we were both

Mormon wives and mothers of young children, sure, but we were both also writers who taught college courses. I wanted to show Eileen the beauty of the Oregon coast, but for reasons I couldn't comprehend at the time, I was anxious about staying alone in a vacation rental with her, so I dragged my mom along as a sort of therapy dog.

It wasn't until many years later, after I had left the church and we subsequently stopped writing to each other, that I returned to that same south jetty and finally understood what I was afraid of. I looked out at the turbulent bar. Rain whipped sideways into my face; I pulled my beanie lower over my ears and watched two ships brave the passing. I had just begun to question the sustainability of my marriage, knowing I was on a crash course with my sexuality. I remembered Eileen on her visit all those years before, our shoulders touching on the same rocky berth, and I finally recognized the intimacy I'd formed with her as more than just friendship on my end. I'd included my mom more as a chaperone than a therapy dog.

One of the boats broached sideways when an exceptionally large wave broke over its beam, and I held my breath until it righted itself. Changing my life, I knew, was going to be as tumultuous as the ride these ships were now on. To go from my old self to my new would require the same kind of vigilance and care taken by the skippers on the water in front of me, and there was no guarantee of safe arrival. But to not make the crossing? That would be certain death.

So I waited.

And at the first sign of a slack tide, I went.

THE SAGEBRUSH SEA

What I am saying is that slack tide is sacred.

When describing slack tide on the Thames River, Matthew Hollis writes, "slack-tide is the river's most hypnotic moment, an occurrence of such serenity that even the terns become temporarily becalmed." I've been present at enough turns of the tide to know this serenity of which Hollis speaks. The whole ocean inhales at the last pull of tidal energy, then holds its breath. One beat, two beats, three beats, four. Do the microscopic sea creatures sense it, too, this pause? Do they hold as still as they can, the entire aquatic world in stasis, like a suspended moment of silence from the universe?

The first six months of my relationship with Katie felt like a sort of slack tide. Falling in love is like that. An invisible hand lowered a frosted glass cloche over me and my beloved, and within that safe enclosure, we were somehow not as vulnerable to the whims of the wider world. The wind blew around the cloche but not within it. Outside, time marched forward, but we didn't age. Sleep was a luxury but not a necessity. Food was indulgence but not need. The air around us bloomed with light the color of salmon and roses; somehow, it was always sunset.

But nobody can live in the slack of the cloche indefinitely. Six months into our fantasy whirlwind, we decided it was time to see if our love could withstand the pressures of the real world, the world that contained school schedules and softball practices and trips to the post office and therapy appointments. We were done with long distance. We wanted to start our lives together, for Katie to start getting to know my kids. Our only problem was that she owned a house in Oceanside, and I owned a house in Portland, and my custody schedule required that I be in the city every other week. It felt too soon to do anything drastic like sell her house, and financially keeping both just wasn't possible. We worked with Matt to come up with a nesting plan for the short term: he would live in the house in the city when he had custody and pay half the mortgage. When it was our turn in the city, we took over the house and he stayed with his partner in Salem.

The Wetlands. That's what I had long ago named the house in the city, because it backed up to protected wetlands that could never be developed. City on one side and swampland on the other. And after fifteen years of owning it, I was going to live there with Katie.

☾

The first order of business was to plant gardens at both houses. Katie had been an avid gardener for decades, and when she'd sold her house in Portland for her quiet life on the coast less than a year before meeting me, she'd said goodbye to a garden that produced thousands of pounds of food each season. For Katie, a garden is both a soul-massaging hobby and a necessity. One of the ways she controlled her digestive pain was by growing her own food.

We embarked on a quest for sun at the Wetlands. The house was in a neighborhood so treed that most residents barely needed air conditioning in the summer. The conifers held their green boughs aloft the way a dancer would a feathered boa, casting long swaths of shade over the roof and the entire yard. Decades-old cherry trees had started to overtake the roof and left woody pits to decay in the soil year-round. We had an arborist gauge the situation and decided to remove six of the most hazardous trees, hoping for just a few patches of sunlight on the ground where we could plant and harvest food for our table.

With the trees gone, the house stood out in a way it never had. It was one of the smallest in the neighborhood, overdue for repairs both inside and out. We spent the coming months following the sun around the yard with our eyes, clocking which spots on the lot got enough light to support the food we wanted to grow. That first spring, we planted rows of thornless blackberries, fall-fruiting black raspberries, and gooseberries in rows along the fences on both sides of the house. In the sunniest tract of yard, a patch that used to sit underneath the towering cherry tree, we moved cherry stones to plant artichokes and asparagus.

We finished the season by digging holes for bulbs, flowering currants, roses, and hellebores. We didn't have the money for the needed cosmetic repairs at the Wetlands, but we could disguise the problem with clusters of blossoms and exotic shrubbery. Daffodils would draw the eye from the stains under the covered walkway from an old leak; Easy Does It, an apricot-colored floribunda rose, would keep visitors from focusing on the fence where it was held up by two-by-fours and rotting on the bottom. We had a long way to go, but I'd never felt so self-reliant. We were making this house our home, and we were doing it without a man.

☾

Humanity, like all good things, was born in a garden. At least that's the story I'd been told so much it felt like it lived in my bloodstream. The Garden of Eden: verdant, lush, abundant. A temperate orchard paradise with perpetually fertile soil and an explosion of oversized plants.

Adam: just glance at the vine you like best, and berries will appear in your hand. Juice drips down your chin and onto your naked body. No matter. What do you care? Look there, to the right: a sheep lies with a wolf. What captures the light in the loose shale under your bare toes? It's a gemstone, a whole rainbow of them. That rushing sound from the north? One of four rivers that run through the garden. Splash in it, Adam. The water is neither hot nor cold. When you finish bathing, emerge onto the banks like the hero of a romance novel—water cascading down your glistening body in sheets to land in that loamy soil that squishes through your toes.

When you get lonely, God makes purchase with your rib, squeezes, pulls. You don't feel pain, just excitement when that rib transforms before your eyes into another person, the flawless, pristine specimen of a woman. (Do you see? It starts already. The binaries through which you are taught to see the world. The destinies that are determined by whether you were born first or as a bony afterthought.) She shakes her hair, maybe, outstretches her hand. Follow the lines of her body as they make their way downward, the sinews of her neck, her round breasts, her smooth abdomen, the tuft of hair just above her sex.

Take the fruit she offers you, even as it leads to your downfall. Hide yourself behind fig leaves when angels escort you both out of the garden into a life of toil and hardship, a world where the ground is rarely fertile and must be tamed with sweat and tears.

The world become wild. The wild as punishment.

What gives more comfort on those dark nights: the memory of the illicit fruit on your tongue, treacly and crisp, or the woman's body moving against yours, skin on skin on skin?

Remember that day in the garden, your hand on the yawning fissure in your chest where a rib once was, when God asked you what to call the woman?

You said, *Eve.*

Her name is Eve.

☾

Gardening at the Castle was entirely different from gardening at the Wetlands. Underneath the lawn and the huckleberries and the invasive Scotch broom, there was mostly sand. I thought of the old children's song from church, about the foolish man building his house upon the sand. No matter how deep we dug, we'd pull up handfuls of the stuff, fine and soft as if our house sat on the beach itself. We paid to have a dump truck deposit piles of moisture-laden dirt the color of expensive, one-hundred-percent dark chocolate. The truck backed slowly onto the property, announcing itself with incessant beeps that barely registered over the book I was reading. When I looked up, I saw Katie had plastered her whole body to the picture window, her tail practically wagging with excitement.

She turned and looked at me. "Do you just not have an inner six-year-old boy?" Her navy blue Carhartt's were slung low on her hips, and she tucked a strand of hair behind her right ear.

"Guess not," I shrugged. We spent the next several weekends spreading a six-inch layer of dirt over the existing lawn, then planted bulbs and other perennials.

The sand-under-it-all problem turned out to be only the first challenge of coastal gardening. The biggest challenge, of course, was also my favorite: the deer. It turned out our delivery of new soil served not only to nourish the ground and kill the weeds and grass beneath it; that dark dirt's superpower was to alert us every time a deer had been in the yard. Their cloven hooves sunk so deep into the sable soil that even the rain couldn't wash away the evidence they'd been munching our buffet. After just a week, we couldn't walk in the garden without stepping on a hoof print.

Katie was outside gardening in early spring while I finished a long writing day at the Castle. From his small bed next to my desk, Marco erupted into fevered barking. The desk was at the rear of the house, where the Castle cuddled against the mountain slope, and through the window, Marco had spotted three young deer perched on the forested incline about twenty feet from the back door. They were almost completely vertical, clinging with their hooves as they munched the veneer of red huckleberry shrubs that covered the mountainside. I wondered if Katie knew they were there, just feet away from where she was pulling weeds.

Marco was irate. The deer lifted their heads when his barks got especially shrill but seemed more curious than alarmed. I picked him up mid-growl and removed him from my office so he couldn't see the animals. Then I opened the sliding glass door to get a better look at them myself. The air was thick with dusk and petrichor, and all three animals raised their heads to look at me, their eyes glowing white. The one in the middle was missing tufts of fur from its coat, a sign the spring molt had begun. I could barely make out Katie's figure around the side of the house. She kneeled in the mud with her back to the deer and pulled on tufts of orange hawkweed. She had buds in her ears and I wondered what she was listening to.

I returned to my desk and stared at the screen. I'd just uncovered something in my research that I'd never known about the Mormon church. In the early 1840s, Joseph Smith traveled to Washington, DC, to demand protection from the mobs angry about polygamy and a promise of religious freedom. According to Smith, President Martin Van Buren told him "your cause is just, but I can do nothing for you," while senator Henry Clay offered only the terse admonishment that "you had better go to Oregon." Joseph himself, in a letter to Clay in 1844 just months before he died, mocked the sentiment: "Why, he is a real giant in humanity: send the Mormons to Oregon and free Missouri from debt and disgrace! Ah! . . . you must go to Oregon, and get justice from the Indians."

Marco still barked sporadically outside the office door, as if he could feel the deer's presence. *Send the Mormons to Oregon.* Despite Smith's open mockery, historical documents suggest that at the time of his jailhouse death a few months later, Smith might have been planning an exploratory expedition with the end goal of settling the Latter-Day Saints in the Oregon Territory.

Katie continued to work the soil, mud up to her knees, unaware she was being watched by curious ungulates. In turns, each of the three deer glanced in the direction of the house and then took off up the mountain to find tastier snacks, smashing sword ferns and weaving around Western red cedars. I couldn't hear them, but I imagined the sound their hooves made on downed limbs as they climbed the escarpment: *click, click, click.*

☾

My own trek to the Oregon Territory was a meandering one. I grew up a child on the move, living the transitory life of a military brat, minus the military. My dad worked for a nonprofit that transferred him to a new state every few years, so by the time I actually landed in Oregon at thirteen, it was the fifth western state I'd called home. Even though my mother was Oregon born and raised, and her parents, cousins, aunts, and uncles still called eastern and southern Oregon home, I'd never been there.

Families are endlessly complicated, and all I knew of my mother's upbringing was that her parents were alcoholics who in adulthood were never active in the faith, although they sent their kids to church with relatives each weekend to get them out of the house. My mother's descriptions of her childhood were as hardscrabble and desolate as her descriptions of that high desert landscape, the arid land windswept and barren, a place where you had to fight to survive.

But she spoke of it longingly, too. Yes, it was true that she and her older sister often had to drag their parents off the torn vinyl stools of the Golden Slipper, the only bar in town. True, too, that she worked tireless days in the barn and sugar beet fields beside her older siblings and surly father. But she also had hours—days, even—of uninterrupted exploration, mapping the parched land with her cousins and getting acquainted with the wild things that lived there. The land gave her the affection her parents didn't. Sagebrush and sunflowers at her feet, howling coyotes singing her to sleep.

This was the version of Oregon that I dragged with me from my birthplace in Idaho through Nevada, Colorado, and two stints in California. Dry but wild, hard but free. When I announced to my seventh grade PE class that I was moving to Portland at the end of the school year, my teacher laughed and said, "Have you ever heard of Oregon mist?" I shook my head, and she stuck the landing. "It's rain that has missed Oregon and hit us instead. Hope you have an umbrella."

I didn't care. I knew Oregon was an adventure and I also knew that we were likely to stay there in a way we had never stayed put before, because my dad was taking a brand new job with roots deep in the region. Before I ever lived there, I knew Oregon was home, even as the childhood I proceeded to have in the state was as different from my mother's as one could get.

☾

Oregon's high desert region has been given many names through the centuries. White pioneers in the nineteenth century gave it the confusing misnomer Great Sandy Desert, despite the region's lack of sand. Some settlers called it the Artemisia Desert, playing with the Latin genus name for the sagebrush, mug wort, and wormwood that dominate the landscape. Other names that didn't quite stick include the Rolling Sage Plain, the Great Wide Open, Oregon's Empty Quarter, and Oregon's Cowboy Country. Today, in addition to being known as the High Desert, some refer to it as Oregon's Outback.

Zoom out.

Oregon's Outback is a small part of the seemingly endless sagebrush prairies worn by the cavernous basins and spacious mesas of the Intermountain West. Collectively, the area is known as the Sagebrush Sea, a conglomerate of sagebrush-steppe habitats stretched over five hundred thousand miles of the United States, from the Dakotas to California, including the southeasternmost swath of Oregon. It is a sea with rolling waves of bluebunch wheatgrass, Indian paintbrush, and mariposa lilies, all adapted to live on under twelve inches of rain a year. An ocean of sagebrush instead of saltwater, where tumbleweed rolls through almost as regularly as the tide, where Oregon pink shrimp become grasshoppers, fish become pygmy rabbits, and sharks become cougars.

It was this sea of sagebrush that Henry Clay likely pictured when he told Joseph Smith to settle in the Oregon Territory and not the lush greenery and rain forests that prevail west of the Cascade Mountains. Oregon must have seemed like a real two birds, one stone situation: here was a wild place that the United States wanted to claim as its own, and the Mormons were causing endless headaches in Missouri. But the prophet's death in 1844 meant that any dreams of a mass exodus of Mormons to Oregon were squelched. Instead, his successor Brigham Young changed course to elsewhere in the Great Basin, deciding to settle instead in Utah.

The US government might not have succeeded in getting the Mormons to leave Missouri for Oregon initially, but the religion spread quickly west from Utah, thanks to robust missionary work. By 1850, Young had sent the first Mormon missionaries over the border into Oregon, and Ft. Lemhi, the first official Mormon settlement in the Oregon Territory, was founded on June 15, 1855. Expansion of Mormon settlements throughout Idaho and eastern Oregon continued for decades; many families (my ancestors among them) were sent there at the behest of the church-owned sugar monopoly, the Utah-Idaho Sugar Company. Today, Mormonism is the second largest religion in Oregon, after Catholicism.

I can claim Oregon as home not just because my dad got a job there, not just because my mom was raised there, but because I am the product of a people who tried to tame the Sagebrush Sea with sugar beets.

☾

I have never touched a sugar beet; I've never even seen one in person. But sometimes it feels like I owe my existence to that giant pallid root.

In the late 1800s, the prophet Wilford Woodruff "obtained a revelation from God telling him to establish the beet sugar industry in Utah," according to Matthew Godfrey's book *Religion, Politics and Sugar*. It turned out to be a profitable prophecy; in a relatively short time frame, Mormons not only created that sugar beet company but wracked up immense dividends for both the church and individuals with land to farm. The resulting Amalgamated Sugar Company in Utah monopolized the sugar industry for almost half a century. A high school in Sandy, Utah, still proudly claims the mascot "Beetdiggers." On the first day of each school year, the students and teachers take bites out of sugar beets still muddy from the earth.

The sugar company spread north to Burley, Idaho, and the Mormons followed. The land and climate in Burley were ripe for farming beets and running the factories that extracted their sucrose and turned it into crystals. My grandparents, Willard Judd and Ethel Ray, met and married in Burley during the Great Depression. As work became scarce, a large portion of the family followed the beets west when a sugar processing factory opened in Nyssa, Oregon, in 1938. Along with the factory, the Utah-Idaho Sugar Company had lobbied for a siphon in the county, which in turn gifted irrigation water to all the newly divided plots of previously fallow land. Willard and Ethel used their savings for a downpayment on eighty acres of that new farmland, visions of sugar beets dancing in their heads.

I grew up with tales of that eighth of a section and the sweet taproots that were planted there year after year. When my brothers and I complained about taking out the trash, say, or helping my mom dust the living room, we were regaled with tales of my mom and her three siblings working to thin and hoe beets during the leanest years when her father couldn't afford to hire migrant workers. She recalled the work as grueling and tedious, the sun scorching into the nineties and above. Twice a summer they tackled the weeds; they'd pull them, roots and all, from the dirt with their hands, and using a hoe, they'd work their way down each long row one at a time. After several rows up and back, Willard would grant them a ten-minute break, during which Ethel gave them each a warm mason jar full of water and a stick of Doublemint gum to keep their mouths moist. At the end of the break, Ethel always recited the same sing-song-y jingle: "Off of your asses, onto your feet; out of the shade, into the heat."

I saw that piece of land once, the old family farm. The summer I finished high school, my mom and I road-tripped to eastern Oregon so she could attend her thirtieth high school reunion. We drove out to the old homestead. When I asked my mom who owned the land now, she shrugged her shoulders.

Where a home and a farm—however destitute—once stood was now simply nothing. The clapboard house was long gone. The stone outbuilding in the back where her brothers slept with the sheep in the winter was gone, too, as was the cattle corral. No sugar beets, no barn cats. No indication the land had ever been tilled or played on. A long stretch of dry dirt that wouldn't feed a single steer, let alone a herd. That night, I sat and read in the only hotel in town while my mom met her classmates at the Golden Slipper, this time to catch up with childhood friends instead of to pull her sloshed parents from the barstools.

We drove home through the most remote parts of the state, quadrants I only knew existed in the abstract. We pulled into the town of John Day for a brief stopover on our way to see some of my mom's cousins. Near a bend in the John Day River, I sat on the porch of a manufactured home with second cousins I'd never met. They talked of long days in the lumber mill and 4-H, and none of them followed my mother's strict rules against double negatives and the word *ain't*. When I told them I had never touched a cow, they were too baffled to laugh. My life in the city was as foreign to them as their rural existence was to me.

We weren't even a half mile down the road when I looked down and realized I was wearing my favorite anti-logging shirt, and I saw myself the way they must have—as a city girl, out of touch with her rural roots.

☾

My future wife grew up in the Palouse, just four hours north of Vale, the tiny town where my ancestors settled to grow sugar beets. And like my ancestors, she was a practical gardener. She wasn't after perfect symmetry, following rules, or curb appeal. She wanted delicious food to eat and as much of it as possible, and some flowers for cutting throughout the spring and summer. She wanted a personal oasis where she could get her hands dirty each morning and lubricate her joints. Fresh air. A conversation with the earth.

After the trees were gone from the Wetlands, our next project was beating back a one-hundred-foot stretch of invasive Himalayan blackberries that measured twenty-five feet deep. It was spring by then, and the brambles reached heights upwards of ten feet. If you haven't spent time west of the Cascades, you might not know of the devil that is the invasive blackberry. It colonizes land that was once wild but has since been disturbed—logged areas, along roadsides and fenced corridors. Left unchecked, its vigorously re-sprouting rhizomes and root crowns will take over an entire yard, encircling garden plants in a thorny embrace and slowly swallowing whole swaths of otherwise fertile soil.

We could grow so much food in that patch of land.

We stared at the meandering shoots, at the leaves with serrated edges, at the density of those brambly canes. And what came to mind was the Great Pacific Garbage Patch. Located somewhere between Hawaii and California, it is the largest accumulation of ocean plastics on our planet. The percentage of the ocean it takes up might be equivalent to the amount of our yard held hostage by the Great Wetlands Blackberry Patch: currently, it is an estimated 1.6 million square kilometers. That means it is roughly six times the size of the state of Oregon. Ripping out our blackberries wouldn't save the planet, but it could save our yard.

We donned long sleeves, boots to our knees, and thick gloves. We stared those briars down and then jumped in, trimmers in hand. We cut the canes close to the ground and pulled them as we went. Some of the stems were rooted in the ground on both ends. Thorns passed straight through the fabric of my work gloves and embedded themselves in my palms. When I stopped to tend to my hands, spots of blood oozed in multiple places over my skin.

And then I wasn't in the Great Wetlands Blackberry Patch or the Great

Pacific Garbage Patch. I was ten years old, near Coos Bay, Oregon, the rural coastal town where Ethel and Willard moved during my mom's junior year of high school. My cousin Andrea and I walked along a wild ridge with a view of the water. The waves roared in our ears. We each had an old mixing bowl in our hands, and we filled them with plump, ripe blackberries. They were dark as obsidian on the bushes, but when we picked them, they left a bloom of red juice that would stain our skin for days.

Wouldn't you know it, I thought to myself. I *had* been to Oregon as a child, before we ever moved there. I remembered it now: a gathering for my grandparents' fiftieth wedding anniversary, one of only two instances in my life that I spent any time with either of them.

I remembered fifths of whisky hidden behind the dishes in the kitchen cupboard. Ethel grumbling to my mom over coffee that *your kids get up too damn early.*

I remembered the plastic mixing bowls filled with blackberries. That we thought we might fall off the cliff into the sea below. The admonition from our mothers earlier that we stay away from that cliff. The scratches on my calves and arms.

The juice on my tongue, sweet and tart. The red on my lips and cheeks.

How Eve must have felt.

☾

Beta vulgaris: that's the name Carl Linnaeus, in his quest to label and categorize the natural world, first gave to the plants we know as beets in 1753. Sugar beets are grown from seed and have the ability to grow in traditionally difficult soils—heavy clay, sandy loam. Above ground, the plant is all green leafy rosettes, while under the soil lies the edible white taproot, a conical, fleshy tuber with an even crown. Photosynthesis in the verdant rosettes creates sugar that then gets stored in the root, and that's what Ethel, Willard, and the rest of the Mormons were after. Fully grown sugar beets clock in at as much as four pounds, up to twenty-two percent of which is pure sucrose.

In 2009, a year after becoming prophet of the Mormon church, Thomas S. Monson gave an address broadcast from the pulpit that he titled "Sugar Beets and the Worth of a Soul." In it, he uses the sugar beet—and its pivotal role in the success of the great Mormon experiment in Utah—to make the assertion that church members should do everything in their power to recover wayward Saints. "Picture with me, if you will, a farmer driving a large open-bed truck filled with sugar beets en route to the sugar refinery," Monson's talk begins. "As the farmer drives along a bumpy dirt road, some of the sugar beets bounce from the truck and are strewn along the roadside. When he realizes he's lost some beets, he [tells] his helpers, 'There's just as much sugar in those which have slipped off. Let's go back and get them.'"

The beets, of course, are a metaphor. Per Monson, I am one of those wayward sugar beets tossed from the back of the open-bed truck. Look at the crown of leaves on my head. Look at my blanched pallor. This is how the church justifies sending missionaries to my house, and the repeated calls from Salt Lake City over the years to ferret out my inactive brothers' whereabouts. Eventually, after I die, this is how they will justify submerging a young girl (twelve? thirteen?) in the chlorinated water of the baptismal font at the temple in my name, believing she is doing the Lord's work of bringing yet another sugar beet to the refinery. I hope when they dunk her in the font that there is a moment before they pull her back up—slack, if you will—when a jolt in her recognizes the woman I was and the person she could be. She'll rise from her immersion, her white zippered jumpsuit wet and clinging to her body, hair pasted to her cheeks. And maybe she'll ask herself if this is something I even wanted, if she even has the right. And maybe a leader will tell her to take that doubt and put it high up on her shelf, to keep moving forward, to be baptized again and again, each time in someone else's name.

Maybe she won't do it.

☾

At the Castle, we asked the only local arborist if he'd be willing to dump his unwanted wood chips on our lawn. We hoped to suffocate the grass and turn the sandy soil into something more fertile. Within a few days, he called to tell us his crew had removed trees from a neighboring property and half an hour later, the truck beeped its way onto our property, engaged its hydraulics, and left a sizable mountain of bark chips.

We tackled the mountain in small increments over the coming weeks. We'd climb to the top of the pile in our boots with rakes and shovels, then slowly spread the mulch until it sat in an eight-inch layer on top of the existing lawn.

Every few minutes, one of us would unearth a whole oyster shell from the pile. This meant our garden beds, as we spread the chips, were scattered with smooth, nacreous shells. Where had they come from? I'd heard that oyster shells make good mulch, but these were whole and not ground, so they wouldn't do us much good on that front. Mostly we were dying to know: how did the removal and subsequent chipping of fir trees result in the skeletal remains of so much shellfish?

I pictured our wood chips *before* they were pulverized. When they were still part of a larger whole, on a mountain that used to be all forest, standing in the way on someone's homestead. Something wild being removed for something cultivated. I pictured hundred-foot-tall Douglas firs, oysters hanging in the place of cones. Full-bodied, alive, thriving as if in water. Ready to be eaten, ready to be pearled. The oyster trees swayed in the wind for hundreds of years, until they were climbed and felled by men with chainsaws. And now the remnants of wood and oysters were in our yard, would help grow our asparagus, our artichokes, our fruit trees.

(Unless the deer got to them first. As we spread the wood chips, we'd come across the remnants of dozens of tulips which the deer had munched to the ground. Maybe that's where the oyster flesh went. Maybe the deer swallowed the pearls.)

What is gardening, after all, but cultivating wildness? Michael Pollen asserts that "wildness is more a quality than a place, and though humans can't manufacture it, they can nourish and husband it. . . . The gardener cultivates wildness, but he does so carefully and respectfully, in full recognition of its mystery."

What greater mystery than pearl-less oysters falling from trees? After a long day of chip-spreading, I climbed into bed next to Katie, too tired to shower. We were both covered in a small film from the Oyster Tree bark. I rolled over, wrapped my arm around my love, and kissed her shoulder through her pajamas.

"Goodnight, my little sugar beet," I whispered.

She pressed her back into my belly. "Shit, I love it when you call me that."

☾

If I can queer the wild enough to make oysters grow on trees, what else is possible? Maybe the Tree of Knowledge wasn't a fruit tree at all. Maybe it was a conifer. Maybe in those seven days of creation, God was able to grow a coastal redwood tree that would have taken a thousand years or more to grow in regular earth-time. And maybe that redwood didn't grow pinecones or oysters. Maybe it grew sugar beets. You can tell me this is a stretch, but listen: if a woman can be created from her husband's rib, why not beets on trees?

Joseph Smith himself wasn't opposed to queering Christian's creation story. I grew up believing the Garden of Eden was located in what is now Jackson City, Missouri. And Adam was more than just the first human: he was also the archangel Michael, who worked with God and Jesus in the "pre-existence" before the world was formed, and was pivotal in planning and executing the Plan of Salvation. I learned the extent of this doctrine that first time through the temple, where as part of the ceremony they play a video that depicts Adam/Michael assisting in the actual creation of the earth and the heavens. Some of the church's apostles have theorized that Adam played a role later in the execution of the plan as well, appearing as the archangel Michael when Jesus was praying and bleeding from every pore in the Garden of Gethsemane.

Adam (Michael): when the woman from your rib takes your hand and leads you to a giant tree, look up. Regard its fibrous red bark, its deep furrows. Note the rounded burls that bulge at its base. Trace the trunk upwards and use your newly created eyes to zoom in on the leaves, arranged in a spiral on the main shoots and resembling scales. And there, on a branch you can reach if you stand on your naked toes, hangs a sugar beet, at once both growing straight from the branch but also covered in dirt, as if pulled from the earth. If the woman says it is good, it must be good.

Name the tree: *Sequoia sempervirens.*

Name the fruit: *Beta vulgaris.*

You know the minute you sink your teeth into the bitter white beet-flesh that the woman has bested you. There is nothing to savor here.

But who is more disappointed, Adam? You? Or the woman who bit into it first, who tasted only hints of sweet beyond that bitterness, who felt duped when no juice dripped down her chin?

Name the woman: Eve.

CLIFFS, SEAWALLS, SALT MARSHES, PEBBLE BEACHES

Would you believe me if I told you that the sugar beet's closest wild relative is the sea beet? When Carl Linnaeus published the second edition of *Species Plantarum* in 1762, he divided beets into wild and cultivated varieties. The cultivated beets, including the sugar beet, kept the moniker *Beta vulgaris,* while the decidedly wild taxon was gifted the subspecies *maritima. Beta vulgaris maritima.* Beets of the sea. And not even the Sagebrush Sea. I mean the one with saltwater and swinging tides.

Sea beets are to sugar beets what gray wolves are to Cricket and Marco. The wild version of the thing we've tamed. These beets-of-the-sea are native to the cliffs, seawalls, salt marshes, and pebble beaches of Europe, North Africa, and Asia. They grow prolifically in rubbish heaps and along roadsides but are never far from the ocean.

What I am trying to tell you is that I am doing what Linnaeus did. I am not the father of modern taxonomy, but I am trying to make sense of the world. I am trying to determine what is wild and what has been domesticated. Which parts of me were meant to grow on seaside cliffs and which parts of me were planted after the fact—by Joseph Smith's own hands, by my parents, by Ethel and Willard, by the youth leader I once deemed safe enough to confide in about my skepticism who told me to lock those doubts up and put them on a shelf in my mind, out of sight.

The cultivated variety—the one they called *Elissa Minor,* then *Elissa Minor Rust,* then *Elissa Minor* again—versus the wild one, the one that is decidedly *Elissa Minor Maritima.*

No.

The one in a garden. The one who goes by *Eve.*

THE SHAME VAULT

My therapist likes to ask me, *What does that feel like in your body*?

Shame sinks in my abdomen, heavy as a log rolling in with the tide. It's taken me years to recognize shame for what it is: a weighted vault that holds a million secrets. Sometimes it feels as if that vault will sink inside me and pin me to the earth. That I will meet my end in a humble river like Virginia Woolf, my pockets filled with shame instead of rocks.

Those things that weigh us down, the things we carry in our pockets or in our palms or in our secret hearts that prevent us from moving forward?

A beached log. A sugar beet. A handful of river rocks. A cup filled with spit.

Shame. All of it.

☾

Concerned about the rise in syphilis cases toward the end of the 1930s, the New York City Works Progress Administration Federal Art Project designed a poster to admonish those with symptoms to seek treatment before it was too late. The design is that of a genderless person, all blue, hiding their face behind their hands.

Above the image, in massive red font:

Shame May Be Fatal.

THE WESTERN INTERIOR SEAWAY

My dad loved Matt. When Matt was on his mission, my father wrote to him almost as regularly as I did. With glass-like clarity, he told me in no uncertain terms that Matt should be my choice. That I'd be crazy to let him go.

Maybe it wasn't that my dad loved Matt (though he surely did), but more that Matt was the kind of man parents begged their Mormon daughters to marry. Kind to a fault, steady and even, slow to temper. Clean cut, committed to the gospel. The kind of man whose coattails a woman could ride to the Celestial Kingdom. My dad loved the things Matt could offer me: the safe temple marriage, a constellation of children. Dad saw in Matt what he never saw in either of his own sons: the desire to stay righteous, to be a priesthood leader and the head of an eternal family, sealed for time and all eternity in the temple.

My grandfather saw it, too. A week before our wedding, Matt and I had dinner at my grandparents' house. We ate our fill of Grandma's lemon chicken, green beans almondine, and ambrosia salad, and then my grandfather—a Bishop himself—pulled me aside and said, "You should know that I see Matt as an important instrument in the gospel. He will be a Bishop, a Stake President, maybe more. The most important job *you* have is to keep him righteous and support him."

When I was little, Grandpa would take me to the swap meet on Saturday mornings. We'd wake early, before my parents and brothers, so we'd arrive at the sprawling asphalt of the fairgrounds right when the gates opened. Between his truck and the entry, he'd tell me to put my hand in his jacket pocket. I knew what I would feel: the waxy rounded skin of an apple so big my small palm couldn't cover it. There was one for him in his other pocket; we lifted them to our mouths for a simultaneous crisp bite.

There were so many ways in which the people I loved most vehemently in the world were complicit in a system meant to silence and contain me.

☾

I spent much of my early childhood in Colorado, the Rocky Mountains as the backdrop against which we went about our daily lives. Looking west from our town, we could see the tallest peaks of the Front Range: Mount Spalding, Epaulet Mountain, Rosalie Peak, Rogers Peak, Mount Goliath, Mount Evans. And my favorite one, only because of its name: Gray Wolf Mountain. We'd drive down the 1-25 corridor and my dad would point out Longs Peak and Pikes Peak. My parents loved the mountains so much that for that brief period of my childhood, each of the peaks felt like a family member.

My uncle Dennis (my mom's brother, who ran early from the church and never looked back, who left the sugar beets for a prestigious career in academia) owned a vacation home in Leadville, an old mining town high in the Rockies. A few times a year, my parents would fill the old silver Volkswagen Dasher with diesel and their three young children, and we'd set out for a free vacation when Denny wasn't using the house. Leadville was only a hundred miles from home, but we might as well have been boarding a rocket and launching to the moon for how different the world felt almost as soon as we left the city.

The Dasher would hug the mountain with every curve, all of us singing along to John Denver and feeling tiny in our metallic wagon against all those mammoth rocks. The peaks were vastly different from the ones I would come to know so intimately in Oregon, though both the Cascades and the Rocky Mountains were formed in similar ways by the dance of shifting tectonic plates in the past one hundred million years. The Cascade Range was built like an elaborate layered cake painstakingly assembled over time; the Rockies, in contrast, were furrowed into being like the satin ruffles of an eighties wedding dress.

In Leadville, we settled into Denny's house. I loved the spiral staircase, the vintage telephone with a functional rotary dial and classic gold bell, the cast iron clawfoot bathtub where my mom bathed all three of us kids at the same time. During the day, we traipsed through snow drifts in Moon Boots, stopping regularly to catch our breath because the ten-thousand-foot elevation was tough on our bodies. I felt the pressure in my chest, the searing pain behind my eyes, that meant we'd gone too high too fast. When it got particularly bad, Dad would carry me on his shoulders.

In a rare picture of him from that era (he was more likely to be the one *behind* the camera), he stands in profile against a snowy street, his eyes concealed by mirrored sunglasses, gloved hands on his hips. He's wearing a bright red puffy ski jacket zipped to his chin. Behind him, a spire rises as if from nothing but snow. It's the steeple of the Catholic church directly across the street from my uncle's house, the one I saw every day when I looked out the window of the second-story bedroom where my brothers and I slept.

☾

I was twenty-eight and the mother of two small children when my dad knocked on my door, disoriented and groggy. He mentioned his right arm had been twitching and shaking earlier in the day. As we talked, he fell asleep midsentence and slurred his words—evidence that something was seriously wrong. In the next few days, we learned that he had been experiencing seizures, brought on by a large diffuse tumor roughly half the size of a banana (why is it always fruit?) that had infiltrated his left frontal lobe. The part of the brain that regulates personality and judgment. The tumor was mean and aggressive, like he would become, and deep. Tentacled into healthy brain tissue, it was hard for his doctors to tell what was tumor and what wasn't. They could treat it for a while, but the damage was irreversible and the tumor, we were told, would kill him.

Those were the years my mom and I became well versed in the vocabulary of brain tumors. Fifteen years later, I can still rattle off my dad's tumor type (anaplastic oligodendro-astrocytoma, grade III) and his daily drug cocktails (Temodar, Dilantin, Decadron) almost as mindlessly as I can call to mind the lullabies I sang my babies.

His brain tumor did more than change the basic makeup of his brain. The tumor's tentacles made their way down the street, invisibly, into my own home, my own faith, my own marriage. I made my decision to leave the church while my dad was in an ICU bed after his first brain surgery. He lived another two-and-a-half years, but he never came back to us after that resection. Not really.

When you become a caretaker for the man who used to nurture you (talking him down from hallucinations, filling in the gaps of his lost memory, administering medication, and steadying him when he walks), you start to examine things, to ask the big questions. In my case, I had been asking the big questions for years, but Dad's decline forced me to find answers. And in answering them, I upset the delicate balance that was my life, my marriage, my foundation. I ripped the crisp white tablecloth from under the dishes, and then I held my breath for years, wondering how many of those dishes would shatter and how many would spin for a bit and then come to a stop, unbroken, on the now-naked table.

☾

My favorite time to visit Leadville was winter; the entire town was covered in an afghan of snow and its attendant silence. The church across the street was dressed in a white skirt, its stained-glass windows wearing an almost invisible extra skin of ice crystals. From the window in the sunroom where we sat and drank our hot chocolate, we would watch the nuns who lived next door walk back and forth between the Victorian-home-turned-convent and the steepled church. Sometimes, their giant cats would follow them through the snow, each long-haired feline closer to a medium-sized dog than any cat I've ever known. For years, I thought high altitudes and alpine air made creatures grow unfathomably large.

If we hit it in the sweet spot between December and March, we had a green light after our hot chocolate to take sleds down Dutch Henry Hill. Dutch Henry Hill was every eighties kid's dream. It didn't look like a hill to me and my brothers. To us, it was a mountain on par with the peaks surrounding it. We were never brave enough to take our sleds to the very top; we'd seen too many others gain enough excess speed to end up thrown from their sleds well before the bottom of the run.

But Dad was brave. And I was, too, when I was in front of him on his sled. It didn't matter how fast we were careening down that giant hill, how blurry the trees and people got, how wind-whipped my nose and cheeks, if I was cradled against his two-hundred-pound, six-foot frame. I trusted him to steer. I trusted him to slow to a stop when the time was right. Like the nun's giant cats, Alpine Dad was invincible. And with his arms wrapped around me as the blinding sunlight bounced off the snow, wasn't I, too?

☾

Whenever I was near Dad, a grisly image lodged itself in my head. I was so close to the vile thing that had taken my father from me. If I could only . . . reach . . . just right there, a few inches beneath his skull . . . and yank . . . then out would come what remained of the damned half-banana-sized growth, snapping tentacles and all.

It might be impossible to see someone you love lying in the intensive care unit (comatose, his head covered in white bandages, a shunt draining fluid from his brain, a feeding tube cascading from one nostril) without seeing yourself in that same bed. My dad was just over fifty. His neurosurgeon answered honestly when my brothers and I asked: yes, his tumor type did have a slight genetic link. The questions came in fits when I took my shifts at his bedside, wondering if he would wake up. Were that me, what would I want to have done with my time? How do I want to have lived?

Some of the answers were easy. Most people run toward faith and meaning in times of crisis. I guess you could say I did the opposite. I saw my dedication to the church of my youth, the church of my ancestors, as the weighty extra that was pushing things in my life out of balance. At any given time, I could easily log ten to thirty hours a week in service to the Mormon church.

And though it was the religion upon which my marriage was founded, upon which my parents' marriage was founded, and theirs before them, it was a religion I could no longer say I believed in. The cracks in my faith had for years been coalescing into a tangled mass not unlike the one in my dad's cerebral tissue. Invisible enough to discount until, one day, it had grown too big to ignore. I could try to address it, or I could watch as I let it kill me.

Of course, with tumors and faith alike, things are always more complex than yank-and-pull.

I told Matt I was done with Mormonism the same week that Dad was moved from intensive care to a standard hospital room, then I swapped out my garments for bikini briefs. I walked past an espresso cart in the local library, and instead of ordering my typical hot chocolate or steamed milk, I shrugged my shoulders and decided that twenty-nine was as good an age as any to try coffee for the first time. I chose a drink based on its picture: a s'mores mocha, replete with whipped cream, chocolate sauce, and graham cracker crumbs. But two sips later, the mocha was in the trash, and I was looking for a water fountain to rinse the burnt, bitter taste from my mouth.

Almost two decades later, I still can't handle the smallest taste of coffee, even in a dessert. A voice always accompanies that bitter taste, loud and angry. A voice I can't hear over. A voice that tells me I am sinful, that I need to get back in line. A voice that also taunts me about never being able to fit in with the world outside of that pioneer-and-polygamy bubble.

The voice is my own.

I will never not be Mormon, much as it is my heart's greatest wish. I will always be the product of a system designed by cisgendered men to keep me quiet, compliant, and solicitous. And I will always be complicit in helping to maintain that system, as were my parents before me, and their parents before them. One serving of funeral potatoes at a time.

My dad's malignancy killed him, but I'm still learning to live with mine.

☾

I am trying to reconcile the man who would never let me fall off his sled with the man who sat me down at sixteen to tell me a cautionary tale about homosexuality.

It was after midnight, and I'd snuck down to the kitchen for a leftover slice of my mom's banana cream pie. The crust recipe was passed down from her mother, who got it from her own mother. Maybe the recipe even crossed the South Pass of the Continental Divide with a Mormon handcart company. However it got to Oregon, I was happy to shovel its flaky, tender pieces into my mouth at all hours of night.

Dad appeared just before my first bite in his striped pajamas. "Great minds think alike," he said and opened the fridge to serve himself a slice. He sat across from me at the table and scooped freshly whipped cream from a bowl onto his pie.

I shoved my plate in his direction and nodded toward the whipped cream. "Hit me," I said. We both settled to devour our midnight snack.

"I've been thinking about a friend of mine," he said. I waited for him to continue. "This guy left his wife and the church because he was gay."

"Sounds brave. Can you imagine being gay and Mormon?" I mused. Dad put his fork down.

"'Lissa. The guy told me afterward that it wasn't worth it and he never should have left."

"Why wasn't it worth it?"

"Sex is never worth losing your faith and your family." He looked at me, hard. I knew better than to push back on the point, and by his seriousness I knew he believed he was imparting important wisdom.

I've wondered in the years since my dad died if there was any such friend. Had he seen the queerness in me that I hadn't yet recognized myself? Or am I reading too much into the past?

☾

One of the terms we learned early on was the phenomenon of "midline shift," when the tumor and swelling brain tissue push the affected hemisphere over into the next, rendering the entire brain off-center and asymmetrical. A shift like this, even a subtle one, can of course have all sorts of untoward effects. It throws off a person's center. By the time of his death, my dad walked slanted forward and slightly to the left. He couldn't accurately track an object and tell you when it was directly in front of his face.

It's a metaphor I still find myself turning to in times of serious searching. When I remember my dad's diagnosis, I see it as a sort of barometer that told me what things in my own life were shifting the midline. Some neurologists implement a test for midline shift in patients who are cognitively unable to respond to other tests: examine the soles of the patient's shoes over time. Wear on the toes of the shoes shows significant anterior midline shift; wear on the heels can indicate posterior shift. It's a strange notion, that you can be so sure you are in proportion to the real physical world, even when your entire inner compass is off. I had begun to feel that way about my life.

☾

At about the halfway point in my family's drive to Leadville, we'd approach a different kind of midline. The Eisenhower-Johnson Memorial Tunnel would appear from a distance, two twin bores under the mountain's tree line into which the road disappeared. We all knew what the tunnel meant, but my dad insisted on making a big show of it anyway. "We are approaching the continental divide! Here it comes!" I didn't understand what a continental divide was, or why it was so cool to be driving across one, but I got just as excited as my parents did.

Every continent but Antarctica has at least one divide. The one traversed by the Eisenhower Tunnel is often called The Great Divide and runs from the western edge of Alaska's Seward Peninsula, down along the crest of the Canadian Rockies, through Glacier National Park and Yellowstone, along the ridge line of the Rockies in Colorado, and eventually makes its way along the Sierra Madre Occidental and into the tip of South America. The Great Divide splits North America in half the way a midline divides two hemispheres of a brain. To the east of the divide, all water flows to the Atlantic—every river, every drop of rain, every ounce of melted snow—while to the west of the divide, all water drains and flows to the Pacific.

Dad would command us all to hold our breath for good luck, as we did through every tunnel. We knew we'd never make it. The dark tunnel was just shy of two miles long, and even if Dad was able to drive it at full speed, our young lungs would never withstand that lack of oxygen. But we never stopped trying. We'd drive that little Dasher east into the tunnel with our collective breath sucked in and held taut, the rivers at our backs (the Columbia, the Colorado) rushing toward the Pacific and re-emerge into a world where the rivers in front of us (the Missouri, the Rio Grande) all coursed in the opposite direction.

Like magic. A sleight of hand. The Rockies' snowy tablecloth ripped out below all those trees.

I used to think the Great Divide was some invisible line that couldn't be shifted or changed at the whims of nature or people, the way I pictured the giant axis upon which the earth rotated. But the divide is really a hydrological feature, a physical byproduct of the earth's volcanic whims, whims that are continuously changing and cycling. But it isn't just that the divide itself is constantly undergoing subtle shifts. Our very understanding of the divide and its importance are the result of cultural and political constructs. James D. Drake says in "A Divide to Heal the Union: The Creation of the Continental Divide" that "geodetic data alone could not produce the divide. It arose as much from the mental maps of Americans who pondered the meaning of secession to national identity, who sought understanding amid bloodletting, as it did from the work of explorers and mapmakers. . . a place where the United States created a national monument in the guise of a geographical phenomenon, a place where the nation turned its history into nature."

In a massive political campaign, the mostly northern, union-loyal operators of the United States during and after the Civil War worked to shape the concept of a country they were once told ended naturally at the Rockies and now would end naturally at the sea.

They quite literally shifted the midline.

I'm doing it here, too. Can you see it? I am making the continental divide the centerline of this chapter, I am building a metaphor around it that suits my purpose. I am making a construct of a construct.

☾

Listen, I am no longer surprised that nothing is as it seems.

When explorer and cartographer John Charles Fremont originally described the area where the Divide runs through Wyoming, he discovered the Great Basin. Drake explains, "The Great Basin belies the existence of a Great Divide, at least conceived as a line through the mountains from which all water on either side flows into one of two oceanic basins. Much water flowing off the west side of the Rockies simply has no chance of making it to the Pacific."

I am forced to reinterpret those long, oxygen-deprived sprints in the Dasher across the Divide.

It isn't that the Great Divide tells rivers which way to flow. The Divide *itself* actually spawned many of those rivers; the Columbia and the Colorado, two of the rivers that run through the narrative of my childhood, can trace their origins to a small trickle somewhere along that mountainous divide, two trickles among millions that never made it past the Rockies.

And because water proceeds all life, in that way, we were passing through the origin of so many things.

A new kind of Eden. An apple-in-your-grandpa's-pocket kind of Eden.

☾

Our frontal lobes do more than just control personality and executive functioning. When damaged just right, they cause a confusing increase in sexual urges and behavior.

In my dad, the hyper-sexuality started immediately after he came out of his post-surgery coma. He would replace words in everyday conversation with sexually charged terms: *They brought me chocolate pudding with lunch,* for example, might become *They brought me scrotum pudding for that hot nurse.* Nurses new on shift would be in the room for one minute before looking at us and saying, "Frontal lobe, huh?"

When we were caring for Dad at home, he once managed to get up in the night and start a fire in the living room that my mom caught just quickly enough to contain. He'd been trying to use the wood stove but had neglected to close the doors after he tossed in the match. When my mom stomped out the fire, she saw what he had been trying to burn: stacks of nudie magazines. Apparently the tumor boring through his frontal lobe did not destroy his ability to be driven by shame. After he died, I felt it for him in his stead. Shame runs deep, straight through generations.

Seeing the impact of physical brain changes on personal and sexual behavior went a long way towards obliterating the constructs I'd been taught about gender and sexuality. More so, it shattered the constructs I'd been taught about an all-powerful and all-knowing deity. It became impossible to go back to believing that we had any control over who we were as people, that there was a god who would judge us for actions that might be out of our immediate control. Mostly, it destroyed any notions I had about the separation of mind and body.

Years after he died, my mom told me that in Dad's youth, he had been repeatedly sexually assaulted by an older male cousin. He had never told anyone but her, and even then, she knew very few details. Psychotherapist Kalie Munro writes, "Survivors of male-to-male sexual abuse have to contend with the additional stigma and impact of homophobia, which increases their shame, isolation, and secrecy. Equating the abuse with gay sex leaves most survivors confused and conflicted about their sexuality. If they identify as straight, they may experience homophobic fear and panic that maybe they really aren't." In my dad's case, it might have led to his distrust of queer people in general. But that's just speculation. I will never know.

There are so many things I will never know, and they all haunt me. But mostly it comes down to this: would he have embraced Katie the way he did Matt? Would I have held my place as the favored daughter, the one so devoted to being good and *doing the right thing,* if he had lived long enough to find out that I am gay?

After his death, my mom never again attended a Mormon meeting. She was done, as were her sons and then her daughter before her. I have no reason to believe my dad would have stayed, either. Our family changed, but also, the world itself changed. A shifting of midline that was at first imperceptible, but eventually undeniable. I have to hope he would have seen it.

That he was wrong, I mean.

About the church, about the gendered way he interacted with his children, about queerness. About who to blame for his trauma-filled past.

☾

It always comes back to the sea.

One hundred million years before the Divide seemingly split water in half, the mountain ridges we hail as some of the tallest in the world were covered in the lapping, salty waves. The Western Interior Seaway was an ancient cretaceous ocean that covered the whole state of present-day Colorado and the Great Plains; it was so large, in fact, that it essentially divided the continent into two land masses: to the east, Appalachia, and to the west, Laramidia. Sediment analysis reveals the Western edge of the seaway was balmy and tropical. As Earth's seas go, this one was on the shallow side, but it was thick with marine life. Larger denizens included ancient sharks and marine dinosaurs such as plesiosaurs and mosasaurs. Early fish and shellfish were well-adapted to life near the muddy oxygen-poor bottom of the seaway, while on its surface, now-extinct birds—some with toothed beaks, some with flightless wings—staked their domain.

Eagle-eyed hikers in the Rocky Mountains can see the remnants of this antediluvian waterway in the fossilized bands of tabulated coral and clam shells that stipple the limestone cliffs. Researchers today believe the Western Interior Seaway had a unique set of operating tides. The giant cormorant-like *Hesperornis* (Latin for "western bird") would have known and lived by the daily high and low tides, making calculated decisions hour by hour as it lowered its lobed toes into the saltwater to swim and used its underdeveloped wings not to fly but to steer in the water.

Is it possible to know for sure how many times a day the water went slack under that ancient bird's flightless wings? Did it feel, too, that silent pause before the shift? Time moves in cycles, with its own slack tides. I close my eyes, and I am in the backseat of the Dasher, hurtling through the Eisenhower Tunnel, waiting for that pause just before the rivers start to flow away from me instead of toward me.

LOST BOY CAVE

Lost Boy Cave is the secret beating heart of the north coast, tucked in a secluded cove between the towering basalt ribs of Maxwell Point and Cape Meares. You can see its adjacent beach from the top of the cliffs if you know where to look: a short stretch of tawny sand that belongs primarily to the deer and the cormorants. If you are lucky enough to gain access to this beach during a low tide, you might get doubly lucky and find that the opening to Lost Boy Cave is also within reach. This little cove got its name—if the century-old legend is to be believed—when a young boy exploring the large salt-encrusted cavern didn't make it out before the tide came in and was swept out to sea.

Lost Boy Cave: toponym and warning in one.

I'd lived in Oceanside for a year before I heard whispers of this secret heart, accessible only a few times a year during extreme minus tides. The night before the lowest tide in August, we brought Clementine to the Castle and climbed into bed by ten o'clock; we'd need to wake by 5:30 the next morning in order to reach the cove just as the tide fell.

I set my alarm and turned toward Katie, who was just putting away her book and reaching for the light, and we made love before falling asleep. The window was open just a crack, and through it the sound of waves breaking and then regrouping in repeated cycles, slapping on sand and rocks, played like a lullaby on loop. I dreamed of rising and falling water, of ebbs and flows. In my dream, I watched the water rise to the second story of the Castle, leaking in through the windows and cracks in the walls, before it receded so low that the sand below the cliffs looked more desert than beach.

Below us, indifferent to the tides of my dream, Lost Boy Cave beat the steady *lub-dub* rhythm of opening and closing heart valves. With each pulse: water in, water out. A cadence so primal, my sleeping body registered it as something that was happening inside me. A valve opened on the right side of my heart, saltwater rushing to my lungs then returning—oxygenated and rich—to chart a course for the far tidal regions of my body.

☾

The tides were created when Thor was tricked into the impossible task of drinking the sea entire.

Thor traveled to the valley of the anti-gods in Norse legend, where he found a locked gate. The bars of the gate were so wide that Thor and his crew slipped right through them and into a colossal stateroom, its size matched only by the enormous men gathered within. In their presence, Thor and his men looked tiny and weak. From his intricate throne, King of the Giants Utgard-Loki laughed at the diminutive men before him.

But Thor wanted to be taken seriously.

"Okay then," Utgard-Loki said. "Prove yourself. What are your strengths?"

Thor told the king that he could drink anyone under the table.

The giant king waved to one of his giant men. "Bring us the drinking horn!" They filled the horn with as much golden mead as it would hold and handed it to Thor, who took it with gusto. The king told Thor that only a great drinker could finish the horn in a single gulp; a man who finished in two gulps was only slightly less admirable, but certainly no person who considered himself a drinking man would take as many as three gulps to drain the horn. (I picture King Utgard-Loki saying glibly out of the side of his enormous mouth, *That would just be embarrassing.*)

Thor accepted the challenge. He held the rim of the horn to his mouth and drank until his lungs forced him up for air, only to find that the mead wasn't any lower than it was when he started drinking. As the king mocked him, he tried a second time, gulping the liquid down his throat until he couldn't breathe. This time when he checked the horn, the level had gone down slightly but the horn was nowhere close to being empty. He gave it a third valiant try, but once again was not up to the task.

Eventually, King Utgard-Loki admitted he'd tricked the hammer-wielding god: the horn's end was secretly connected to the ocean, and while Thor hadn't succeeded in emptying the horn, he *had* consumed a good portion of the sea. In doing so, the water levels of the world's oceans had lowered, and would forever be stuck in a cycle of high tides and low tides.

Look at the rising or ebbing tide, according to the Norse legend, and you'll witness the result of Thor's courageous effort to complete an impossible task.

The tides, then, are a reminder of all the impossible tasks of this world. Even a strong warrior like Thor can carry on when looking failure in the eyes. Even an impossible task is sometimes still worth doing.

☾

I woke before my 5:30 alarm on my left side, the covers taut in my fist. Katie's back was against mine and as I felt the slow rise and fall of her breathing, I matched it with my own as a sort of meditation before the time-pressed adventure began. Oxygen in. Carbon dioxide out.

Katie let out a whimper and yanked on the covers. I'd somehow done it again: gathered all the blankets in the night and wrapped them around myself like a burrito, leaving her shivering. I undid my wrap and flipped half of the covers in her direction, then turned off my alarm before it could ruin the peace.

"So cold," Katie said without opening her eyes. "All night."

"Sorry, baby," I said as I sat up and touched my feet to the wool runner that ran the length of the bed.

"Not moving," she said, the covers now wrapped tightly around her. "This is literally the only time I get any covers in bed." When I switched on the light to dress, she pulled the duvet over her eyes in protest.

I stumbled downstairs into Clementine's room; through sleep-crusted eyes, she produced a litany of all the reasons she should be allowed to sleep in and be excused from our early morning spelunking.

"The only people excused are the dogs," I told her, tossing her waterproof pants on the bed and putting music on her speaker to force her up.

"*Bruh,*" she said, her eyes still closed.

"*Bruh,*" I echoed back to her.

"Dogs aren't people," she said.

"Tell that to them." Just for good measure, I added a second, thoughtful, "*Bruh.*"

When I got back to our room Katie stood at the foot of the bed in boxers and a tank top, wrestling with a pair of brick red nylon pants that were still muddy from our jaunt in the forest the day before.

"Did you get her up?" she asked, standing on her toes in order to zip the pants.

"The child is awake," I said. "It's a miracle!" Katie pulled on a black cotton sweatshirt and added a striped cowl for warmth. Then she came up behind me as I rifled through the dresser and rubbed her hands on my lower back.

"Morning, baby," she said into my ear.

Miraculously, the three of us were buckled into the car twenty minutes later with beanies pulled over our ears and windbreakers zipped to our chins. While I drove, Katie sipped on hot Earl Grey tea; I caught whispers of bergamot every time she titled it against her lips. When we pulled up to the parking lot at Oceanside Beach, the sun had just emerged over the eastern horizon as if pulled by an invisible thread; small beams broke through the twilight. It would have been awe-inspiring if we'd been less tired.

Getting to Lost Boy Cave is akin to playing Russian roulette with Poseidon. In any given year, a window opens to reach the cave on average three times and for less than an hour. An approach from the north would require scaling steep rocks on a basalt cliffside adjacent to Short Beach, past a churning punchbowl of foamy seawater that filled and emptied depending on how much Thor swallowed. An approach from the south, if timed just right, *might* get us to the cave's entrance, but our lives depended on our ability to remember that we would have limited time in that secret heart of the sea.

The empty twilit beach sprawled before us like a vast question. We walked at a clipped pace around the end of Maxwell Point, newly exposed by the low tide. Ocher sea stars, gooseneck barnacles, and yellowish-brown nudibranchs clung to the rocks, but we didn't stop to admire them. Our mission was to reach the cave's entrance at the exact moment of slack water, which would give us a twenty-five-minute window before the tide swished its skirts, twirled, and reversed itself. If we missed our return window, we'd be left to spend eternity under those skirts with the lost boy.

We waited.

We watched the water.

Lower, lower. It continued to recede until the one-foot-wide path between us and the cave was revealed, and then it stood still. The newly risen sun glistened on the water that stilled at the edge of the sand.

It had happened: the tide held its skirts back for us, the sea's stillness a go-ahead nod. It was then I knew: the secret heart was hers. Slack tide was the sea's invitation for us to witness what it held in its deepest chambers. "She sat still, trying to hush her secret heart," writes Margaret Landon. She was talking about Anna and her illicit love for the King of Siam, but it could just as easily have been written about the tide in front of us, the way she gathered those petticoats until the fabric made no sound. I felt the resulting slack as both invitation and desperation.

Katie, Clementine, and I nodded at each other over the still water, then made a single-file break for it. Around a bend, the lost boy beckoned us into his vast cavern. The cave was taller than I expected, its ceiling reaching at least thirty feet. We stepped over small profusions of sand separated by pools of standing seawater. The rocks at the base of the cave were a distinct reddish hue, home to hundreds of aggregating anemones, limpets, and black turban snails.

"Look at that," Katie pointed to a horizontal line about fifteen feet above our heads, just above a cluster of orange and white gooseneck barnacles.

"What is that?" Clementine spoke for the first time since we had climbed into the car.

"The teen awakes," I said.

Clementine shot me a look while Katie answered her in earnest. "It's the high tide line," she said. "So in a few hours this cave will be filled with fifteen feet of water."

Clem stood with her neck tilted back, staring at the line. "That's low-key terrifying," she said, before wandering off to explore deeper into the cave. I watched her crouch on a low mound of sand and lean over a pool of water, using the flashlight on her phone to expose tiny mottled sculpins that swam in sharp movements where they were trapped until the tide returned. Katie wandered off next, toward the light of a hidden third entrance. She squatted on a boulder and held her phone in macro mode against the bedrock wall. She wore the same blue striped beanie that she wore the first time she took me to Oceanside Beach, a hat she'd bought as a college exchange student in Cambridge in the early aughts.

While I watched Clem and Katie, large drops of water fell indiscriminately on my head. If I walked close enough to the walls, the creatures there emitted a high-pitched, almost ultrasonic squeal. I knew it was just the water leaving their shells, but I couldn't shake the thought that they were angry, screaming at the intrusion of strangers.

Time disappeared. When Katie told us the tide had turned, it felt like both no time at all and an eternity had passed since we walked into this secret heart, and I had managed to forget the present danger, the lost boy. The water had indeed started rising, so we rushed through to the other side and walked south, the cave and its screaming creatures at our backs. We were silent, all equally in awe of what we'd just witnessed.

I pictured Clementine where she had squatted over that pool of water. I wondered what the sculpins meant to her. I wondered about her own secret heart, wondered if she knew what it was yet, if I had taught her well enough to guard it and give it away in equal measure.

☾

Actually, no.

A different origin story.

The tides were created when Raven found an old woman in a sea cave and tricked her into letting the water go.

Many tribes of the Pacific Northwest tell stories about Raven, a trickster with sleek black feathers and deep russet eyes. In the Tlinget telling, Raven's meal of choice included oysters, clams, and other delectable crustaceans. Back then, the ocean was more like an immense stagnant lake whose deep waters covered most of the planet and made retrieving Raven's favorite delicacies hard work. Raven was as notoriously lazy as he was tricky; he didn't want to swoop and dive for his food. He'd stand on the shore of the ocean, trying to will shelled creatures into his mouth.

Wait, Elissa. Take a beat.

Storytelling is sacred. Is this your story to tell?

By virtue of loving a place, do I have the right to its stories? Even if—most certainly—I'll get them wrong?

"If I could get the waters to pull themselves back, imagine the bounty I would have to feast on," Raven thought. He asked the black bears, cormorants, sleek bald eagles, and otters if they knew who controlled the waters. Each one pointed him to a woman older than time who lived somewhere on the edge of the sea and controlled the flow of the water.

Raven set out to find her. He flew along the coastline, growing tired, until he discovered her hiding in a cave just at the water's edge. She held the tide line tightly in her hand. The woman ignored Raven when he entered the cave and gripped the tide line tighter. No matter what he said to her, no matter how he swooped his tail feathers and pleaded with his beady eyes, the woman looked straight past him as if he wasn't even there. The only indication that she knew of his presence was her increasing grip on the line in her hand.

A better question: Do stories belong to a place*—in the magnetite sand, in the basalt cliffs, in the spruce roots—or do they belong to the people who first told them there?*

Are stories the secret heart of a landscape? Do they begin with the first telling, then with each subsequent telling are etched into the crags, streams, and bedrock of the place? Subtle shifts in the energy of a landscape that can be decoded by the literate?

Raven grew impatient. He plucked a sea urchin from the wall of the cave where they stood and stabbed her in the backside repeatedly with its spines. She shrieked and begged him to stop.

"If I stop, will you release the tide line twice a day so I can feast?"

Reluctantly, she released her grip. The ocean receded as if pulled back by an invisible force. The line hung slack in her hand. Raven and soon all the people along the coast enjoyed their first access to the intertidal zone, where the crabs and mussels were easy pickings.

I am the progeny of early racist colonists who called themselves "saints" and preached that American Indians were descendants of lost Israeli tribes. Joseph Smith gave himself permission to tell—nay, to invent—their stories in the Book of Mormon and pass them off not just as fact but as doctrine directly from God. I am the progeny of prophets who preached that Indigenous tribes were "cursed" with dark skin, the mark of Cain, because of their sins and misdeeds. It's a revision of history that justified significant violence, both physical and otherwise, against Native people.

Erasing someone's humanity, especially by taking control of their story and making it your own, changing it to suit your whim, is the worst kind of violence.

Those early saints told me a story about my *existence, too. They told me a story about what I was and who I should become.*

Tricksters, by their very nature, are boundary-crossers, creative rule-breakers, urchin-ass-stabbers. This is how they enact change. Look at the rising or ebbing tide, according to the Tlinget legend, and you'll witness the result of Raven's out-of-the-box thinking.

The tides, then, despite their reliability and regularity, are a call to question the way things are done, to challenge the status quo. Raven saw a better way and would not be cowed into believing it was impossible.

☾

One year to the day after we made our first successful crossing into Lost Boy cave, we prepared to repeat the experience. (Twice the previous winter, the tide was supposed to recede low enough for another possible chance at the entrance, and twice she denied us passage: she swung her skirts wide and tossed foamy breakers against the rocks where a path would have opened.) This time, we brought both my daughters and my mother, and we passed easily at slack tide. When we looked up and saw the cave's entrance, a hush fell over the group that was punctuated by the quiet reverence of slack water.

I wondered if it said something about the sacred nature of generations, of time and its attendant cycles, that our best luck with the cave was always when we were flanked with the children or my mother. But that too is part of the awe-inspiring nature of sea caves, their ephemeral connection to time. Every sea stack we witnessed on the coast, including the ones we stared at daily from the Castle windows, got its start as a cave churning with salt water. First comes a headland with small cavern-pockets near the water. Those caverns get bigger and wider with each passing tide, the seawater slowly eroding the basalt until it burrows straight through the headland, creating the rocky arches our coast is so famous for. Each arch stands for just a hot minute in geological time before the surrounding basalt becomes too weak to hold the arch erect, and then the arch careens into the waiting arms of the sea.

Entering someone's secret heart calls for reverence. Not the obedience-couched-as reverence of my youth, the kind that required crossed arms and hushed lips in every square inch of a church building. This reverence has nothing to do with pipe organs and annotated scripture, and everything to do with the old woman's clenched fist around the tide line, with Thor's breathless gulps of mead. A secret heart is akin to how Stephen Dunn describes a secret life in his poem of the same name, something that "begins early, is kept alive/by all that's unpopular/in you." It's the thing we keep when "the government said you can protect/one thing, all else is ours." It's the queerness in a person that starts earlier than puberty, the questioning of a parent's truths. It's what turned Raven into a trickster. It's what led me to the Castle for the very first time on a windy

August day. It's whatever Clementine learned about herself in that pool of tiny, mottled fish and their sharp, nervous movements.

And what of the lost boy's secret heart? I found a different version of the story that says the cave was *not* named for a boy who drowned, but instead after a pair of brothers who lived. The two went exploring at low tide, and while they made it out of the cave in time, they were stranded on the sandy cove. The whole town fretted about the missing boys, but search parties turned nothing up. Twelve hours later, when they believed the boys had been lost to the sea, the tide ebbed again and the brothers made it safely along the beach in the dark and then back home, tired and hungry but no worse for wear.

Like the boy who cried wolf, their story became a cautionary tale. It is a story that, like the cliffs where they were lost, ossified and changed over time, with all the important pieces lost to tidal history. Pieces like how wet their clothes were when they showed up that night at the back door, shaking and tearful. How their mother might have wrapped a blanket over their shoulders, how their father might have thrown more logs on the fire, his own heart bursting at having them home but his outward appearance stoic, managed. How they might have eaten bowls of soup reheated by that fire, how they might have stared into the flames and thought about the cave they discovered, that always-beating secret heart, how the flames danced in the reflection of their eyes and for the first time they wondered about their own magnificent, terrifying, secret desires.

What would I tell those boys, given the chance?

A secret heart holds the keys to who you really are. To find yours, look to what you hold sacred. What you protect. What you reveal. What you guard fiercely.

What stories you tell.

What kills you to guard in silence.

What you want more than anything. More than belonging, more than comfort. What you hold tightly in your fists.

UNGULATE WOODS
(Tillamook: *Nascowitzen*)

What you hold tightly in your fists.

I clenched the eighteen-inch elk bone in my hand and planted my feet in the thick copse of leaning firs and gnarled snags. Next to me, a deep amber bog rippled with the breeze. The trees' upper canopy was a congested tangle of needles and leaves so thick the sunlight barely made it through. I lifted my arm above my head, and with it the bone I had found lying in the elbow of one of the dead snags.

Katie was several paces ahead of me with both dogs at her heels. "Babe! You aren't going to believe this," I yelled. She turned and looked over her shoulder.

"What do you have now?"

"Elk femur!"

She laughed. "Yeah, looks like an elk femur alright," she said as I nodded my head enthusiastically.

I smiled and cocked my right hip out seductively, then let out a whoop that was part wolf-howl and part eagle-screech and sent Cricket running for her life through the cascara.

"Minor," Katie said, "you are an adorable, fucking weird little creature."

The first time we'd accidentally walked into this eerie place where the forest seemed to be swallowing the trees, we'd named it Spooky Bog (what's spookier than a marsh the color of strong tea, large swaths of darkness during a summer noontime, a giant bone in the crook of a mostly-dead tree?). And we called the forest within which Spooky Bog lived Ungulate Woods.

Ungulate Woods—complete with its mysterious bones—was my own secret heart.

☾

Forgive me. I should backtrack.

When I first started staying at the Castle with Katie part-time, we looked for alternative ways to exercise the dogs when the beach was too stormy. We settled on a defunct road at the top of a nearby mountain, closed for years and overgrown in all the right places. On the west side, the road was sinking with the crumbling mountainside. *Post-apocalyptic*, we described it. After a few months, we noticed a break in the salmonberry just below a collapsed section of asphalt.

"Should we?" Katie asked.

"Do you even need to ask?" I followed her through the prickly shrubs and down a steep hill. Barely more than an elk trail, it looped over nurse logs and around the glossy green leaves of Pacific wax myrtle. We walked—as if on stepping stones—over tree roots that stuck out of the spruce needle duff like buried ribs. In the distance: the boom and crash of the Pacific.

We named the trail Minor Arcana Loop.

We explored the forest for hours at a time, naming each new discovery. We found Prednisone Pond the day after I tapered off the steroid and had returned to a reasonable version of myself; the Village of Moss People had thickets of skinny Douglas firs who wore moss like clothing; Red Rock Falls was a tiny trickle of water on vermillion rocks from an upper stream to a lower. And Future Wife Point was a vista through the trees that overlooked the raucous ocean and stretched so far that we could see a lake, a bay, a spit, and the lights of three different coastal towns.

It felt so much like falling in love, probably because we *were* falling in love with the forest. Each curve in the trail, new misshapen stump, pile of cougar scat, and plume of goatsbeard felt akin to walking through a new lover's rooms, rifling through cabinets and drawers. I liked pretending we had discovered something no one else had, a secret we needed to protect at all costs.

☾

Katie and I leash our dogs whenever we are in the woods, and I'd like to say it has always been that way, but we needed to be taught a valuable lesson first.

We could usually smell the elk off Future Wife Point long before we saw them. Anyone who has had a significant encounter with the creatures can tell you about their earthy musk that rises from the understory and sits in the air like an invisible cloud. During rutting season, the scent profile included an undertone of bull-elk pheromones. Katie and I were careful to leash the dogs up whenever we approached the spot.

Until we weren't. In late autumn, after the rut was over, after the leaves had fallen and only the firs and pines remained, the forest took on a sparse look. We walked toward Future Wife Point; Cricket and Marco ran ahead, but Katie and I were too deep in conversation to pay close attention.

That's when the whole mountain shook.

"Grab the dogs!" Katie yelled, and we ran after them. We reached Future Wife Point just in time to see the heart-shaped asses of over twenty elk stampede down the cliff, while Marco and Cricket gave chase. We didn't even have time to blink and suddenly the vista was as it had been: no elk, no dogs, just the two of us.

"Well, shit," Katie said.

"I guess we're doing this," I said.

We scrambled over the side of the cliff and slid down the muddy mountain on our backsides. Sometimes from miles away we'd hear a distant bark; we knew the dogs would chase the herd until they absolutely couldn't anymore, and we wondered where that would take them. As we hurried toward the ocean, we were in truly untouched territory. I couldn't shake the sense that I had entered a world that was not mine, a world where I did not belong. We found ourselves in knee-deep mud, sloshing through swampy grasses and beside ferns that stood at what seemed to be twice our height. Was it a trick of the light? Had we shrunk, or was everything in this world simply *bigger*?

We were there to rescue our dogs before they found themselves at the business end of an ungulate's hoof. But I couldn't turn off the part of me that wanted to take in every inch of this new discovery. I knew we'd never be down here again; it wasn't safe, nor was it easy. But it was pure prehistoric magic, as if we'd been dropped into an earlier era where giant things ruled the day. We waded through the waterlogged terrain and pushed past plants that were intimately familiar yet massively oversized: red elderberry, horsetail, and wild cucumber that grew taller than our heads. What was this place? How was it real? I half expected a triceratops to round a bend in the trail.

Our dumb little dogs chased the herd for more than two miles, when they finally gave in to their exhaustion and chill. We found them trembling and contrite. Cricket had a black eye and long scratches on her belly, but Marco was mostly unscathed. We leashed them up. By the time we climbed and crested Future Wife Point, something inside of me had changed. My blood pumped with adrenaline, but it wasn't just the excitement of the Great Elk Chase. It was the sense that we had stumbled on something extraordinary and untouched in Ungulate Woods. Katie sat down on the edge of the cliff with Marco in her arms. He leaned into her shoulder, vibrating with both the cold and the elation of what he'd just done. Cricket sat leashed just next to me, calm and ready for a nap as if she'd already forgotten what had just happened.

"You know, these hidden trails," Katie said, "make me think a lot in terms of queerness. Like a person can go her whole life staying on the road, never trying to find a better way through these woods. They're fine seeing it from a distance. But look! Look at what you get if you just step away from the road."

I sat in stillness. I thought about the thirty musky, hoofed creatures that stampeded down the cliff where we now sat. The evidence of their departure was all around us in the form of six-foot-deep hoof impressions in the wet forest floor. Was this why these woods had so fully captured my attention? And how many other humans have had the absolute joy of this experience?

It was the queerest thing ever. I was falling in love with a place and a person at the same time.

☾

More to the point, I was falling in love with two bodies: Katie's fleshy one, which she pressed against me day after day, and the earth's body, as told in this little slice of the north Oregon coast.

The church had tried to scare me away from pleasures of the flesh. They divided the world into another impossible binary: things of the flesh and things of the spirit. We were to ignore the things of the flesh as lesser than spiritual pursuits. Sometimes also called "things of man," things of the flesh had directly to do with the fact that we are bodies, living and relating to other bodies. Any potential pleasure found therein was explicitly forbidden. Sex, of course. But food and drink, too. We weren't supposed to drink alcohol at the end of a hard day, or drink coffee at the beginning of a long one. Eventually, my brain took it to an extreme: I couldn't eat and enjoy food, and I couldn't tap into my sexuality.

I couldn't even walk outside and commune with nature in a way that felt authentic. Instead, I buried my head in books. Reading about nature was safer than walking through it. The shame of purity culture was that I completely separated myself from my body. It wasn't until I came out, left my marriage, and met Katie that I saw my body as something worth celebrating, as an extension of the natural world.

Terry Tempest Williams writes that "our lack of intimacy with each other is in direct proportion to our lack of intimacy with the land. We have taken our love inside and abandoned the wild."

I decided that day on Future Wife Point, mud-covered and breathless from chasing stampeding elk, to take my love outside and abandon every damn thing I had been taught about my body.

☾

So it was that I'd discovered the femur, after we walked into Spooky Bog with the dogs pulling at the end of their leashes to kick up the litter fall of bark, leaves, cladodes, and needles at our feet. I had leaned my arm on the barely living tree next to me and felt something odd: there, in the hairpin-curve of the tree's trunk, sat the largest bone I had seen outside of a museum. I was caught off guard by its weight when I lifted it with my right hand, though I shouldn't have been. The thing was almost two feet long and as thick around as my wrist. When we walked out of the forest that day, it was with both pooches and the femur of the long-deceased elk in tow.

Katie had the skull of a cow outside at the Castle; its mandibles were falling apart and lay with the skull in a heap on top of a retaining wall, just behind a thicket of blackberries. I added the elk bone to the pile.

In the next two years, our bone collection grew. We found what looked to be another femur at the junction where The Village of Moss People and Hidden Vole Valley meet. And then what looked to be a tibia appeared on the Green Road, a grown-over logging access road where we sometimes ran the dogs. We found the crown jewel of our collection perched precariously on a rotting log: an elk's full skull and upper mandible, complete with a full set of teeth that had been ground down to their nubs. We added it to the top of our growing bone pile, which we moved to a more remote location on our porch, because for some reason, people get weird about piles of bones. They were the *memento mori* of the Castle, a reminder not of the life after death, but that death comes for all of us.

In those moments when I felt the most disembodied, it helped to think about the wild animals of Ungulate Woods as creatures with physical bodies not so different from mine. At least this is my best explanation for why the elk bones I collected along the way felt so sacred to me. When I held an ungulate bone in my hand, I was reminded of my own marrow. That I was an animal species walking this planet alongside other animal species, and that when I am gone, another animal might look at my tibia, say, or my scapula, examine it, and think about their own animate body.

☾

Landscape-based environmental artist Adam Kuby played with this idea of the human body as a metaphor for the land. The body in question was the city of Portland, and in 2010 Kuby sculpted acupuncture needles as tall as buildings that he left in "points" across the city. Along the heart meridian, he placed a needle in a point at 4th and Couch Street in Chinatown. He placed another on Swan Island, an attempt to cleanse the liver channel of the heavy metals and pesticides of the notoriously toxic spot in the middle of the Willamette River. Yet another giant needle on 122nd Avenue and Reedway was meant to mimic the meridian of the small intestine and balance inequities in far Southeast Portland. "Using the body as a metaphor for the entire city," Susan Anderson, then director of Portland Bureau of Planning & Sustainability, said, Kuby planned to identify "those places in the landscape that are important to us as a community, drawing attention not only to the significance of each focal point but also to the interconnectedness of them to each other as well as to ourselves."

When I had trouble navigating the elaborate trail system hidden in Ungulate Woods, Katie told me to think of the forest as a person's body. "Picture a woman lying on her left side, her left arm outstretched at the shoulder," she told me. Mapping the forest as a body this way gave me new insight into how even the most distal parts of the woods were connected. Minor Arcana Loop ran along the woman's entire left arm; the spot where we parked at the old road sat in the curve of her left elbow, and her palm cupped Cape Meares beach. The vista at Birthday Point sat level with her breast, and at her abdomen, the trail split off into Spooky Bog. If we stuck to the right, we passed Diesel Donkey

Trail at the level of her hip, which opened further down her thigh and calf into Prednisone Pond, Slice Slice Bay, and Red Rock Falls.

Seen this way, our woods were the connective tissue of this fictional woman's body, a mycelial network of desire up one limb and down another that infused itself into the mounds of detritus on the forest floor and the upper tree canopy above.

☾

Some nights, I asked Katie to hit me with the elk hide flogger we kept in the closet.

If by nature of having a body I am a physical extension of the land itself, shouldn't that manifest most in those moments when my wife and I met flesh with flesh, those sweaty rutting beats of time punctuated by the catch of our breaths?

On those nights, the flogger landed with a thud on my left hip, the supple leather both sharp and velvety on my skin. A thump, then, on my ass, and then again. Katie switched up the intensity, so that sometimes it landed with a sting and sometimes with the grace of pure butter, the leather as soft and delicate as down.

The flogger's falls smelled so much like our herd of elk in Ungulate Woods. Under the piquant natural leather were other earthy notes, these coming from our bodies, as resinous and musky as the forest beasts themselves.

The more Katie struck my skin, the more grounded I felt. With each blow of the elk's hide against my bodyscape, I grew roots. The leather landed like a thunderclap in the swale between my breasts and abdomen, sloughed like water off my skin. And I swear, in the spot on my head where a friend in second grade had rubbed her hand to look for "Mormon devil horns," I felt the tiny eager push of antler buds.

I swear to you.

☾

This is the story of how Spooky Bog became Elk Hollow.

Almost two years after first discovering Ungulate Woods, Katie and I were startled by a lone elk in the bottom of the ravine that held Spooky Bog. We were on the return arm of the Minor Arcana Loop, and we'd just followed the dogs through the Fairy Grasslands and past the turnoff to Birthday Point. It had been more than half a year since we'd seen another human in these woods, so when the loud rustle and then snap of branches echoed through the ravine, there was no question we were dealing with a creature of the forest.

"Shit," Katie mumbled under her breath as she reached down and lifted Marco into her arms. Once the other dog was safely leashed, we all stood in silence. Held our breath. Waited.

Is there anything better than standing still in a crisp autumnal forest? Then that stretch of anticipatory silence while trying to out-wait a wild creature? When the understory cracked again, the outline of a stately female elk appeared, making its way into the ravine through the hemlock, as if in relief against the woodsy backdrop. She wasn't more than thirty feet away, and she made eye contact with me as she descended toward the water. She was five feet tall at her shoulder. As she walked, musk floated away from her in pungent waves.

She crossed the bog, then went straight up the other side of the ravine toward the cliff and disappeared from view. Katie motioned to me to wait; I saw her eyes scan the ravine for evidence of other herd members and then land on the forest floor. I followed her eyes. She was staring at an elk bone, larger than any we had previously found, stuck out from the litter of leaves and decaying fungus. We had hiked halfway back to the car, the heavy bone gripped in my right mitten, when we decided through a vote by the committee to change the name of that dip at the bottom of the ravine. There were two people and two dogs on that committee, and the vote was unanimous.

☾

I wasn't so naive that I missed the shameful undercurrent of our forest. The old road had been closed after erosion caused landslides and sinkholes that wouldn't stay patched, the depleting soil a testament to the mismanagement of our coastal forests. Always looming in Ungulate Woods were the vestiges of logged old-growth giants, their severed stumps taller than my head. Like streetlamps, they lit the forest with an untouchable ache.

But there was so much left behind to love, even if it was the result of past misdeeds. It doesn't help any of us to see nature as perfect, unchanging, pristine, and free of shame. If Ungulate Woods could be imperfect and bring us so much joy, then I could learn to accept the parts of myself that have been permanently scarred by the chainsaws and harvesters of a religion that wanted me to disappear.

It was this imperfect wilderness, not a deity, that saved me. And it saved me mostly with its indifference: to who I was, to what I believed, to who I loved, to whether I lived or died. Put differently, someday that bone in the crook of a sun-starved tree could be mine, and knowing that one simple fact brings me more joy and peace than anything from the thin gold-edged pages of scripture ever has. The wilderness taught me that I wasn't special. Instead, I was *lucky*: to be on the beach just when the sun set, to be in a deep rainforest when the bats arrived with the twilight, to watch from a cliffside overlook as a black bear searched for forage.

I had come from a system that tossed the phrase "eternal life" at us like it was a bomb we had mere moments to defuse. It was a system where obedience was the best and only way to earn worthiness. But in the wilderness, everything I could see and even things I couldn't—cell, bone, leaf, insect, bear, thistle, grass, me—were worthy simply by being part of the whole. It was a place where death and life touched everything equally, and nothing, not the voles under the pine duff, not the thousand-pound elk, not even the old-growth Sitka spruce trees, escaped it.

THE PLANET KOLOB

(Southern Paiute: *I-u-goone*)

In September 1993, Lynne Kanavel Whitesides, president of the feminist group Mormon Women's Forum, was summoned to a formal church disciplinary council. Her crime was speaking publicly about Mother in Heaven and encouraging other Mormon women to have a relationship with the woman who sits on a throne next to God. Official doctrine *does* maintain that God has a wife, and that she lives with him on the planet Kolob, but Heavenly Father has refused us any further details. Heavenly Mother is so sacred, in fact, that members are warned not to speculate about her and especially not to pray to her. In other words, she is closely guarded by her husband, who doesn't want to introduce her to his friends, and no, you can't call her.

(Katie and I once hiked Kolob Canyon, a lesser-known area of Zion National Park in Southern Utah. It was breathtaking, a canvas of reds and pinks that stretched as far as the eye could see. If I were a god tasked with designing my own planet, as Mormonism promised my husband he would be, I might create something similar. But I'd tell the whole goddamn world about my wife.)

Whitesides was disfellowshipped. Five others were disfellowshipped or excommunicated that same month, all left-leaning scholars with an eye toward gender equality in the church, many of them discussing the existence of Heavenly Mother or openly advocating praying to her. They are known as the September Six.

Renowned psychology researcher Brené Brown writes, "Shame derives its power from being unspeakable." If as women we are a reflection of a Heavenly Mother, then doesn't that make *us* unspeakable too? Maybe the shame starts before we are even born, in the exact instant an X-chromosome-laden sperm fertilizes an egg.

X marks the spot: the buried treasure on a map, the third-to-last letter in the Latin alphabet, the voiceless consonant cluster that follows a stressed vowel, an unknown variable in an algebra equation, a horizontal axis, Roman numeral of the number ten, the rating for a movie I would never be allowed to watch. The sex chromosome that will always, always, always carry a terroir of shame.

BEVERLY BEACH
(Siletz: *Nestucca*)

When Katie moved in with me and the kids at the Wetlands, remnants of my old life were everywhere. When Matt and I separated, he had moved into the guest room, and I had tried to reclaim the main bedroom as my own. I rearranged the furniture. I scrubbed. I purged. I got rid of the California king bed that had been the dominant presence in the room for the last decade, a bed large enough for two grown adults, a few small children, and a dog. Without a husband or kids young enough to climb into bed with me, it felt like a waste of space; I opted instead for a queen platform bed and expensive mattress to help my constant back pain. New bedding. New rugs. New dresser.

But you can never burnish a place clean of a marriage. Not completely. It sticks in the cracks and furrows. The damaged molding at the base of the door that our old cat had used as a scratching post; the bamboo floors Matt spent a sweaty spring break installing; the rainbow of stains on the bathroom vanity from when Chloe at ten had used a hair dryer and crayons to "make art." At the end of the day, Katie and I still slept in the same place where I had slept with my ex for all those years. When we opened the windows at night in the spring, I fell asleep to the same high-pitched mewing of the peacocks who lived on the rooftops a few neighborhoods over.

With the peacocks vocalizing and the walls the same latte-brown as they had been for the past fifteen years, my body enacted old patterns. My system had spent over a decade bracing itself for the unwanted possibility that my spouse was interested in sex, so now, in this room with Katie, I had to work hard to remind myself that I no longer needed to sleep on the very far edge of the bed with my back to her, that I didn't have to lean in to my back pain or my migraines as an excuse not to engage physically. At night, in that room filled with the ghosts of the past, my body wanted to keep me safe the way it had for so long. It became clearer than ever the level to which I had duped myself my whole life, and the toll my body and mind had taken by trying so hard for so long to be someone I wasn't. Lisa Taddeo captures it perfectly in her book about women's desire, *Three Women*: "We pretend to want things we don't want so nobody can see us not getting what we need."

At the Castle every other week, where we fell asleep to nature documentaries about animal homes, I held the soft pelt of my animal body against the soft pelt of hers. There, Katie became my den, my nest, my web, my cave. But in the city at the Wetlands, the young Mormon girl inside me pulsed with shame.

☾

One Saturday night when I was fifteen, I was forced to kneel on the cement walkway just outside the west entrance of the stake center, the largest Mormon meetinghouse in the Portland metro region. Three adults circled me to scrutinize my legs and the hem of my skirt. Dani, my best friend, stood off to the side and waited for the verdict.

It was the first Saturday of the month, which meant Mormon teenagers from all over the area were gathering to attend a church-sanctioned dance. Dani and I had parked just minutes earlier; we watched as clean-cut teens in crisp ties and ankle-length skirts poured into the building, passing the checkpoint with flying colors. But when I got to the door, two of the women clucked their tongues.

"Your skirt isn't long enough, Sister . . ."

"Minor," I filled in for her. "But it hits my knees. I thought that was the rule?"

They talked to each other instead of addressing me. Dani and I, blocked from entering the dance, watched as more kids streamed into the steepled church ahead of us, unchallenged by their wholesome wardrobes. I could smell the vapor pouring from the fog machine inside, and I was sure I caught the rise of the duet coda between Meatloaf and Lorraine Crosby in "I'd Do Anything for Love (But I Won't Do That)." The female chaperones waved over a man I recognized as a member of the Stake Presidency and asked him what he thought of my skirt.

"Kneel down for me," he said, politely, as if he was telling me to pass him the salt.

"Right here?" I wasn't wearing any tights and winced at the thought of my bare knees on the cold concrete. The man in the suit nodded. If the hem of my skirt didn't touch the back of my legs all the way across when I kneeled, they'd send me home. It seemed to me that kneeling would only make my skirt ride up more, so I tugged on it as I bent my knees. The three adults exchanged glances. The hem of my skirt touched not just the back of my legs, but the ground in front of me. A group of cute boys Dani and I knew from Beaverton filed past us, avoiding eye contact to pretend they didn't know us.

But I met the eyes of the Stake President in his suit. The other chaperones looked at him, too. We were waiting for instructions. Dani stood as far away from the walkway as possible, trying to disappear. Finally, he spoke. "You're okay tonight, Sister, but please take care to be more modest in the future."

All my life, in bed with my lovers, I'm sidetracked by the unbidden sensation of my knees pressed against the concrete. By the memory of the suited man circling above me, by being called *Sister* in a way that made me feel small and dirty, by the vaguely maple scent of propylene glycol pouring from a fog machine, by Meatloaf's plaintiff insistence that despite being willing to do anything for love, even he has his limits.

☾

Therapist Jenny McGrath explains the disembodiment that often results from purity culture. "When sex, desire, arousal, or any other normal thing about being a body fires together with shame, fear, and guilt from a young age—often the safest place for folks to go is away from themselves."

Going away from myself. The duality presented by the church was straightforward: I was made of both flesh and spirit. My job was to ignore the flesh and nurture the spirit. Every Sunday lesson and official church publication reiterated the fact that disembodiment was perhaps the best and only way to be spiritually safe: "Those who keep themselves sexually pure will avoid the spiritual and emotional damage that always comes from sharing physical intimacies with someone outside of marriage." It can't be both. Unless you are a cisgendered woman married to a cisgendered man, the only way to remain pure is to shut down the signals and needs of your physical body and focus solely on your spiritual well-being.

Careful, though. According to the Mormons, even your mind can turn on you and lead you into sexual sin. Their website offers this ominous warning: "Control our thoughts. No one commits sexual sin in an instant. Immoral acts always begin with impure thoughts. If we allow our thoughts to linger on obscene or immoral things, we have already taken the first step toward immorality. We must flee immediately from situations that may lead to sin and pray for constant strength to resist temptation and control our thoughts."

Going away from myself. The Law of Chastity reveals that sexual sins are so serious, so transgressive, that *only murder* is worse in the eyes of God. In my young mind, that meant succumbing to bodily temptations would put me right up there with Ted Bundy and Hitler. McGrath elaborates, "I see purity culture as a system of disembodiment that enables folks within that system to remain compliant and complicit in the system."

So my body decided to keep me safe. It turned off. And in doing so, I was doing exactly what the system hoped I would. I went away from myself.

☾

Some of the ways I went away from myself.

1. At seventeen, my older brother's friend asked why I wore clothes two to three times my size. *Why do you dress like a fat girl* is what he actually said, and it took me months to understand he meant my baggy overalls, my full-length sleeves, the thrifted cords that sagged on my hips and hid the shape of my legs. The way I treated my body like it was a bomb with the potential to detonate and shielded the world from it with layers.

2. My food aversions started in earnest in adolescence, and most of the items on my do-not-eat list contained strong, unmistakable flavors. Mushrooms, seafood, garlic, cilantro, gamey meat, aged cheese, cheesecake. Food that reminds those who eat them of the fact of their soft animal bodies, the way they touch the earth. Going away from my body meant I didn't like any reminders that I was in one. I could put down processed food like nobody's business, famous in college for my ability to down a box of Twinkies in just one sitting. Because when you are disconnected from your body, you are disconnected from the living earth and the living things that feed it. Hostess snacks and Cheetos feel safe in a way whole foods, still dirty from the earth, feel threatening.

3. My high school friend Miles pointed out that *you don't walk like other girls.* At the time, I thought it was a compliment. It meant I wasn't sashaying my hips

for male attention. But until he'd said it, I'd never noticed the way other girls walked. Or boys, for that matter. Legs were for getting you from place to place. Why would anyone think to pay them extra mind? Three years later, I briefly dated a guy in college who told me that his favorite part of a woman's body was her legs. He described the perfect leg: hairless, the calf muscled, slightly tanned. I saw the image of myself as a disembodied head, floating in the air next to him as we talked. My life would have been so much easier if I didn't have to lug a body around.

4. Those shame-filled scratch-an-itch orgasms that I tried not to have, tried even harder not to enjoy, tried harder still not to crave.

5. Ivy, the flaxen-haired girl down the hall from me in the BYU dorms, used to bounce around the halls without shoes on, then come into my room (that place so off limits to men, at the penalty of expulsion) and lament about her bad decisions with boys, her yellow head on my pillow. She glowed. All that flax. All that shine. My body said reach for her. I hugged myself instead and watched her stream out the door to do mushrooms with a local boy who passed bad checks and wasn't even Mormon. What I wasn't consciously asking, but my body was: if Ivy can break the rules for him, why can't she break the rules for me?

1. (reprise) When he said *Why do you dress like a fat girl*? he wasn't asking if I was dissociated from my body and how he could help me. He wasn't asking me anything at all. He was *telling* me how I should behave inside my body, how it should look, how I should use it for attention. And he was dragging down other women's bodies to do it. But his voice wasn't the first in the swelling chorus of men who made my experience of my body about *their* experience of my body, and he wouldn't be the last.

☾

I walked to the bathroom in the dark, tripping over the rug and hoping I didn't wake Katie. The door was open just a crack, but through it, I could see shafts of gleaming May moonlight coming through the skylight above the toilet. I pushed open the door and stepped into the celestial stream. Through the glass above my head, the moon was round and thewy. Full-to-bursting.

After I peed and rubbed the sleep from the corner of my right eye, I turned to the sink and was hit with more light: the pint glass next to the faucet glowed neon blue. Had I woken into some sort of fluorescent night-world? For a quick moment, I longed for the reading glasses on the nightstand by the bed, but then I squinted and saw it.

The silicone dildo we'd used the night before sat in the same pint glass we'd used to warm it and apparently its neon blue core was glow-in-the-dark. The moonlight must have been enough to activate it. I'd caught moon and dildo speaking the furtive language of full-bodied desire.

Not long after that August day when I'd walked up the steps of the Castle for the first time, Katie had asked me, "Since you're new to this, do you want a hot tip?" Her face gave nothing away, and I didn't know if I was in for a joke or something so real I should get ready to tattoo it on my skin.

I gulped, wanting it, yes, but scared for what was coming.

"Never drink from a full pint glass next to the sink." She practically winked. I took a few beats and still didn't make the connection until she pointed to the glass of water in question. "That's where the dildo was last night." I made a gagging sound and Katie laughed.

We'd used a strap-on for the first time the night before. More specifically *I'd* used a strap-on the night before, surprising myself with how much I liked the control that comes with giving pleasure, with taking someone almost to the brink and then backing off. For the next three days, until it was time for me to return to my parenting duties and leave the Castle, that pint glass and the dildo it warmed up stayed next to the bathroom sink. I stared at it every time I brushed my teeth, washed my hands, or grabbed a cotton swab, a pit of shame in my stomach.

Here was such a visceral reminder of the sex we'd had, of the passion with which we'd grasped at each other's flesh.

But Katie was nonchalant about it. A strap-on next to the bathroom sink was no different from leaving out the shearing scissors we'd use to trim the fur around Marco's face, or taking a few extra days to return a bottle of vitamins to the medicine chest. How must it be to look straight at last night's sexual accessories and feel not an ounce of shame? To accept sex as one of the body's basic needs, even as one of life's greatest pleasures? I would soon grow used to the way Katie liked to wake up each morning and reflect on the sex we'd had the night before, despite how much I didn't want to acknowledge what we'd done between our gray sateen sheets. I didn't want to look it directly in the eyes. The sex, I mean.

Back at the Wetlands, the moon and our sex toys had less of a dalliance. The sex we had there was clandestine and quick, a necessity born of having teenagers in the house. This was not a place you could leave used dildos in a pint glass of water next to the sink. What was the trick, then? How could I embody the full version of myself—the one who gave and took pleasure in turns, who could make a case for orgasm as spiritual enlightenment—there in the city, in the house where for the better part of two decades I'd avoided sex at all costs?

James B. Nelson, professor of Christian ethics, believes that religion misses the mark in its body messaging: "If I do not realize the profound sense in which I *am* a body, if in a false spiritualization of my selfhood I deny my embodiedness, I will also tend to minimize the personal significance of activities which I carry on through my body. When my body ceases to be fully personal, my relationships to other body-selves are diminished in their personal meanings. The world becomes external and foreign."

The answer, sitting in the dark at the Wetlands, was to make my body fully *personal*. I wanted to live in a world where moonlight washing through an open skylight and the remnants of sexual passion from the night before make me *more* fully embodied, not less. Where I felt every pang of hunger, every yearning for orgasm, the relief in every deep breath that fills my lungs. Where my body was the somatic sum of everything I had done and felt.

☾

Ivy was the first female crush I'd even remotely acknowledged. But she had her predecessors, girls I now understand I was desperate to hold. Every queer woman, especially those of us who came out later in life, looks back on her childhood to play the game, "Was she my best friend or did I have a crush on her?" Often, it's an unanswerable question.

Take Dani. Before she was my best friend, she was the Cool Older Girl, who always wore her hair in a chin-length bob, tucked behind her ears. Her ears themselves had never been pierced, because her parents were stricter than most of the other Mormon parents. Even without the chunky earrings of the nineties, though, Dani was one of the most popular kids in our ward.

Somehow, she managed to find just the right loopholes to always have a cute boy on her arm without breaking any rules. She hung out with the group of Cool Older Kids who didn't register my existence, the older siblings of the kids in my Sunday school classes. One of them was Matt, tall and slim in his black leather jacket, pushing Dani playfully in the hallway outside the chapel after Sacrament Meeting. They stood always with the other high school kids, and although my entry into their world was only a year away, the chasm between us felt impenetrable.

I watched Dani from a distance when our ward took its annual Memorial Day camping trip to Beverly Beach State Park. The entire campground was nestled against pebble-rich Spencer Creek, in a patch of forest hidden between the aptly named Cape Foulweather and Yaquina Head. I spent time with the middle school crowd that weekend—including long beach walks with Matt and Dani's younger siblings. We circled the older kids at a distance when they sat in portable folding chairs and roasted marshmallows; Matt sat on Dani's left, laughing and trying to start a singalong, and on her right was Nicholas, her latest romantic conquest.

Nicholas was a year older than Dani, which meant he felt light years older than me. The night before, I'd rounded a corner of the wooded trail, looking for the bathroom, to find Dani and Nicholas nuzzled up against a scraggly shore pine, her arms around his neck, his mouth firmly on hers. She wore pajamas and her feet were bare. I veered with the trail to the right, away from my family campsite, to avoid being discovered.

I walked deeper into the forest, until the clouds covered the moon and the trails were shrouded in darkness. Beverly Beach was made up of miles of these serpentine footpaths, flanked on both sides by blackberry and manzanita. I was in the middle of the kind of coastal old-growth forest that would one day save me: standing snags of dead wood interspersed with nurse logs, woody vegetation, and conifers forced sideways by the wind, their top branches and needles swept dramatically backwards like a distressed damsel's hair in a blowing storm.

Half-lost in that moonwashed forest, I wasn't wondering what it would be like to be in high school and have a boy as tall and athletic as Nicholas want to kiss me. I wondered how it felt to *be* him, to be the focus of Dani's attention, to have her soft elbows around my neck. Too, I wondered how it felt to be the pink redwood sorrel blooming under her bare feet.

Dani bored of Nicholas a few months later, and that's when she started calling me. School wouldn't start for another two months, and we had nothing but time on our hands. We slept in the queen-sized waterbed at my house, and on the trampoline outside at hers. We shared a toothbrush, ate Tang powder straight out of the jar until our fingers were the neon orange of traffic cones, baked cakes for local fire fighters, drove aimless late at night in the July heat, stopping only for a cheap midnight snack at the Taco Bell drive-through. Three weeks into this daily routine, the phone in my bedroom rang.

"I'm so annoying, I know," she said, "But there just isn't anyone else I want to call."

A flutter in my chest, a soft fist over my heart.

Unthinkable. This girl I found so shiny and alluring seemed to think I was shiny and alluring, too. Her words played over in my mind, even as she talked through the receiver about a boy from the Tigard ward she hoped would show up at the dance that weekend. I knew boys like him and Nicholas would always get a part of Dani that was off limits for me, but I didn't yet understand why.

☾

My body had the uncanny ability to bring God-fearing men to their knees.

1. When I turned twelve, I met with the bishop alone for the first time, standard practice for each child when they come of age. He told me that since I was now twelve, and since I lived with two brothers, my job was to avoid being a temptation for them. *Always wear a robe in the house,* he said, and *be careful not to let them see you in your underwear.* The bishop was a bit older than my father. My only interaction with him thus far has been to line up with the other children—only through age eleven—outside his office when church ended, where he stood in the doorway passing out handfuls of candy from a bulk grocery bag. My younger brother and I were always the first ones in line, because the licorice we loved went quickly. But there must have been something about turning twelve that shifted me, overnight, from the kind of girl who waited in line for licorice to the kind of girl who could destroy a man with lust. I didn't even *own* a robe. Was I supposed to wear one over my clothes? I didn't ask for clarification, opting instead to fold deeper and deeper into my tiny self, wondering how many times I would need to fold the weaponry of my body until it simply disappeared.

2. In high school, I slept in the leftover fundraising shirts that my dad brought home from work. They fit like oversized dresses on my one-hundred-pound frame, covering my knees in a way that would make any dance chaperone happy. But if I came down for breakfast still wearing it, my dad would turn to my mom and say, *I don't want her sleeping in T-shirts. It creates bad habits.*

I never asked what the bad habits were, but I did remember to toss a pair of sweats underneath when he was around.

3. The Sunday before Matt left on his mission, his parents hosted the traditional missionary Open House. Earlier in the day, Matt had given his farewell talk in Sacrament Meeting, and now every member of our ward was gathered in his parents' house, eating their fill of his mom's white-chocolate-covered grapes (the same ones we'd serve at our wedding two years later) and trays of Costco quiche. His grandmother had flown in from Utah for the send-off, and she made sure to pull me aside near the kitchen island to tell me, *Matt needs to focus on his mission and on the Lord these next two years. He doesn't need a girlfriend to distract him from that.* It was the first time I had ever met the woman, imposing in her stature, and I could see what I was to her: the potential downfall of her grandson. He was flying three thousand miles away for two full years. We wouldn't be allowed to talk on the phone or write more than one letter a week. And yet—even when he was too far away to see or hear or touch me—I was the temptress. When I pulled Dani aside to tell her about the exchange, she popped a white chocolate grape in her mouth and shrugged. *He needs to focus on the Lord.*

4. I could blame Eve and her nasty fruit-picking fingers. Except I hadn't offered fruit to any man—not because it was forbidden but because it simply didn't look worth eating.

That.

That right there was the *real* original sin.

☾

Dani and I got a bonus vacation two months after Beverly Beach, this time to the equally alliterative Black Butte Ranch, where our Young Women's leader and her dentist husband had a large vacation home. Black Butte was less ranch and more private resort, at the base of an extinct stratovolcano and surrounded by the sprawling Deschutes National Forest. I didn't know it until much later, but the day before we left, Matt pulled Dani aside and asked her to put in a good word for him. *You know, if it comes up in conversation.* I don't recall it ever coming up, and she didn't reveal how he felt until much later. It was the last time she was loyal to him instead of me.

We shared a bed in a room of doubles and bunks and spent the week mostly with each other. We rode bikes through extended cow pastures, took a watercolor set to the edge of the forest, and swam in one of the many chlorine pools. We reveled in the wildlife, and even back then, I spent a good portion of my time trying to decipher between the golden-mantled ground squirrels and yellow-pine chipmunks that we watched dart in and out of the leaf litter where the cow pastures met the dry forest. The two are almost identical, except the stripes on a golden-mantled stop at the shoulders, while similar striations on a chipmunk's body go all the way to their noses. I learned that summer that to differentiate between the two, I only had to look at the creature's eye makeup.

In the evening, we huddled for prayer with the rest of the girls and listened to reports about everyone's day. Someone had inevitably fallen off her bike in a particularly humiliating way, another had come face to face with a black bear; several had used the house phone to call and hang up on her crush back home. On the fourth night of our trip, during one of these download sessions, our friend Mandy posed a question that sucked the sound right out of the room.

"Is everyone here a virgin?" We froze. We could have heard the drop of a single pine needle outside. What a strange question. *Of course* we were all virgins. She might as well have asked if any of us had murdered a man that week. At the insistence from the entire group that we were all, indeed, virginal, she dropped her bomb in the most casual way, as if continuing a boring conversation that she was only halfway interested in.

"Well," she shrugged, "because I'm not anymore." At this point, God himself could have swung two hundred golden-mantled ground squirrels from the rafters and we wouldn't have moved a muscle. We had already known that she and Natalie had met two boys at the pool earlier in the day, and that they had rendezvoused with them after dinner. What we hadn't known was that the boys had asked them to meet near the cow pastures that only existed to make wealthy guests feel more authentically like they were on a ranch. Mandy told us one of the boys had laid on top of her in the pasture's forage, her back pressed against bluebunch wheatgrass.

Later, Natalie will tell us that she didn't know what to do when she looked across the pasture where she sat talking to the younger of the two boys and saw only Mandy's knees where they were raised up on the blanket.

Here it was, the thing we'd been warned against our whole lives, the thing that would destroy us. The thing we were on a crash course with.

Our sexuality.

I don't recall who thought to ask the question that could right the ship, but someone from the group said, "Did you *want* to do it?"

"Yeah, did you say no?" another girl probed. Mandy paused, looked around the room. Deciding. Then she nodded. Yes, yes, she had, in fact, said no.

Relief rolled through us, not unlike the wind that ran through the sagebrush steppe's overstory of rangeland grasses.

We were kind enough to reassure Mandy that she had been raped.

Sometimes, when I conjure this memory, Mandy looks confused at our assertion. Sometimes she looks relieved, other times scared. The truth is I have no idea what happened in that pasture in July 1991, apart from the munching of ruminants. I do know that by midnight, we'd told our leaders, and they'd called the police, and the boy Natalie and Mandy met that day in the pool had been handcuffed outside of his parents' fancy resort house. I do know that by the next morning, all charges against him had been dropped.

I do know that every girl in that group and especially our leaders were thrilled that Mandy had been raped when the alternative was her actively consenting to the same act. I knew, even then, that the distinction we were making was not about consent versus coercion. We were making a distinction between sinner and victim. Like golden-mantled ground squirrels and yellow-pine chipmunks, the two things looked so similar.

Did I know then that no matter which story was the truth, Mandy hadn't done *anything* worth being ashamed of? That we were none of us sinners, all of us victims? That with just a trick of the light, the tawny cape that stretches over the golden-mantled squirrel might be undetectable to the human eye. That when I saw a rodent scamper across bike paths on that pseudo ranch, there were two *other* possibilities, the least chipmunk and the Allen's chipmunk, indistinguishable from each other and from the yellow-pine chipmunk except in a post-mortem exam. They all run up the same conifers, pilfer the same cones for seeds.

That when the world presents us with binaries, there is always an obscured third option.

☾

I crammed my high school classes into three years so that I could graduate the same time as Dani and Matt and all of our friends. Dani and I got our acceptance letters from BYU on the same day. We each came home from school to thick manila envelopes, ripped them open, and learned that we had accomplished the Mormon Dream: BYU was a stepping stone to the temple, the only person, place, or thing we were taught to actively want.

Dani drove to my house with her envelope and together, we cut the first sentence out of our acceptance letters: "Congratulations! You have been admitted to Brigham Young University to begin Fall 1994." We taped that sentence onto plain T-shirts, right where a name tag would go, and wore them for the rest of the day and night. We went to the mall and bought trinkets, stocked up on Tang at Safeway, jumped on the trampoline at her house. We had done it. We were going to BYU. We daydreamed about what our dorm room would look like and how much fun we were going to have as roommates.

The next day for our Young Women's activity, we baked cookies for less active members of the ward. After mounding snickerdoodle dough on baking sheets and letting them cool, we arranged the cookies on floral paper plates, covered them in plastic wrap, and finished off each plate with a pink ribbon. We were given addresses for five members who had stopped attending church; our treats were an incentive to come back to the fold. Dani and I piled into an old Ford Escort with five other girls. To fit everyone, I sat on Dani's lap in the passenger seat.

Had I sat on another girl's lap before? Surely, I had. But not Dani's. Our physical intimacy stayed in the realm of chaste shared beds and shared toothbrushes. But on this day, racing headlong to annoy people likely fed up by the church, something shifted.

The Escort was tiny, so not only did I have to sit on Dani's lap, I also had to fold my body against hers so my head didn't hit the roof of the car and I didn't get in the way of the driver's stick shift. I balanced two plates of cookies on my lap, their ribbons smashed against the plastic. When the car turned too quickly, Dani put an arm around me to keep the cookies and me from careening sideways.

Flint rubbed against steel in my abdomen. Sparks first, then an ember. I wanted Dani to wrap both arms around me and squeeze. I wanted her to bury her face in the back of my neck. The sensation came on so quickly that I froze. A distinct, fully formed question echoed in my head: *Is this what it feels like to be gay?* And then: *Am I a lesbian?*

A memory surfaced from a deep recess of my brain behind a door marked Do Not Disturb.

Sixth grade. San Jose, California. My best friend lived directly across the street from me. Her parents had set up a camping tent in their backyard as a playhouse, and for months, she and I would unzip the tent flaps directly after school and make out inside all that white nylon fabric, sometimes stripped to our underwear. We were just practicing, we told each other. As evidence of such practicing: we each took turns being The Husband.

But remembering it from the vantage of Dani's lap, I wondered if it really had been *practice* for me after all. I wondered if I was just practicing now. If Dani pulled me close and let me hold her, could we write it off as that? We stopped to deliver the first batch of cookies, and when I got back into the car, I squeezed into the backseat instead of reclaiming my place in front with Dani. The moment passed the way I hoped it would, and I wouldn't think of it again for at least a decade.

I never really wanted Dani, not in the way I know now that I want other women. Not the way I wanted Ivy, or The Poet, or especially Katie. But as a young queer girl closeted even from myself, the lines between friendship and romance were blurry at best.

☾

Our ward spent two other Memorial Day weekends at Beverly Beach State Park, and then the tradition was banned altogether when the Stake Presidency intervened. While my parents were an exception in Mormonism (they never went to church while on vacations), most of the other families had gone into the nearest coastal town to attend Sunday meetings. But there were a few other families like us who stayed behind at the campground to cook breakfast and read while the other families went to church. The Stake Presidency decided our entire ward was taking too many liberties by having a church-sanctioned camping trip that fell over a Sunday.

I wouldn't have known it at the time, but just months before that first camping trip—Dani kissing a boy against a shore pine—ground broke on an ocean-view lot on the corner of Drawbridge Drive and Knight's Armor Road, just fifty miles north of Beverly Beach. Newly cleared of trees, the lot's construction probably happened over a few months: a poured concrete foundation, rough framing of the simple two-stories, bare sheetrock on the inside, cedar siding on the outside, stuffed between with insulation. Twenty-eight years later, Katie bought that house and gave it its Castle moniker. And just two years after that, thirty years after I watched Dani and Nicholas longingly, I would walk up the steps that would become my home.

Late at night, when the window is open at the Castle and Katie sleeps soundlessly beside me, it feels like I can reach out to Beverly Beach and stroke the hair of that young camper who had been taught that *want* was a dirty word.

Want. Want. Want.

The years roll from the ground underneath the Castle. The Castle disappears and so do all of the homes around it. We roll past the thirties, the twenties, the entire village of Oceanside evaporates. But the peaks and cliffs it was built on remain, densely forested and stippled with rusty diesel engines and pulleys, the landscape become extraction for old-growth wood. Farther still: see the native Chinook tribes, living among those giant trees we will one day raze. This is what the earth looks like thousands of years before Joseph Smith will claim an angel's revelation that all Native Americans were visited and ministered to by Jesus after his death, that they share a cultural heritage with anyone who accepts the teachings of the Book of Mormon.

I touch a bare foot to the earth.

I am taking my body and this forest back to a time before men with scriptures and chainsaws told us how little we were worth, then padded their pockets with profits.

CAPE LOOKOUT
(Salish: *Nasitselz*)

It was jarring to go from Portland's creeping urban blight to the verdant health of the coastal communities in just under two hours. Something shifted in me whenever I approached the summit of the Coast Range near Lee's Camp. The summit was only sixteen hundred feet above sea level, and it felt like a distinct boundary between two worlds. Once crested, I was closer to the landscape where I was settling into my natural self, as if fibers of my body's fabric were already weaving themselves into the coastal terrain. And yet behind me was the city, more fibers being stretched: my teenage children, happy and safe with their father, but still always in my rearview mirror.

By November, there were traces of frost already on the summit and along the sides of Highway 6. I was heading west for a three-day visit, following the highway all the way into Tillamook, which announced itself with the stench of cattle. This was the point where Cricket always sat up in her little booster seat and lifted her snout toward the window: she knew the reek of off-gassing cows meant the Castle was just fifteen minutes away. There were heifers to both sides of us, some casually hanging with egrets in the field, some eating in the barn. A lone bull I named Bernard always greeted me on the right-hand side of the highway just before we hit Tillamook. A year later, our out-of-town wedding guests would speculate about the local cow population, and Katie's old college friend would look it up: cows outnumbered people in the county by about twenty-seven thousand head of cattle.

(My mom told me once that her father had given her brothers each a calf when they turned fifteen, something they could raise and then sell to help pay for college. When my mom and her sister asked for the same thing, he told them that since an education is wasted on women, he wasn't about to squander a cow for them. She worked in that shrimp factory instead, just a few years away from the BYU Halloween party where she would meet my father and move into a cow-less life.)

Cricket panted in excitement when we pulled up to the Castle on a wet day in February. By the time she'd wagged her way up the slick wooden steps, Katie had opened the front door to greet her. She used an old towel to wipe each of Cricket's paws off—no small feat as Cricket squirmed and contorted herself to get her tongue on Katie's face.

I paused to take in the scene. "Is that a Boston Terrier on your face or are you just happy to see me?"

Katie laughed. "Both. Hey, baby." She released the hound and gave me a quick kiss on the cheek. She was in stockinged feet and her thick cable-knit cotton sweater brushed against my arms as I walked past her.

We planned to hike Cape Lookout, a forested headland located on the sandy Netarts Spit. The cape was left over from an ancient Miocene lava flow that jutted two miles into the sea. It was a popular hike, and we'd gotten so spoiled by our empty beaches and forests that we couldn't stomach hiking in a congested throng of people. Crowds were for my other life, my city life. We'd chosen today on purpose: cold, wet, and blowing sideways, the type of weather that would scare most people away. Not us. We donned parkas and waterproof pants (men's, of course, because pockets) and loaded into Katie's Outback, the dogs in the backseat.

When we arrived and leashed Cricket and Marco, they gave us unhappy snorts.

"Still thinking about that elk chase, I see," Katie said. There was a lull in the rain when we set out on the trail. Cricket pulled me along behind her; at twelve months, her bulk had grown faster than I could teach her to heel. The clouds to the west had cracked open, revealing large swaths of blue. And yet there were no other hikers to be seen. We'd gamed the system.

Soon, we were calf-deep in mud. We entered a section of the trail where exposed tree roots acted as steps and propelled ourselves uphill in the sludge; the dogs plunged into the mud and then back up onto each root. We laughed when a curve in the trail revealed a newly felled spruce that had landed in the mud and overtaken the path. The dogs stood in front of it and looked to us for ideas. Marco's face was smeared with brown sludge.

Katie found a detour up and around the fallen giant, through a dense tangle of evergreen huckleberry, Western sword ferns, Oregon grape, and Scotch broom. To the right of us was a sheer five-hundred-foot cliff; at the base of it, ocean water sparkled in the dappled sunshine. Against the hillside to our left, two surgical masks clung to huckleberry bushes, streaked with dirt. An older couple with a yellow lab emerged through the chaparral and startled our dogs, forcing us closer to the edge of the cliff. It was the first time Katie witnessed my fear of heights. She took Cricket and Marco and found the trail where it continued on the other side of the downed tree while I flattened myself against the mountain and baby-stepped my way in their direction.

When we reached the end of the headland, a startling eight hundred feet above the ocean, the four of us sat and looked at a horizon that stretched so far you could see the curvature of the earth. The trail was to our backs, and in every other direction, our eyes were drawn to that far horizon where the sky meets the sea. Two eagles made cliched circles overhead. Below us, three ships bobbed like fishing floats in the water.

Katie snapped a picture: our legs at the edge of the world, absolutely coated in muck. The toe of my muddy hiking boot rested gently on the sludgy heel of hers.

☾

As we sat, I thought about a Walt Whitman poem I'd taught my literature students the term before, one that made many of them squirm in their seats. In section twenty-eight of "Song of Myself," he writes about a man caught in the throes of self-pleasure: "Is this then a touch? quivering me to a new identity, / Flames and ether making a rush for my veins, / Treacherous tip of me reaching and crowding to help them . . ." As his excitement builds, the man uses the metaphor of a headland to convey the moment of climax: "I went myself first to the headland, my own hands carried me there. / You villain touch! what are you doing? my breath is tight in its throat, / Unclench your floodgates, you are too much for me."

Until I spent time in Oceanside, I didn't understand why Whitman's lustful speaker imagines himself at a headland, which is just a fancier word for a cape—a long abuttal that juts out into the ocean, high and with a sharp drop, surrounded on three sides by water. As I sat there on Cape Lookout, contemplating Whitman, it became clear to me that a headland—and the person standing on one, by extension—tests the limits of the boundary between land and water. It is the meeting place where any roots that keep you connected to the earth start to give way, where with just one movement you will have left one world and entered another. It is there, on just that sort of precipice, where you can surrender yourself to a touch that is also a limning of two states: shame (that villainous touch) and pure ecstasy (the floodgates). Whitman wasn't the first to equate orgasm with water, with riding, cresting, and then crashing a wave, and he certainly wasn't the last.

Perhaps it isn't shocking that I was taught Satan controlled the water. In 1831, Joseph Smith and ten of his disciples were traveling by canoe down the Missouri River. On their third day, the men stopped to rest at McIlwaine's Bend, when one of the men had a vision, "the destroyer in his most horrible power, ride upon the face of the waters." The other men didn't see the destroyer, but they claim to have heard the thunderous noise of its ride. Later, Smith included warnings about Satan's dominion over water in the religion's official scriptures: "Wherefore, the days will come that no flesh shall be safe upon the waters. . . . And now I give unto you a commandment that what I say unto one I say unto all, that you shall forewarn your brethren concerning these waters, that they come not in journeying upon them."

My beloved and I stood and held gloved hands at the tip of the Cape Lookout headland, gaping at the enormity of the ocean hundreds of feet below us. If those waters are controlled by Satan, I thought, Lord, make me a Satanist. My fear of heights was abated by the ropes that separated us from the actual edge of the towering drop-off. The day had become so clear that we could see Cape Foulweather thirty-nine miles to the south and Tillamook Head forty-two miles north. Behind us, red alders and Sitka spruce formed a safety net; they hugged us close, reminded us, even as we looked out at the endless sea, of the importance of being grounded.

Look, they said. Take it in. But don't forget you are in a border zone where there is only a thin veil between amazement and death.

We heard a noise from the trail behind us and dropped each other's hands.

Three men in their twenties, one with a dog, had reached the top and whooped with delight. I shifted my weight and Katie busied herself with Marco's collar. It was a safety thing. Whitman's speaker might give in to ecstasy at the headlands, but here, in conservative Tillamook county, it was survival for us to look like sisters, to hide the ease we had with each other that only comes from physical intimacy.

It was survival for us to pretend we wanted nothing, as we stared ahead at the opaque blue stripe that formed on the horizon between ocean and sky. But really I wanted the whole damn thing. The earth, the sky, and everything in between.

☾

I've always been drawn to borders, boundaries, the places where two or more disparate things meet. Where water meets sky. Where ocean meets land. Where boat meets water. Where eagle meets sky. I'm especially drawn to the spaces *between* the two things that butt up against each other. I have a love affair with the word "and," with the commas of the world that link two otherwise disparate things together even while holding them as separate. It's that word *and* that shows us the world is simply not binary.

I'd been diagnosed in my late twenties with a painful autoimmune disease that caused the interstitial tissue of my bladder to eat away at itself until the inside of the entire organ was a raw bleeding wound. It was the first time I'd paid attention to the word *interstitial.* Taken broadly, it describes a space that intervenes between things, especially one between closely spaced things. Those minuscule gaps into which any number of surprises can be tucked. Microscopic fauna live in the interstices between grains of marine sand. Spiders hide in the interstices between wood stacked in a shed. Advertisers make billions of dollars a year off of what they call "interstitial ads" that are placed between content.

But it doesn't have to only apply to closely spaced things. If you zoom out enough, almost anything will become closely spaced. On the headland that day, the space between our feet on the cliff and the water below seemed so small as to be interstitial, too, even at that height. Viewed from the moon (she was visible, barely, a shadowy white apparition in the south that day), the sandy beaches that mark the space between headlands are also interstitial.

I knew firsthand how profoundly a seemingly benign interstitial space could turn the natural order of things on its head. There is magic in the interstice between what we *say* we want and what we *really* want. Or in the space between words in a spoken sentence that holds the weight of an entire language: in that beat before the next uttered word, anything might be said, anything is possible.

The blue ribbon on the horizon that drew our eyes as we sat, muddy and exhausted, at the end of Cape Lookout is what we call *the offing*. The offing is just another kind of interstice, a glowing stripe that seems to hold the potential for boundless magic. According to the ancient Egyptians, the offing is symbolic of the human condition. Alvin Boyd Kuhn posits that since the ancient texts consider the sky to be the spiritual realm and the planet beneath it the material realm, then the horizon becomes the perfect metaphor for human existence as a union of the two. He writes, "And the horizon is halfway between heaven and earth, tying, as always, spirit and matter, the two ends of being."

I'd been indoctrinated to only look up toward the sky, toward the spiritual. We were told to fear the "natural man," someone who lives in the material realm ruled by the desires, passions, and appetites of his physical body. Instead, we were to tend our spiritual selves in hopes of one day returning to the spiritual realm with God. In Sunday school we were taught a *Book of Mormon* scripture from Mosiah 3:19: "The natural man is an enemy to God and should be put off."

That call from the horizon asked me to broaden what I allowed in. I'd spent my first three decades solely focused on the things of the spirit. I'd renounced those things of the spirit fifteen years ago, but I still had little access to lived experience in my own body, against the earth, against other bodies. Natural woman.

Both. I want spirit and body. *And.* I want the space in between.

☾

On our first date, Katie traced her fingers along the hummingbird tattoo on my left arm. "Pretty," she said absentmindedly as the pads of her fingers landed on the bird's reddish-orange wingtips, its glaucous body and black beak.

"That's for my mom," I told her. "She's bird obsessed."

She met my gaze, so close I could see the faint freckles along the bridge of her nose. "That's right on the pericardium channel," she told me. I blinked and blinked again.

"Come again?"

"The pericardium channel forms a pathway straight to the heart. It's about protection." She told me more. The channel was named after the sac that surrounds the heart; in Western medicine, the job of the pericardium is to act as mechanical protection for the heart and its bigger arteries. In Chinese medicine, it is considered (like the heart it is sworn to protect) an organ of fire; the heart, then, is as fiery as it gets—fire within fire. In addition to physically protecting the heart, the pericardium protects you emotionally. It's responsible for maintaining boundaries in intimate relationships, standing sentinel to clearly delineate where you end and your loved ones begin. It keeps you from getting too enmeshed with the wrong person, maintaining a healthy distance between the heart that beats in your chest and the heart that beats in someone else's.

Katie skimmed her index finger slowly from the palm of my hand, up through the tattoo, and on toward my elbow. I could feel my heartbeat in my chest, could hear it echoing in my ears.

My oldest child, Chloe, was just two days old when I held her on the bed that Matt and I shared. She had just finished nursing and was swaddled against my chest, and I felt the weight of many sleepless hours crush down on me. I turned to Matt and asked him, "Could you please scratch our back?"

Equally sleep deprived, he tilted his head and looked at me. "Your back or the baby's back?" This was the first moment since her birth that she became a person separate from me. Of course my back was no longer "our back," and it would never be again. But in those early days, the boundaries between mother and child were nebulous. My body was her body. She grew inside it. She lived there. She emerged from it, and now it sustained her with the substance vital to life. As the philosopher Iris Marion Young points out, pregnancy is the "most extreme suspension of bodily distinction inner and outer."

And yet. My back was *not* her back. Just as my dreams would not be her dreams. Just as my decisions would not be her decisions. And if we were two separate beings, if only at this point barely, what would lodge itself, over time, in the interstice between us?

When I stood atop Cape Lookout that day, the mud to my knees, I couldn't help but wonder about that interstitial space between me and my beloved. Even still today, it sometimes feels like we are the same person, but the truth is we are always two separate beings, with separate emotions and separate needs. I can't always see or touch the space where she ends and I begin, but I know it is there, a metaphorical piece of connective tissue that gives us what I crave.

Both.

And.

☾

The sun came out fully and families with golden retrievers arrived in droves. We were still at the top, taking in the 360-degree view with a reverence that I once reserved for taking the sacrament at church. From that height, the coastline was perfectly festooned, the sandy beaches strung U-shaped between the headlands like decorative garlands.

We were right between what geologists call "littoral cells," sections of the coast marked off between large headlands that act as closed compartments for sand supply. Cape Lookout is the interstice between the Sand Lake littoral cell and the Netarts littoral cell. In other words, the sand to our right would stay to our right, and the sand to our left would stay to our left. But neither cell would ever look exactly as it did that day. The coastline is as cyclical as the tides, just on a larger time scale. The headlands formed here initially due to bands of rock with alternating resistance that ran perpendicular to the coast. Where the rocks were weaker, the sand and clay was eroded. This left bands of stronger rocks—chalk, granite, and limestone among them—to form the capes, like the one on which we now stood. But the headlands are shrinking. Through the deposit of sediment within the bays and because of the erosion caused by wave surges and tidal actions, capes have a relatively short geologic lifespan. The Oregon coastline will eventually straighten itself out before starting the whole process again.

Where the tide goes from high to low and then back again each twenty-four-hour period, so the coastline goes from straight to scalloped and back to straight over a period of thousands of years. But as sea levels rise, as the frequency and intensity of storms continue to increase here and in other parts of the world's coasts, the erosion will escalate and happen on an increased time scale, leading to irreversible changes and loss of habitat.

A couple emerged from the trail with a husky so hyper it bounced at the end of its leash. Marco, who has hated huskies since he lived in the same neighborhood as a particularly grumpy one, barked hysterically, and Cricket followed suit. We apologized as we made our way around them through the mud. Cricket's leash got caught on a piece of wayward salmonberry, and then she stopped and stood completely still. Marco, too. They lifted their noses to the air and breathed deep.

We smelled it about thirty seconds after they did. The wind must have been blowing in the perfect direction, because the odor from twenty-seven thousand Tillamook cows filled our nostrils.

☾

"Do you know what that smell is to a farmer?" my dad would ask his city-dwelling children on road trips when we were little. We were too busy covering our noses and complaining to answer. He'd laugh and exclaim, "It's the smell of money!"

My dad took me on a solo road trip to San Diego, where my grandparents lived, when I was eleven. I'd never taken a trip without my brothers before, and I felt chosen and excited. We loaded our bags into his black VW diesel Rabbit and blared John Denver through the stereo. Half an hour down Interstate 5, he asked me how many cows I thought we'd see on the trip.

"I guess two hundred," I said. I knew I was overshooting.

"I think we'll see more," dad said. "Wanna place a bet?"

"What kind of bet?"

"I think we'll see more than five thousand cows on this drive. Whoever's guess is closest wins."

"Five thousand cows? No way." I was annoyed by how easy he was making this. I hated when anyone purposely let me win. "What's the winner get?"

Dad was ready with a response. "A magazine and a candy bar."

I shrugged. "You're on."

We drove south and the weather was perfect the whole way. I didn't even open my book because the cow counting kept me occupied. By the time we were three hours in, I had counted 254 cows, but I was still certain my dad wouldn't get close to the five thousand he had placed his bet on.

And then it hit. The smell of money.

The aroma of manure filled my nostrils, coated them from the inside. We crested a hill and then saw nothing but fields of back-to-back cows. I counted frantically while my dad laughed, but it was impossible to keep up. They were almost one on top of another in field after field, but I still had hope for that candy bar and magazine. My dad exited the freeway and drove to a small guard booth at the entrance to one of the fields. The guard—a young man in what looked like a ranger's outfit and hat—nodded at my father as he rolled down the window of his Rabbit.

"About how many head of cattle do you have here?" my dad asked.

"Somewhere around ten thousand?" the man said, though it sounded like a question. My dad grinned, and then I knew: I'd been set up. I'd played right into his hands, and now I owed my dad an issue of *Car and Driver* and a Butterfinger from my allowance.

Sometimes, I think about how it felt to watch him die while I held his hand. I feel relieved that I never had to tell him I left the church, or that I'm gay. But mostly I just feel cheated that I was never able to give him the chance to love me for who I am instead of how good I could be.

☾

The mud forced our legs to work twice as hard, made us twice as winded. Katie had a stripe of sludge on her right cheek, but I thought it was too cute to tell her it was there. Cricket sat down just off the trail and wouldn't respond to my pull on her leash. Marco sat down next to her. The dogs were on strike.

The dogs had plopped down in front of a metal plaque covered in foliage. Etched into it were the words, "On August 1, 1943, a four motored Army Air Force plane crashed 500 feet west of here. This marker was erected by the Oregon State Highway commission in commemoration of the members of this flight crew that perished in the line of duty." We'd read about this plane when we researched the Cape Lookout hike. In the middle of World War II, the bomber had been making its last routine patrol flight along the coast before its crew shipped overseas to fight in earnest. Instead, a particularly overcast day forced the pilot to fly close to the water, and eventually the low visibility sent them barreling into the side of Cape Lookout. Nine men were killed on a day so cloudy there was no horizon, no seeing the way forward. Nothing in the offing. Supposedly there were still old plane parts in the understory off trail, but it was too dangerous to go looking for them, especially in the mud.

My eyes closed. I was dizzy from the careening nose of the plane, then jolted by the impact.

The same way zooming out to view the coastline from space makes the cells between headlands hardly discernible, zooming out against the backdrop of time makes the boundaries between events murky. In the grand scheme of things, there was only an interstitial space between those dead airmen and me, there on that basalt cliff where they once died and I now stood. Viewed from that timeline, there was even less distance between my father, now dead fifteen years, and myself.

Every so often, time can change and cavort the way the tide does.

And what of the interstice between my mom in her family's barn in 1961, kittens mewing at her ankles as she squeezed milk from the udders of a cow belonging to her older brother, and me here today, smelling cattle on the wind? If I kept my eyes closed, maybe I could catch the difference between the two smells, between the cows in the valley below me and the one in the barn with my mother, the one that would not, could not, send her to college.

THIS STORY HAPPENS EVERYWHERE

I'm not the first queer thinker to see time as nebulous. My teenaged mother in a freezing cattle barn. The impact of a B-17 plummeting sideways into Cape Lookout. The moment I sit here typing, right now, looking out the window of the Castle onto the Three Arch Rocks. None of these necessarily happen on a chronological plot line, although our brains experience them this way. Engaging with our personal history and the history of humanity through the nonlinear is the essence of what scholars call "queering time." Queering time doesn't need to be anti-science. Albert Einstein once wrote to a grieving family that "For us believing physicists, the distinction between past, present and future is only a stubbornly persistent illusion."

So although I was sitting in the living room of the Castle when I saw on social media that Mandy had lost her teenage son, I felt like I was sixteen again.

He'd been her second born, and he'd played sports at the same high school we had attended as teenagers. My children went there, too. Had our kids ever walked down one of the school's long hallways and unknowingly passed the specters of their parents, carrying our geometry textbooks towards the math wing? Or had we ever stopped at the drinking fountain near the library and experienced a sense of deja vu that we quickly shook off, not knowing that time had folded and our progeny had just entered the cafeteria, or been called to the attendance office, or were gathering their sports gear from their lockers?

Mandy became a parent long before any of us, if we are following a linear timeline.

☾

I came home from school, dropped my bookbag, and made a beeline for the sodas in the fridge. My mom was waiting in the kitchen. Sister Moneyhan,

Mandy's mother, had just called her with the news that Mandy was pregnant. True to who I knew my mother to be, both while she was in the religion and long after she'd left it, there wasn't a hint of judgment in her voice. There wasn't pity, either. She'd seen before, growing up in a rural farm town, how easily girls fall prey to the hungers of boys and men. And how fully girls were always left to shoulder the sexual consequences on their own. "She's going to need her friends," mom said. Sister Moneyhan had told her how sick Mandy was, that she was throwing up at home instead of attending school.

I wanted to tell Dani, but I knew Dani abhorred gossip. She prided herself on her obedience; gossip was one of the sins we were warned against, despite the fact that our parents indulged in gossip regularly in whispered hushes outside of sacrament meeting and over the telephone lines. So I waited to bring it up until our Laurels presidency meeting. Dani had been called as Laurels President a few months earlier, and she chose me to be one of her two counselors. (*Laurels* was the name for the group of oldest girls in the Young Women program, between the ages of sixteen and eighteen, named for the laurel wreaths that were often given as a symbol of significant achievement.) We spent most of our presidency meetings planning upcoming activities and tracking the attendance of less active girls, always on the lookout for ways to bring them back into the fold. I knew it was a confidential space.

"One of our activities this month should be to drop in and see Mandy," I offered when the time was right.

Natalie jumped in just as I was expecting. "What's up with Mandy? She sick?"

Dani looked away and squinted, as if examining something far away.

"Pregnant," I said. Natalie sucked in a breath. I secretly delighted in being the one to offer this juicy piece of news. Natalie and I started talking about putting together care packages and a potential baby shower.

Dani interrupted us. "I've already talked to the bishop," she said. "We aren't allowed to do anything. Mandy isn't a Laurel anymore."

"What do you mean she isn't a Laurel?" I asked. "She's sixteen."

"It's a rule from Salt Lake City," Dani said with a shrug. "If a girl gets pregnant, she is out of the Young Women's program and moved into Relief Society with the women. Mandy is their responsibility now, not ours."

"I don't want to be *responsible* for her. I want to be her friend. Are you saying we aren't *allowed* to be friends with someone?"

"I'm saying we aren't allowed to include her as a Laurel."

"That's ridiculous," I said. Natalie looked from Dani to me and then back again. It was the first time we'd had any sort of conflict. I continued, "So Jesus says love everyone, but a random Bishop in Oregon gets to override that?"

Dani wasn't having it. She was—and still is, to this day—one of the most compassionate and service-oriented people I had ever met. But she is also a rule follower. If the Bishop had spoken, so had Dani. Mandy wouldn't be coming to our weekly activities anymore, and she wouldn't be joining us in Sunday School each week. She'd contracted a vile plague, terrifying in its potential for contagion. The church had decided it was more important to protect the rest of us from Mandy than it was to protect Mandy from the harsh world she was about to enter. A shrug of the shoulders. She'd had her shot, and she'd blown it.

☾

When Mandy had the baby, Mom and I brought gifts and well wishes. We walked into Mandy's parents' living room to see my friend lying on the couch lengthwise, her sleeping infant pressed against her body. They looked like two pieces of the same whole. My mom disappeared into the kitchen to talk to Mandy's mom, and Mandy, her infant, and I regarded each other.

Mandy and her baby reminded me of the mother ducks I'd seen in lakes and wetlands each spring, the way they tucked their babies inside their feathers for warmth. It seemed so natural for Mandy to have her baby tucked there under her invisible wing. I wondered how she knew to do it. I wondered if I would know, too, when it was my time. This was the whole thing, after all. This is what they wanted from us. Whenever I'd asked in Sunday School about women not holding the priesthood (especially since every member of the church assigned male at birth received the priesthood at age twelve), I always got the stock answer: women get to have children; men get the priesthood. In this way, they are equal. What I didn't think to ask at the time: Why is it, then, that men and their priesthood get to tell us when and how and with whom to have children?

Mandy shifted when the baby cooed and smoothed her hand over his downy head. But for a wrinkle of time, I could almost feel that parallel moment, seven years later, when I would sit with my own newborn tight against my feathered body and ask my husband to *scratch our back*.

Time is as much a construct as the Continental Divide, as gender, as the notion that an all-knowing god has given us a blueprint to live by. The suggestion that time moves in multiple directions, and that, as Philip Cheung asserts, "we just happen to inhabit a section of the cosmos with a single, locally defined arrow of time," has been around as long as the discipline of physics has.

☾

I wish I could say the rumors didn't swell and churn through Mandy's pregnancy and after. During a scripture scavenger hunt during one Youth Activity Night, while we were busy paging through our Bibles (mine had my name engraved in gold on the black leather front), Natalie told us what she'd overheard in the school cafeteria, keeping her voice low so the boys wouldn't hear.

"Mandy's had sex with *so* many guys," she said, her eyes wide. "And they said she just lies there. Doesn't move or anything."

Don't have sex. And if you do, don't enjoy it. But do enjoy it just enough so that it doesn't have an adverse effect on your partner's enjoyment.

Becoming a mother is the ultimate divine goal for a woman, they said. Nothing is more sacred than motherhood, they said. But become a mother the wrong way, and you'll be removed from the community in a shame-cocoon of your own making.

The game. It was rigged the whole fucking time.

FORT STEVENS

(Chinook: *Katielaát-sop*)

Matt proposed marriage in my parents' driveway after we'd seen a Jurassic Park sequel in the theater with friends. We sat in his parents' taupe 1980 Subaru sedan while the engine ran. He didn't have a ring to offer me, though he did sing me a short rendition of Billy Joel's "She's Got a Way" over the metallic double-knock of the old car's idle. We kissed, and he held me for a bit, and then I went into my parent's house where my mom was folding laundry on her bedroom floor. It was a moment I had imagined differently my entire life.

Sometimes I can queer time enough to superimpose the two engagements on one another. Twenty-year-old me in a long-sleeved dress looks like a transparent ghost over forty-five-year-old me in a T-shirt, cowl, and hiking pants. The dirty upholstered front seats of that old Subaru are a strange overlay on the dense forest understory of Ungulate Woods, where I kneeled before Katie twenty-five years later. Seen this way, the version of me who does the asking sits like a thin veneer over the version of me—all those years ago—who did the answering.

Matt and I celebrated our engagement with a day trip to the north coast. En route, we picked up the half-karat diamond solitaire he'd ordered for my left ring finger and drove the same Subaru out of Portland and toward the Pacific. It was late spring, and the highway through the Coast Range was buffered on both sides by five-foot-tall foxgloves blooming in shades of fuchsia and white that the towering forest wore like ankle socks. We talked as Matt drove; sometimes after shifting gears, he covered my newly bejeweled hand with his and squeezed it tightly, a loving gesture that made my stomach flip in a confusing amalgam of elation and dread.

Our future ahead of us, we delayed talking about the wedding and instead played hide-and-seek at Fort Stevens, the old military ghost site that sits on

Point Adams near the Columbia River bar. We were the only people exploring the old garrison that day, and we ran from room to room like the children we mostly still were. We guessed where the guns had been mounted, where the soldiers slept, how they got from one level to another. We kissed in a small concrete room that used to be the officer's quarters but now smelled mostly of urine and sea spray. We pretended to be gunners in what used to be the control room, aiming for the sea through a slit in the concrete at eye level. We ignored the vulgar graffiti that adorned a good portion of the walls, at least the ones not overtaken by vegetation.

A picture from that day still sits in a box at the bottom of the closet I now share with Katie: Matt and I stand on the spiral concrete stairs that lead from an interior chamber to the gun emplacement on the upper deck. Matt holds the film camera at arm's length above his head, and it captures us against the steps where they curve to the right and out of frame. I am wearing a loosely knit hat with a brim and a patched denim jacket; Matt wears a color-blocked polo shirt with long sleeves and Teva sandals. I'm smiling, pressed against his side. Around us, the concrete blooms with sepia water stains and moss.

It's the mossy film of time. Time moving backward and forward, stretching out to infinity and also not moving at all. What you can't see in that picture: the natural world closing in on the garrison, salt-tolerant shrubs like kinnikinnick and salal reclaiming the infrastructure in the last breaths of a long-ended war.

☾

And six weeks later, we posed for a wedding photo. It's a picture every Mormon couple has in their wedding album, of the moment they exit the intricately carved doors of the temple in their finery and the tuxedoed groom dips the white-clad bride for a kiss. I am still impressed, when I see this photo, how well I played my role. I am just another happy bride, lifting her wildflower bouquet in celebratory relief against the mahogany double exit doors, Matt leaning me back for a kiss. The doors were each carved with the Star of Bethlehem and were flanked by massive walls of finely veined white marble. Our friends and family members lined up in rows along either side of the walkway that led from the doors to the temple's reflective pool. Many of them, like my brothers, had not been allowed to see us get married just moments before because they weren't deemed worthy enough to enter that giant block of granulated marble.

Matt's kiss was chaste and sweet, exactly what everyone lined up before the doors expected to see. Prophet Spencer W. Kimbell famously said, "Kissing has . . . degenerated to develop and express lust instead of affection, honor, and admiration. To kiss in casual dating is asking for trouble. What do kisses mean when handed out like pretzels and robbed of sacredness?" Kimball encouraged unmarried Mormons to restrict each kiss to a "clean, decent, sexless one like the kiss between a mother and son."

(Time queers again. Katie presses my back into a small indent on the side of a rock bluff, out of view of other beachcombers. She stands on driftwood to give her several inches over me; her breath smells faintly of coconut. The swells slap the sand behind us again and again and again while we kiss, her tongue in my mouth. Lust. I become part of the rocky scarp and raise my hips to meet hers, our waterproof pants pressed together, my hands in her hair.)

The kiss outside the temple doors was our first presentation as a married couple, and the weight behind it was different from any of our previous kisses. It wasn't dangerous. It was sanctioned. We could relax our constant vigilance about our morality and our eternal souls. And every person who cheered for us as Matt dipped me was really cheering for what was to come in a few short hours, when we'd be having sex for the first time.

But we didn't.

We didn't have sex that night.

We didn't have sex the next night, either, or the next morning, or the following day, or the entirety of our honeymoon in Hawaii. After our wedding reception send-off, we drove to the Hampton Inn near the airport in my mom's Volvo station wagon, "Just Married" sloppily painted on the rear window. In my overnight bag, I had packed a red silk teddy that I'd purchased for the occasion, my meds, my toothbrush, and my stuffed sea lion, Walter, whom I'd rarely slept without. I don't remember if the lingerie even came out of the bag. I just remember I lay in bed next to Matt, started to undress, and then broke down in tears. I moved to the floor to sit on the mildewed carpet, my back against the wall, and sobbed. I couldn't name what I was feeling, except that it felt like immense grief, as if I'd lost something irreplaceable.

"What's wrong?" he asked over and over.

"I have no idea," I said through tears, mascara bleeding down my cheeks.

It was the truth. I had just done the one thing I'd been groomed my whole life to do. I went to the temple and became someone's wife. We were now sealed together for time and all eternity. I had no idea why I wasn't the happiest woman in the world, or why I didn't want my doting new husband to touch me.

☾

Purity culture was full of tips about how we could avoid being touched by men. How to dress, how to sit, how to say no, how to withhold, how to avoid being caught alone. Boys were crazed and sex-obsessed; our job was to help them avoid sin by constantly rebuking the advances they couldn't help making. Our virginity was our most precious asset. It was the greatest gift we could give anyone, which meant every boy—and man—around us wanted it.

And yet there I was, newly married, completely unable to give my husband this gift I had so painstakingly and carefully cultivated over the last twenty years. Turns out keeping men out of my pants was the easy part. It was a game I could usually win because I didn't want it the way they did.

Every time he came close to penetrating me, the muscles in my vagina would erupt in spasms of pain and revolt. I had never heard of vaginismus and had no way of knowing that I was experiencing a documented medical condition, one far more common in women raised with purity culture. My vagina reacted to attempts at sex with complete lockdown.

My virginity was a construct I'd obsessed over my entire life, worried I would lose it too soon as if it were something always on the verge of being shaken loose from me. I'd been Matt's wife for four months when we drove to northern Arizona for a hike and the winding road left me shaky and nauseated. I threw up in the forest service visitor center's bathroom. Another English department teaching assistant kept asking me if I was pregnant and encouraged me to take a test when I got home. I didn't want to tell her that there was no scientific way I could be pregnant, because although I was a newlywed of four months, I was still a virgin.

I don't remember when it finally happened. At some point, we successfully overcame my body's stubbornness and consummated the marriage. I've disassociated completely from the event. All I know is that for so long I *couldn't*, and then, somehow, I finally *could*. I had succeeded at being normal. I had packaged and wrapped my gift, signed, sealed, and delivered with a card apologizing for its tardiness. And the prize I'd been promised, the whole reason I had so carefully guarded this gift, was that God would still love me.

But I could no longer love myself.

☾

I was elected to speak at the school district board meeting when I was fifteen, a whole five years before I failed to lose my virginity to my husband. The debate was whether the school district should begin using an "abstinence only" sex ed curriculum, stemming from the same nineties purity culture that had kept my sexuality on lockdown. Those promoting it believed teaching sex ed in schools only *increased* teen pregnancy, STDs, and the psychological damage caused by having sex out of wedlock.

Amanda spoke before I did. She wasn't a Mormon, but she was a close friend of Dani's whom I respected and admired. The only thing I remember from Amanda's speech was her rallying cry at the end: she passionately told the board and the hundreds of spectators that teenagers will have sex regardless of whether they were taught to do it safely or not, so "Please do not bury your heads in the sand." I've never forgotten Amanda's words. They reverberate still through the thirty years between then and now, overshadowing the speech I half-heartedly gave next about the virtues of abstinence.

It's easy to preach abstinence from intercourse when you are uninterested in sex with men. I thought I was successful as a good Mormon teen for resisting temptation, but I was mostly successful because I didn't want to have sex with boys and wouldn't let myself explore having sex with girls.

When I got home that night, there was a single white rose resting on our doormat. Tied to the stem with a white ribbon was a note that said, "Thanks for being brave and doing the right thing and fighting for morality." A woman in our ward, someone I babysat for frequently, had heard my speech and left it for me as a token of her appreciation. No, of my goodness. I picked it up and held it to my nose, surprised by its smooth stem. It was the first time I'd held a thornless rose to my face. I don't remember how the rose smelled. I *do* remember that all I could focus on the rest of the night was Amanda's line about heads buried in the sand. I had a sense already that in doing what I'd been told was right, I'd done something wrong. After all, what was a rose without thorns if not an ostrich with its head in the sand, a complete denial of the natural state of things?

I hid the rose in my jacket and snuck it into my bedroom. I didn't want my mom to see it. I knew where she stood on social issues, and her stance was always at odds with the church. She believed in sex education, she voted Democrat, she rallied for gay rights. She must have wanted me to question the messages we received every week in church, but she'd never pushed me to do so.

There was no rose on my doorstep during those long, frustrating months when I was trying to consummate my marriage. The thing that I had been so afraid of *accidentally* happening had become an insurmountable task. And the most confusing part of all was the fact that my body just didn't respond to his. I could have used a dose of temptation. My mind wanted to have sex with him as if I was marking off a checklist, but my body was uninterested. It would be well over a decade before I knew what it felt like to truly *want* someone, to have to talk yourself into slowing things down.

I wish I could queer time and tell my fifteen-year-old self these things. I'd ask her to take that thornless white rose and bury it bloom-down in the sand right here off Oceanside Beach.

☾

Our actual wedding—our temple sealing—exists in my mind as snippets and flashes, a collage my brain can't quite make sense of.

Your dress is not white enough, says the Temple Matron. I'm asked to change out of the wedding gown I'd dreamed of and so thoughtfully selected because the ivory is just not quite pure enough for God. And to think I'd been so careful about the length of the sleeves, the covering of my shoulders and décolletage, the fabric to my ankles.

As the bride, I stand on one side of a floor-to-ceiling pleated curtain, a representation of the veil that separates earth from heaven. My husband-to-be plays the role of God, checking my worthiness to pass from earth into eternal life.

Three sharp knocks of a wooden mallet. Don't mess this up, Elissa.

What is wanted? Matt-as-God asks me.

An elderly woman in full temple garb stands next to me and whispers the phrase I am to repeat in my ear. *Eve, having been true and faithful, desires to converse with the Lord through the veil.* Once I've said it, Matt-as-God's hand appears through a slit in the curtain; he takes my right hand in a secret grip.

What is that? he asks. I recite the name of the handhold, or token, and the quiz from God continues. Handshakes. Passwords. When I've answered all of God's questions satisfactorily, Matt-as-God pulls me through the veil, at which point I whisper my new secret name, the one I am to never utter out loud outside the temple, the one only my husband will know. I don't get to know his.

The Celestial Room, the place that is supposed to bear the closest earthly resemblance to the highest level of heaven. Gold light fixtures with long crystal prisms hang from the ceiling, like stalactites in a cave. They are the only part of the room not a stark, fresh-after-a-blizzard white. Our clothing. The walls and ceiling. The upholstery of the couch under our thighs where we sit, waiting for a temple worker to guide us into the sealing room.

Abject terror on each inhale.

Wait, wait. Not all white. Around our waists are the bright green aprons embroidered with leaves in equally verdant thread. They represent our nakedness. That we now bear the closest earthly resemblance to Adam and Eve.

Another couple sits to the right of us, on a white couch the exact replica of ours, also waiting their turn. *Please let them be first* loops in my mind on repeat.

You could run. You could hotfoot it right out of here. Just stand up. Take off the green apron. You could run.

I am on one side of a white altar, kneeling. Matt is on the other side. He takes my hand.

Halfway through the sealing, my grandfather, serving as witness, stops the ceremony. He's concerned Matt isn't holding my hand in the Patriarchal Grip. It would make the whole sealing null and void. Grandpa, too, wears a green apron layered over a white pleated drape that resembles a toga. A string on the drape is attached to the colorless cap on his head. From my vantage, it is almost impossible to discern him from Matt, or from any of the other men seated in the room.

You could still run. This break in the action, you could use it. Get off your knees. Blaze out of here. You could run.

The Patriarchal Grip or The Sure Sign of the Nail: Matt' right hand in my right hand. Our pinkies intertwined. Our index fingers pressing against the inside of each other's wrists.

No aisle. No flowers. No rings. No kiss. No mention of the word love.

Matt promises to obey God. I promise to obey Matt.

Matt-as-God.

Lois. My secret name is Lois. I won't speak it out loud again for fifteen years.

I don't run. As much as I queer time, I will never be able to force myself to drop the hand of Matt-as-God and simply follow my gut and run.

☾

Why didn't I run?

☾

Matt and I left the church ten years after we were sealed in celestial marriage; soon after, we spoke our temple names out loud one night in our bedroom. Nothing to that point in my life had felt like a greater transgression than learning my husband's temple name.

And today I don't remember it.

I could find out what it was. There are charts published online now that show what names were universally given out to each gender on specific days in the temple, which means that every person assigned female at birth who went through the temple the same day I did is *also* a Lois. I wonder if they, too, think about Lois Lane and her mild-mannered reporter when they remember their secret name, like I always have. But something stops me from looking Matt's name up, even to include it here. I could also ask him on our daily text thread, and he'd tell me without hesitation. Again, something always stops me, though, some piece of my brain etched with a fear that borders on superstition about my salvation. Part of me doesn't want to make waves, wants to leave well enough alone, the way Lois Lane never, ever would.

But Matt-as-God knows my name. I whispered it to him at the veil. How else will he call me forth on the first morning of the resurrection to usher me into heaven?

And if I'm in bed with my wife at the time, do I have to go?

BARRED OWL SPRINGS

The first time Katie and I went to visit her parents on the Olympic Peninsula, I discovered a cache of owl figures in the top drawer of the dresser next to the bed. There were small ceramic owls with painted dots for eyes and a slightly larger cedar one, finished only with wood stain, its face devoid of features. I held one of the ceramic owls up for Katie.

"These are adorable," I said.

"I had a thing for owls as a kid," she told me. "My mom keeps *everything*." We were leaving that afternoon, so Katie was rolling her shirts for maximum packing efficiency.

"I can't believe you never told me this," I grabbed one of her newly rolled shirts and snapped it at her playfully.

"Really?" she asked, walking toward me, her eyes squinted. She wrapped one arm around my waist and pulled me against her. "Owls? All the things I haven't said and you choose owls?" She leaned back a bit to look into my eyes.

"Wars have been started over lesser offenses," I told her.

She grabbed her shirt back from my hand. "Really? Are you going to stand by that statement?"

"We talk about owls all the time," I reminded her. "Remember our erotic owl serenade?"

I walked into the adjoining bathroom to gather the toiletries, but I could hear her resigned "*touché*" through the open door.

☾

Once, Katie and I made Clementine watch *The Matrix* with us on a school night and then went to bed. We lay on our backs with pillows propped behind our necks and admired the bedroom. We'd spent the day brushing primer on all the walls and trim in the Wetlands. The bedroom had been a dark brown since Matt and I bought the house; I didn't like living in a room the color of barely creamed coffee, and more, it felt as if the past clung to that old paint like the goose-neck barnacles clung to the walls of Lost Boy Cave. Just one coat of primer had changed the entire vibe of the bedroom.

The windows were open to air the fumes, and the crisp, early May breeze wafted into the bedroom. It was just after eleven. I turned to Katie where she lay on the bed next to me in plaid boxers and a black tank top, both of which were still covered in drying primer. White paint was streaked along the underside of her chin in the shape of a small lightning bolt. The sight of it triggered something in me. I became an electrical tangle of wanting.

Within thirty seconds, we'd removed our clothes, quietly so we wouldn't wake Clementine. Katie's soft animal body was downy against my flesh as she climbed on top of me, the full weight of her physique pressed against mine. As we moved together almost soundlessly, our breaths quickened; a sudden screech pierced the room, followed by the rhythmic, unmistakable low barking of a pair of barred owls either mating or defending their territory. They must have been sitting in the redwood tree whose oversized trunk sat ten feet from the open window. Katie's teeth closed over my earlobe as the owls' duet raised to a fever pitch of monkey-like howls and gurgles. My own primal moans played in my head against the backing track of the owls' distinctive nine-note hoots.

☾

We were only slightly less intimately acquainted with another barred owl pair, one that occupied a small urban park surrounding a protected natural spring. We named the park Barred Owl Springs; it was our nightly four-minute walk from the Wetlands. The park occupied just three-and-a-half wooded acres surrounding the spring and the stream it created, and we could find the owls there every time, with their mottled brown and white feathers and almost-jet-black eyes. For three years running, the month of May brought with it two to three owl fledglings. We timed our walks so that we'd get to the park just as dusk opened its hasp; in that otherworldly light, the barred owl parents taught their juveniles how to fly, and then how to hunt, and then how to leave the nest altogether.

We watched as three owlets used their wings like climbing grips, their entire bodies splayed against the trunk of a Douglas fir. Below them, their father patiently waited until he saw just the right movement; he pounced into the ivy-covered ground four feet in front of us and then lifted a shrew out of the green leaves with his talons. His kids would eat tonight.

☾

Before I met Katie, I went on a date with a biologist who was appalled when I told her how much I loved barred owls. Barred owls are an invasive species in western North America, she told me. Colonizers of our forests, their very existence in Oregon drives down the population of the northern spotted owl. My delight in these birds became a conflicted guilty pleasure. Like so many before them, these mottled brown and white creatures were claiming land that wasn't rightfully theirs. Another theft in the long history of a region built by taking.

It frightened me, on my quest to feel my body and its desires, that wanting was a precursor to taking.

SLAB CREEK GHOST FOREST

(Tillamook: *Neskowin*)

Slab Creek's three-mile beach stretches from the mouth of the Nestucca River to Cascade Head (*Nastucco* in Salish), which rises twelve hundred feet above the water. And on that beach, during especially low tides a few months out of the year, the ghosts come out.

These are not human apparitions but over one hundred stumps and snags in the sand, the remnants of a stand of Sitka spruce trees that once stood over two hundred feet tall. Buried for close to two thousand years, this ghost forest was once merely legend. A few people—separated by decades—claimed to have caught a glimpse of the stumps, but when the tide turned, the sand covered them as quickly as they'd been uncovered. Then came an extreme *El Nino* in 1997, and with it a turbulent squall that swept a good portion of the sandy beach out to sea. Once the white caps calmed and the sun returned, there they stood: hundreds of stumps of varying sizes, teeming with barnacles, anemones, and sea stars. Far under the sand, these petrified trunks are perched in the original soil where they germinated. Some of them have shallow pools in their centers, worn down by erosion and salt water, where sea life gets trapped when the tide is out.

And when the tide water comes back in, it gently covers these ghost trees to free the stranded intertidal creatures, a vanishing act that stands as a reminder that there is very little space, if any, between today and yesterday.

Bliss Cua Lim writes, "Ghosts call our calendars into question. The temporality of haunting, through which events and people return from the limits of time and mortality, differs sharply from the modern concept of a linear, progressive, universal time." The ghost trees that once made up a coastal rainforest are proof of this.

☾

Here I should admit that I am terrified of ghosts.

I'm afraid of so many things, really. Airplanes. Road rage. Aliens. Spiders. Toxic nerve gas. Brain-eating amoebas. Communicable diseases. Noncommunicable diseases. But ghosts top the list.

It isn't a rational fear. I am a skeptic to my core; I don't actually *believe* in ghosts, even a little bit. I once went on a date with a woman who revealed halfway through the meal she was a medium, and that she was picking up on some real supernatural activity around me. There was no second date.

And yet.

When Chloe was fifteen, she and her best friend begged me to take them to see *The Conjuring*, a horror film whose entire premise was malicious ghosts. The movie was rated R, so they wouldn't be able to see it unless accompanied by an adult. My need to be a cool mom outplayed my fear of ghosts, and I bought the tickets, the popcorn, the drinks. I've since blocked it out (to be fair, my eyes were closed for most of it), but I do remember the reverberations of those two hours. It was weeks before I could walk downstairs alone after dark. I dreaded blind corners. Every slant of light, every shadow, every movement, transmogrified into the spectral.

Ridiculous? Absolutely.

Deep breath, step back. Maybe not so ridiculous.

I was raised to believe in ghosts.

Worse—I was raised to believe there was a ghost actually inside me, whispering directly into my head. Like other Christian faiths, Mormonism holds sacred the trinity of the Father, the Son, and the Holy Ghost, though the three are wholly separate individuals. Of particular note, the Holy Ghost, like the other two, is portrayed exclusively as male, and according to the LDS website, "is a personage of spirit, without a body of flesh and bones." In other words, true to his title, he is a *ghost-ghost*.

After Mormon kids are baptized, another ceremony follows in which they are given "the gift of the Holy Ghost." For me, this meant that with my father at the helm, eight priesthood holders in suits piled their hands on my head, closed their eyes, and pronounced me a new host for the Holy Ghost. As long as I remained worthy and followed the tenets of the faith, I'd keep him with me every second of every day. I'd be able to hear him whisper to me, feel him sometimes physically within me, prompting me in my decisions and my daily interactions.

(You see it, right? The women all sat in their Sunday best in the audience while the men surrounded me, a little girl, and gave me the gift of a ghost who would accompany me everywhere—a *man ghost*—and tell me to do things.)

This ghost worked differently from Bliss Cua Lim's ghosts, who challenged linear temporality. The Holy Ghost haunted me on the strictly heteropatriarchal, white colonial timeline drilled into me since birth. In the LDS faith, everyone is on the same chronological trajectory. Any deviation from that norm is dangerous, an indication that you aren't living up to God's standards. We all met the same benchmarks: getting a CTR ring ("Choose the Right") to wear at eight when we were baptized, entering the young adult program at twelve, dating once we turned sixteen, marrying preferably in our late teens or early twenties, and birthing as many babies as we could make. The same blueprint, a factory farm of righteous, identical lives.

☾

Ghosts are everywhere, especially on the northern Oregon coast.

In late 1907, the *Emily G. Reed*, a sailing schooner out of New South Wales, carried over two thousand tons of coal toward the docks along the Willamette River in Portland. The Downeaster was two hundred feet long and the fastest of its kind. Copper sheathing on her underside protected her hull from barnacles and other marine growth, and four full masts rose in peaks from her deck to propel the wooden ship forward.

The *Emily G. Reed* never reached Portland. Before the clipper could try her hand at the Columbia River bar (that graveyard of the Pacific), an intense storm and an error in judgment capsized her on Rockaway Beach, just ten miles north of the Castle. It was Valentine's Day, 1908. Midnight. No stars, only wind and sideways rain. The ship instantly broke apart, pitching crew members as she went. All two thousand tons of coal disappeared into the ocean. The captain and his wife survived by clinging to the poop deck and then swimming to shore at low tide. When the captain reported the wreck, he told officials that the accident had claimed eleven of his crew members. But three days later, another vessel discovered a lifeboat drifting in Neah Bay, Washington, two hundred miles north. Aboard were the first mate, the cook, and two other seamen; the cook was dead, but the rest were rescued. All told, the shipwreck claimed eight lives.

But the seamen aren't the ghosts I am interested in.

I'm interested in *her. Emily G. Reed.*

She haunts Rockaway Beach. Every few years, the sea sweeps enough sand away for her ribs to emerge. Passersby would be hard pressed not to notice just how large she was in her prime; those ribs seem to stretch the entire length of the sandy beach. It's impossible not to imagine her at her finest, when those ribs attached to her outer planking and inner sheath, and her mainsail stood proud above the other three masts. Like any good ghost, you can't go looking for her. She decides when she appears, when she wants to show her ribs to the world.

Queer temporality. She last sailed over a hundred years ago. She last sailed yesterday. She'll sail again tomorrow. I think of what Stephan Feuchtwang wrote: "Ghosts are unwanted reminders. Ghosts are traces of repressed desires. Ghosts are discarded dreams. Tied to a place. Ephemeral but also eternal."

Repressed desires. What or who did Emily G. Reed *want*? And what of those spectral ribs? What vital organs, what secret heart, are they sworn to protect?

☾

We were trained to use the gift of the Holy Ghost. I worked doggedly at it—to listen and recognize his voice in my head, so I could obey his promptings. I am nothing if not steadfast when I put my mind to something. At the start of morning recess one day in fourth grade, I ran out the classroom door toward the four square courts, my daily ritual. Vincent Takahashi and Billy Mason were already tossing the dull red nylon ball; I'd known both boys for years and we played every recess. But this day I stopped short: I felt the Holy Ghost like a chill in my body. He said, *Do not play four square with Vincent and Billy today.* I recognized it right away—a prompting! Something terrible would happen if I didn't turn and change course. (I was, admittedly, surprised how much the Holy Ghost's voice sounded like my own.)

Let's not dwell on the California sun that day, how it gleamed pointedly on the four perfect squares made up of two intersecting lines where Billy and

Vincent stood, or that red ball I was expert at hitting with my palms clasped together. Or how I would have spent most of the recess in the top square, the server's spot, because of my precision and accuracy. But instead of playing, I sat on a hard concrete bench with two girls who swapped lip gloss and talked about who wanted to "go around" with Vincent and Billy, girls who prodded me to tell them which of the boys I thought was cuter; it was one of my early brushes with the heteronormativity that would keep me in the closet until I was over forty years old.

That night, lying in bed underneath the posters of the space shuttle I had taped on my ceiling, I envisioned all the horrible things I probably avoided that day. Clearly something awful would have happened had I played. Maybe a bolt of lightning would have struck right where I was standing (never mind the fact that there were no clouds that day). The D.A.R.E kid in me thought maybe I would have been offered drugs. Or simpler: Vincent might have hit the ball too hard in anger and it would have broken my nose. (Vincent had a penchant for meanness. He once told me my ears looked like flowers—long pause—*cauli*-flowers.)

☾

The French philosopher Derrida said of the construct of time, "What is happening is happening to age itself, it strikes a blow at the teleological order of history. What is coming, in which the untimely appears, is happening to time but it does not happen in time. Contretemps. The time is out of joint."

The time is out of joint.

Elias stayed at the Castle with us a few weeks before the wedding to celebrate his twentieth birthday.

"What are we going to do today?" he asked the minute he arrived, ever in need of entertainment.

"Depends," I said. "How do you feel about finding secret military bunkers?"

"I'm down," he replied casually. Katie and I had read about an old bunker from the Second World War hidden in the hills behind Oceanside village. But the actual location of this bunker seemed to be a well-kept secret. Our first try took us down a trail of wooden steps to a narrow beach with a waterfall; we looked deep into the underbrush to the right and the left of us and found nothing. The next day, we parked on the shoulder opposite a viewpoint. We found a break in the fern understory and climbed straight up the side of the mountain. I took up the rear, and I could make out scraps of the conversation Katie was having with Elias.

"You're telling me that Yeat, a rich white boy from Lake Oswego, is the *greatest rapper or hip hop artist that ever lived*?" Katie spoke to Elias's back as they climbed. Elias lost his footing and stumbled forward before he regained his balance.

He said, "No, I said *Drake* is the GOAT and Yeat is number two." He lifted two fingers in the air to punctuate his case.

"And you don't think that has anything to do with the fact that you used to be best friends with the dude's brother?" Katie was operating on Patience Level Gold. "What about Atmosphere? Kendrick Lamar? The Weeknd?"

"Not as good, not as good, and not as good." Katie turned to roll her eyes at me. Elias came to an abrupt stop; the elk path we'd been following up the mountain had narrowed and we all felt like we were being watched. This mountainside belonged to the elk herd and felt untouched by humans. There was no way this path would end in the discovery of clandestine vestiges of a long-over war. My main thought as we climbed was how hard it was going to be to descend after we ran into the inevitable dead end.

And then.

We climbed just high enough that the moss-laden top of a concrete radar tower rose out of the forest canopy. And the closer we got, as if in direct response to my feeling that we were the first humans to scramble up this mountain, the more we could see a dazzling array of bright colors spray painted over each of the walls of what used to be operations or officer's rooms. Now these rooms were open to the elements, the roof long since replaced by crashing tree limbs.

A pink butterfly the size of my entire body had been spray-painted to the right of an open doorway; to the left was a graffiti tag of whites, purples, and greens in large letters that I couldn't make out. We took turns ducking through the concrete doorframe, Elias first, then Katie, then me. The butterfly, as it turned out, pointed the way to a series of rooms being reclaimed by the forest. Since the end of World War II, dozens of spruce and alder trees had fallen into the bunker, and new growth had sprung from them. Ivy, manzanita, and the berry-covered branches of salal grew in vines and tangles around these trees. I watched Elias navigate the apocalyptic maze where American soldiers had been tasked to watch for Japanese Mitsubishi bombers from the west. We followed him in silence from room to room, sometimes climbing downed trees to the tops of the walls. Ferns grew right out of the sides of the concrete; red graffiti tags co-mingled with shoots of green snaking moss.

The time was definitely out of joint. Elias and Katie kicked aside discarded Snapple bottles and beer cans to climb into a concrete chute that might have been part of a generator; I took pictures of them with their faces peeking out of tiny square windows. It felt as if I could close my eyes and see this place as it once was, camouflaged on the side of the mountain to avoid detection, bustling with men. Was there carpeting on the floor? Linoleum? Were there tables for eating and radios for calling in suspicious planes? Did the elk mind the disruption in their stomping grounds? That August day, we could see the imprints from many thousand-pound elks, a series of flattened weeds and ferns to the bunker's left where a herd had recently bedded down.

Queer time says: ghost elk.

When we got back to the Castle that night, my back was in spasm from the steep hillside climb, so Katie put me on the table for an acupuncture treatment. While she gently placed needles along my spine, in the side of my hand, and in my ankles, we talked about ghosts. I reiterated my belief that ghosts weren't real.

"Well, what *are* ghosts?" she asked. "What if they are something different than we think they are?"

"Like what?"

"Like the sense memories of trees maybe?" Katie said she believed in the ability of a space to retain the energy of its previous occupants, and trees have extremely long memories. What if forest ghosts, for example, are just trees that remember gunshots and chainsaws?

I paused, my head face down in the cradle. "Did you think there were ghosts in that bunker?"

"It felt *sticky*. And like we were invaders."

She adjusted a needle in my piriformis. I felt the *chi* flowing upward toward my spine and neck. More needles went into the flesh above my sacrum. She continued, "I mean, ghosts come up in Chinese medicine."

She told me problems with neurology and mental health are considered a result of "ghost invasion," called *gui*. *Gui* scatters the spirit, unsettles the mind, and enervates the will, a recipe for behaviors that are self-destructive and compulsive in nature. Treatment for these disorders—which range from seizures, lockjaw, nightmares, addiction, mania, paranoia, and even headaches—consists of careful needle application in thirteen regular meridian points called Ghost Points. Katie turned my left arm and ran her fingers across my hummingbird tattoo. "Pericardium 7 is a Ghost Point," she said. I felt my stomach flip. A Ghost Point, right on that channel whose job it is to protect the heart.

In the original Chinese medical texts, dating back to the seventh century, Sun Si Miao said that Ghost Points could be used to transcend time and space. I wondered what the Ghost Points of a *place* were, whether this might be used to bridge the gap between timelines on the earth's body instead of just a human one. Perhaps time *must* be out of joint to lead to healing.

☾

By the time I was a teenager, I learned to listen for promptings from the Holy Ghost when I felt chills up my legs. The voice always followed the chills (it was my own voice, but *also not my own voice*). Dani and I once drove downtown in my mom's burgundy Volvo 240 wagon to browse the poetry section at Powell's. As I steered toward the entrance to the parking garage (a tight, dark place where I'd park twelve years later to give a reading for my first book), I felt the chills and heard the voice: *Do not enter that garage.* I seized with fear and did as I was taught, which was to give the voice credence and act accordingly. Thanks to the prompting I now knew that evil lurked in that parking structure. We passed the entrance and parallel parked seven blocks down Burnside Street instead, walking along the cold sidewalk at twilight. For years I held as absolute certainty that by listening to the Holy Ghost that evening, Dani and I had avoided being brutally attacked, raped, murdered, shoved in someone's trunk, reduced to a bag of bones in a suitcase tossed off the Burnside Bridge.

It's not a surprise that I was diagnosed with an anxiety disorder at twenty, only months after I'd been married "for time and all eternity." As my new husband and I drove into the desert so I could attend graduate school in Arizona, I must have brought the anxiety and panic, my constant shadows, with me, tucked into the rear of our small U-Haul (the fight-or-flight snuggled next to the wedding gifts, the constant-sense-of-dread under the garage-sale queen mattress). These unwanted guests masqueraded, always, as divine gifts, as constant ghostly whisperings, as much a part of me as the rattlesnakes are a part of the barren desert.

This was a stretch of time when a series of road rage incidents in Phoenix saturated the nightly news. I can't accurately assess if there was *actually* an increase in road rage in Phoenix in the late nineties, or if my disordered brain just latched onto them as the major threat of my life. It seemed as if on every evening newscast, another unsuspecting driver had been shot, stabbed, or beaten to within an inch of their life for transgressions as simple as failing to signal a turn, or driving too close to the car in front of them, or simply being in the wrong place at the wrong time.

The Holy Ghost started working overtime. When I drove, he would prompt me to turn a certain direction to avoid an angry truck driver with a gun, or he would prompt me to pull into a library parking lot and turn off my engine for three minutes. More often, he just prompted me to stay home and not leave. I'd have my keys in hand, ready to go to the post office, and it would arrive clear as day: the tell-tale tingling legs, the intonation in my head: *You will not be safe if you go right now*.

I stopped driving altogether. Matt drove everywhere instead; he dropped me off to teach my classes, sat in the waiting room while I was at the dentist. The promptings didn't stop, but they became more confusing. Once while I rode in the passenger seat, the Holy Ghost told me to look in my rearview mirror at a stoplight. Through it, I saw the driver in the car behind me reach into her bag, and I knew with certainty—the tingling legs! the voice!—that she was reaching for a gun. Like so many other times, I removed my seatbelt and curled onto the floor of the passenger seat, only to have Matt tell me that she'd pulled out a tube of lipstick, not a gun, that she was painting her lips bright red while she waited for the light to change.

☾

The ghosts of sea otters splashing in the salty waters off our coast. But for a trick of time, I should be able to look out at the stretch between Oceanside Beach and Three Arch Rocks and see furry bodies bobbing in the surf, a whole raft of otters floating on their backs, using stones to pry open otherwise stubborn clam shells for supper.

Before John Meares and other fur traders arrived by ship in the eighteenth century, the Pacific off the north coast was thick with otters. Their feeding habits helped keep the ecosystem thriving. When they snacked on crabs, for example, they encouraged the growth of eelgrass in estuaries. Their taste for urchins similarly buoyed the health of the kelp forests that ran all along the coast of the western United States, critical highways for countless marine species. As the sea otters were hunted to near extinction, the kelp forests, too, began to disappear.

Historian Shane McCorristine speaks of "ecological hauntings," the notion that the ghosts of species and places past still haunt landscapes and human memory. He writes of the tangible nature of absences: " . . . they inspire action, trigger memories and contextualize presences." This place that has healed me contains spectral traces of animal and plant species that used to be but are no more—not just sea otters, but whole pods of whales, kelp forests, diverse reefs, Steller sea cows, Labrador ducks. The list of endangered animals in the region is long and growing: the short-tailed albatross, Chinook salmon, blue whales, gray whales, leatherback and loggerhead sea turtles.

Even our old favorite the California brown pelican, whose return to Oregon each year marks the start of the spring for me and Katie, spent several decades on the endangered species list. It almost disappeared entirely until a pivotal decision by the Environmental Protection Agency in 1972 to ban DDT. It was a reversal that likely saved the species, and by 2009, the birds were no longer classified as endangered. Bald eagles, too, those majestic birds whose almost daily appearance above the Castle inspires awe, were nearly obliterated by the insecticide.

Is the DDT still in the birds' intergenerational memory all these decades later? A distant traumatic retelling of near extinction? If so, here is what is written on the DNA of both the pelican and the eagle: the DDT didn't actually kill the birds outright. Instead, it altered their ability to metabolize calcium so much over time that they laid eggs with thinner and thinner shells. Eventually the shells became so attenuated that when the pelicans and eagles sat down to incubate their future offspring, their eggs were crushed underneath them.

It's in my DNA, too. When my mom hoed sugar beets in her family's small field as an adolescent, crop dusters flew regular routes above her to coat the fields—and my mom and her siblings—in a profuse film of DDT. There's no way to definitively know the effects all that DDT exposure had on my mom, aunt, and uncles, though each of them experienced chronic health problems and autoimmune disorders starting in young adulthood. And who's to say how much of the chemical was passed on to their children; what has it left in my own cells, the human equivalent of a thin shell, a fragile life, a threatened species?

Brown pelicans and bald eagles were once just as much ecological ghosts as the sea otters off coastal Oregon are today, proving that what was *once* here, what is *now* here, and what *will be* here in the future is in a state of constant flux. It's that ecological absence that McCorristine speaks of, absences that "are everywhere, if you know how to look for them. Absence is therefore relational and actionable: like the play of shadows, absences provoke the imagination and can structure experience and memory by sending ripples through what remains present."

Ecologically speaking, ghosts serve a warning. A clarion call. Tell their stories around the campfire; there is so much to fear.

☾

Cracks appeared in my logic as the anxiety mounted. First: Matt was as worthy as I was. No. *More* worthy. Why would I get promptings that he didn't? Why would I have access to the voice and protection of the Holy Ghost in moments when he did not? Matt was the priesthood holder in our family, which meant that the gauge on his Holy Ghost meter should be more finely tuned than my own. For the first time, I started to question my instincts. It wasn't until he convinced me to see a campus therapist and accept the anxiety meds that the intractable doomsday thoughts calmed down.

But if the Holy Ghost hadn't been telling me to be afraid, if I hadn't been listening to something life-saving those thirsty months in the desert, did that also mean that I could have played four square with Vincent and Billy? That I could have parked in the Powell's parking garage? That I should start to impugn everything I'd believed?

How was I supposed to parse out my own anxious thoughts from the whisperings of the Holy Ghost?

Every person assigned female at birth is inhabited by a cis-male voice at one point or another; it's the very crux of the patriarchy. Take the concept of the male gaze. Who among us hasn't made a decision about what to wear, or how to style her hair, or whether she should venture to the drugstore without makeup on, without the whispers of men (those she knows and those she doesn't) dominating the internal conversation? And in catering to those voices, we are slowly being driven mad. The diagnosis of female hysteria as a medical condition dates back to the ancient Greeks and took a major foothold in the eighteenth and nineteenth centuries; it was one of the most commonly diagnosed disorders for hundreds of years. Men used it to explain a number of ailments in women, among them anxiety, depression, infertility, and PTSD.

It's a chicken-and-egg scenario. My anxiety disorder seemed to be the direct result of being told I had a male voice inside me, dictating each decision I should make. And the catalyst that pushed it over the edge was my marriage. My therapist at the time told me that often the onset of anxiety disorders occurs after a major life change: marriage, divorce, childbirth, loss. But my marriage was weighted. Even though I married the kindest of men who saw me fully as his equal, we'd married in an institution that saw me as a second-class citizen. Our temple marriage ceremony asked only this in the form of vows: Would I promise to obey my husband? And would he in turn promise to obey God? It is no surprise that my anxiety disorder kicked into overtime when I promised myself I'd be subservient to a man.

The woman in the car behind us, the one I was so sure was pulling a gun out of her glove box, *reached for her lipstick*. She, too, was performing her gender. She, too, was a victim of the male gaze.

The treatment for the intrusive thoughts of my anxiety disorder was to learn to do the exact opposite of what I'd done my whole life. I was supposed to be actively distrustful of each thought that came through my head. Getting my mind back took years, and it meant learning to doubt every thought I had until I had thoroughly interrogated it, moving me from steadfast blind faith to a more healthy skepticism that centered my own knowing above any outside force.

When I left the church almost a decade later, those promptings remained, even though I didn't believe in them. They still exist as a sort of muscle memory, although now instead of listening, I pause. Each thought is fragile as an egg, and just as full of potential. I notice as it passes, pluck it from my brain, and hold it in my palm. Rub its smooth shell. Turn it over and inspect it for thickness, for viability. Then decide: toss it or grant it incubation. This is how I have learned to rely on my own intuition and to trust my own inner knowing, eschewing the idea that someone outside myself knows better than I do how to live my best life.

☾

Early in our romance, holding gloved hands and walking our dogs, Katie and I discovered a ghost forest a stone's throw from the Castle, in the mudflats surrounding Netarts Bay. While Marco and Cricket chased each other through the quicksand and muck of the low tideline, my beloved and I went from stump to stump, touching what we could only assume were the remnants of old trees.

Elsewhere on the edges of the same bay, geologists have discovered a ghost forest that, at eighty thousand years, is one of the oldest in the world. These ghosts are not huddled along the tide line but rather preserved in the clay cliffs that guard the bay like Chinese Foo dogs. I've seen pictures, but its actual location is kept secret, meant to protect these ancient trees from careless humans. And with good reason. When these trees were living—taking in sunlight and breathing out carbon dioxide—they hadn't met a single human. It was the cusp of the last ice age, as the planet was just starting to cool, long before the migration of homo sapiens along the Bering Land Bridge brought the native tribes to what we now call Oregon.

Robert M. Pirsig writes that the entire world as we know it is full of ghosts:

> Laws of nature are human inventions, like ghosts. Laws of logic, of mathematics are also human inventions, like ghosts. The whole blessed thing is a human invention, including the idea that it isn't a human invention. The world has no existence whatsoever outside the human imagination. It's all a ghost, and in antiquity was so recognized as a ghost, the whole blessed world we live in. . . . Your common sense is nothing more than the voices of thousands and thousands of these ghosts from the past.

That's what I trust these days—my common sense, built layer-upon-layer of everything that came before me and everything that will come after me.

It's why a year after first arriving at the Castle and falling into Katie's arms, I knelt in Ungulate Woods on a moist padding of pine needle duff with a ring box in my hand. To my back was a drop-off overlooking miles of riparian forests that led to Cape Meares beach. And in front of me, sitting on a log-and-rope swing suspended between two Sitka spruce trees a hundred feet tall, was Katie.

With those trees as my witness, I asked her to be my wife.

Marrying Katie was just good old common sense. Not a magical predestined fate, not something God or a higher power was urging me to do. Good old-fashioned common sense, in the form of whispers of ghosts that have come and gone. The ghosts of my first marriage. The ghosts of giant old-growth trees in our coastal forest. The ghosts of all the queer people who had come before me and decided to embrace who they were instead of who the world wanted them to be. They all bound together and told me to grab tight and not let go, because time is a tricky, tricky sleight of hand.

WASHINGTON, DC

(Piscataway: *Nacotchtank*)

We woke early on Katie's forty-second birthday because we'd planned a long hike. Our friends Sam and Sophie were staying downstairs, and I could hear the patter of their dog's feet on the hardwoods. When Katie rolled out of bed to use the bathroom, I wiped the sleep from my eyes and grabbed my phone. The breaking news alerts came hard and fast. *Supreme Court Strikes Down Roe v. Wade,* said one, and I dropped my phone onto the duvet cover, hoping I could make the news go away by unseeing what I'd just read.

"Well, shit," came Katie's voice from the bathroom, dashing my hope that she had left her phone near the bed. "Happy birthday to me."

The draft of the Supreme Court decision, which had been leaked six weeks before, should have prepared us for this. But how do you prepare a woman for the moment her country insists that it can decide what she does with her body?

On the other side of our bedroom blinds, the sun had started its slow arc westward. The rocky outcrops in the water were irradiated with a golden hue that we knew was there but could not see. By the time Katie climbed back into bed and pressed her forehead into mine, I could almost see the dense interplay of light and shadow against the basalt and the seabirds circling above. It was almost as if the planet were indifferent to the daily whims and laws of its apex species.

☾

My anger was familiar.

Each year when the snow arrives in the mountains surrounding us, the forests are covered with a blanket the color of bone that draws the eye to swaths of recent clear-cuts. I can see through the trees into stripped land that I'd otherwise assumed was still forested. Every winter, without fail, I am reminded anew of the hunger of chainsaws and log loaders, and the futility of human interference against the jaws of harvesters and skidders.

My therapist likes to tell me that anger is the appropriate response to injustice. But I wonder about its utility. My anger has never stopped a logging company from ripping trees off a mountainside, and it certainly wasn't going to reinstate legal abortion in the United States. My anger has never taken a greedy politician from power, released a hostage, or stopped a genocide. But I feel it anyway, growing, here in the center of my chest, at the thought of my daughters being forced to carry an unwanted pregnancy to term even if they are in danger.

The reality of extractive economies is that women's bodies are no less a commodity than the trees or precious metals or oil that are being stripped and sold at breakneck pace.

☾

We tried to focus on Katie's birthday and not the news that had dropped that morning. Our plan was to go deep into Ungulate Woods, and we dressed accordingly: water bladders in shoulder packs, beanies, cowls, hiking boots. When we got to the decommissioned road, the dogs pulled toward the forest at the base of the Queen of Swords, and we let them be our guides over Two-Step Log, through the Fairy Grassland, past Birthday Point, and through Spooky Bog. From there, we took an intentional right up a riparian knoll where an ancient sign was still partially nailed to a tall pine tree. *Diesel Donkey Trail* was burned into the wood: a place in our forest that came with its own name.

"What is a diesel donkey?" Sophie asked.

"Probably logging related," Katie guessed. We were used to finding the rusted loops of old logging cables lodged into the forest floor. They were thick as a grown woman's thumb, resembled metal rope, and barely budged no matter how hard we pulled on them. Our group pushed forward as the trail climbed higher and higher. We crested a fern-covered berm, and below it a piece of corroded machinery sat half-sunken into the woods.

"There's your diesel donkey," Katie said. Almost eight feet long, the hunk of archaic logging equipment was rectangular with old belts still mostly intact. It flaked red with rust. On top was a series of cogs, wheels, and arcs of steel that must have once powered hoists and winches in these woods. The side of the engine was riddled with bullet holes. Moss grew in the crevices between cogs, and several deer ferns and sword ferns rose from the center where it had been filled over time with wet soil.

I removed my glove and took Katie's hand. Our friends stood silent across from us and even the dogs weren't moving. Our little group would have looked to passersby (be them elk, cougar, or human) like we were in the midst of some preternatural ritual. Like we were harnessing the energy from last night's waning strawberry moon.

Like we were trying to raise the dead.

The trunk of a red alder, tall enough to have grown there for as many as fifty years or more, had been split into two by the machine; both white-barked sides straddled the axles of the back two oxidized cogs. The tree was inseparable from the diesel donkey. Remove one, and a person should be ready to remove both.

☾

I was thirty when my gynecologist told me I needed a complete hysterectomy. Clementine was just over a year old. On the day of the procedure, the receptionist refused to check me in without giving me a pregnancy test. I argued with her for about ten minutes, knowing full well how unlikely it was that I was pregnant, but also knowing that if I was, they would halt the procedure and I would be faced with a different future than the one I was now imagining.

"Ma'am, it is protocol that everyone who checks in for a hysterectomy gets a pregnancy test," she said.

How did it take her so long to see what I was saying? How didn't she see the words hanging like invisible weights in the air between us? *I want them to take my uterus whether I am pregnant or not.* Or, maybe closer to the truth, *I want them to take my uterus* especially *if I am pregnant.*

☾

There was never any cell service in Ungulate Woods; we carried our phones solely for their time-keeping and cameras. So how did my phone ring and flash Chloe's face as I stood next to a patch of creeping Oregon grape overlooking the sea?

I froze. My twenty-two-year-old daughter, no doubt, wanted to talk about the Supreme Court's ruling, and I didn't know how to comfort her. I could not comfort myself. Cirrocumulus clouds stretched their long fingers toward me against the late-morning sky. A peregrine falcon circled the copse of alders that ran from just below the cliff to the water's edge.

My phone stopped ringing.

There were only a few hours of daylight between this moment and the moment *before* Roe v. Wade was overturned, but it felt fragile and ephemeral. If "the boundary between sea and land is the most fleeting and transitory feature of the earth," as Rachel Carson asserts, what of the boundary between yesterday and today?

☾

In *A Field Guide to Getting Lost*, Rebecca Solnit details the skills a person needs to survive in wild spaces, skills like watching the weather, tracking landmarks, and orienting yourself with the sun, moon, and stars. These are part of what Solnit calls "the thousand things that make the wild a text that can be read by the literate."

At fourteen, in the final months of junior high, I felt a dull ache in my abdomen that came and went in waves. I was the last of my friends to get her period, and still I was surprised when I unzipped my acid-washed jeans and found the reddish-brown spots on my underwear. In the coming years, I learned each month what it meant to close my eyes against the sharp prostaglandins-mediated contractions of my uterus, to sink into the fiery pain that was my body. Eventually, I knew by the smallest of signs (a slightly sensitive nipple, a crash in my mood, a shift in digestion) when my menses was about to start.

My own body, with its wild inclinations, was also a text to be read by the literate.

In those final throes of junior high, while I adjusted to the cyclical changes in my body, my mom handed me a newspaper at the breakfast table and pointed to a headline. It was an opinion piece about the urgency of preserving a woman's right to choose. I shook my head and grimaced, knowing only the party line I had learned at church about abortion being murder, about it being the worst sin a woman could commit. But my mom held firm and told me that as a woman, I should have a say in what I do with my body. She told me about the days pre-Roe, with coat-hanger deaths in back alleys and twelve-year-olds being forced to carry the babies of their rapists to term.

I had never heard a Mormon express a nuanced view of abortion before. It wasn't lost on me that by taking this position, she was in open defiance with the elders of the church. She was essentially saying *the prophet himself was wrong,* despite the church's repeated adage: "the prophet can never lead the church astray." This moment with my mom in the kitchen was the start of a golden thread that I would follow into adulthood, a thread that collected evidence against the divinity of the church until one day it was too heavy for me to carry and I decided to put it down and walk away altogether. In that way, I was ultimately saved by the quiet defiance of the woman from whose uterus I had sprung.

☾

After our birthday hike, we returned to the Castle and settled into a comfortable silence. Sam had made a cake from scratch that was safe for Katie's allergies, and he placed it on the dining room table where we sat watching the whitecaps pummel the sea stacks below us.

I looked at the stand on which the cake rested, a gorgeous piece of kitchenware with a glass top and a solid wood base. It brought to mind the diesel donkey from earlier. Where did this stand come from? Who cut the tree down, and how? I shifted my eyes and looked around the room. The oak coffee table held a shallow hickory bowl where we liked to keep our fruit; on the maple end table by the sofa sat a smooth bowl of turned pine where we kept the local tide schedule. Next to Katie's recliner was a hexagonal mid-century accent table inlaid with crisscrossed arches.

Downstairs, I knew the cherry four-poster bed sat ready for Sam and Sophie to have another cozy night's sleep. Outside, three separate piles of neatly stacked firewood, cured and ready for the next winter, stood sentry in the corners of the yard. My favorite stack, nearest the bird feeder in the front, boasted a center log with a heart-shaped design that looked exactly like an elk from behind, the telltale heart shape of light hair etched into darker. This, I knew, was the complexity of extraction: I wanted people to leave our forests alone, but I also wanted the treasures those forests held for myself.

☾

Those in power feel entitled to the land the same way they feel entitled to women's bodies. All people assigned female at birth in America live at the intersection of our extractive economy and the patriarchy, an intersection where we are forced to acknowledge the truth: our bodies are merely commodities, ripe for the taking.

As a newly engaged couple, the Supreme Court decision on Katie's birthday left us petrified about our ability to eventually marry and have it be legal. Were they coming for *Obergefell v. Hodges* next? Had I just stepped into this new life only to be told I wasn't worthy of marriage because I didn't love who I was expected to love? And even if our right to marry wasn't at risk, Vanessa Raditz, co-creator of the Queer Ecojustice Project, asserts that "Liberation doesn't end with overturning the sodomy laws if we're still living in a settler state that's extracting resources from the planet that's ultimately our larger body."

Confession: I didn't write the whole story. After we woke up but before we left for the woods, I fucked my wife. Not only because it was her birthday, but because we were two women with bodies, and we wanted to *feel* those bodies. We fucked in a way that could never end in pregnancy, our kind of sex now eminently safer for people with bodies like ours.

The kind of sex that is of the earth. I felt roots sprout from my skin and dive into the soil beneath the Castle, which had risen up to hold us the way detritus from a woodland understory cradles the flared base of a Sitka spruce.

MINOR ARCANA LOOP

I didn't know how long the Queen of Swords had been dead. A Sitka spruce who stood more than twice the height of the trees around her, she'd somehow avoided the sawmills that had destroyed the other old-growth trees in Ungulate Woods. Katie and I nodded at her several times a week, whenever we dipped off the decommissioned road and onto the trail that led into Ungulate Woods, which we'd named the Minor Arcana Loop. The Queen of Swords got her name because she felt like the matriarch of the forest, the lynchpin around whom every rhizome, fungus, and microorganism spun.

Like many ex-Mormons, I was highly skeptical of anything I couldn't see with my own eyes. I'd lost Santa at nine and God in my twenties, so I refused to be pulled in again by the promise of magic or augury. But you can't be on the dating market as a queer woman in Portland without familiarizing yourself, at least a bit, with astrology and tarot. I owned a few tarot decks full of gorgeously rendered cards, and I really *wanted* to believe in their powers of divination.

The Queen of Swords is typically associated with older women: crones, widows, divorcees. Like my wife, she has remarkably high standards and is so self-critical that she is, in turn, her own worst enemy and her own greatest cheerleader. In my favorite decks, the queen is depicted with one hand extended and the other holding her steel rapier high, her hand tight on the hilt. Sometimes she is seated on a throne, her crown or robe made up of swirling butterflies, and sometimes the skyscape drawn around her is rife with clouds and wind.

But I did believe in the power of *this* Queen of Swords. Wherever I was in the forest, as long as I looked for her looming barkless trunk where it rose high above the rest of the tree canopy, I could find my bearings in Ungulate Woods. She marked our entrance into the woods and she always, always made sure we could find our way out. If that isn't divination, I'm not sure what is.

☾

Just before I graduated from high school, I drove to a multimillion-dollar home in the hills on the west side of town in my mom's maroon Volvo station wagon. I parked beside a double tennis court, smoothed my dress, and walked around to the front of the house. When I knocked, the Stake Patriarch's wife answered the door and ushered me in. The Patriarch himself was waiting for me in his office, his back pressed against an overstuffed leather chair.

I was there to receive my "patriarchal blessing." Like most Mormon rites of passage, this one was spoken of little and often in hushed tones. I knew that the words he spoke when he placed his hands on my head were meant to give me a small glimpse into the rest of my life. The blessing was a guide of sorts, and we were told to study it regularly and follow the advice it offered for ultimate blessings in this life and the next. "Patriarchal blessings may contain promises, admonitions, and warnings," says the church. "Those who follow the counsel in their patriarchal blessing will be less likely to go astray or be misled. Only by following the counsel in a patriarchal blessing can one receive the blessings contained therein."

We weren't supposed to share our patriarchal blessing with other members, though I'd heard whispers for years, of course, of people whose blessings told them they would never marry or they would face major trials of their health. I'd heard rumors of abundance, too: one boy in our ward claimed that his blessing told him he'd be wildly successful in business. We all hoped for a concrete answer, for a glimpse of a spectacular future we couldn't have even imagined.

The Patriarch set a tape recorder on the mahogany desk so that his secretary would be able to type my blessing up later and mail it to me. Then he put his hands on my head, closed his eyes, and channeled the Holy Ghost to tell me who I was that day and who I should be in the future.

☾

The Queen of Swords in contemporary decks has a decidedly feminist bent; she represents autonomy, intellect, and self-sufficiency. "For a woman in our culture, this could look like a pretty enviable show of power," says American tarot expert Tiffany Lee Brown. Brown says boundary enforcement is key with the

Queen of Swords, and those who draw this card should look at "the boundaries, the physical ability, the power to completely lay out the terms under which we will parlay . . . to say how words are spoken in front of us, who does what to or toward our person."

Our Queen of Swords, the colossal snag that was once a vibrant evergreen, was also a keeper of boundaries. When we walked into the forest, we knew when to dart off the path by her looming presence. On the other side of the woods, the side that wraps around the mountain like a deep bowl, whenever I lost my way, I would scan the upper tree canopy until I found the top third of her skeletal silhouette, its branches long since stripped of their glory. And when I had her in my sights, I knew which direction to head. From Future Wife Point, the Queen of Swords was due south. In Elk Hollow, she cast a long shadow from the west. I could never orient my own body in space, but I could always orient hers.

☾

The Patriarch pressed down harder on my head as he spoke, which didn't help the headache I'd walked in with. *Sister Minor, it is your duty and responsibility as a Latter-Day Saint to set an example for all who know that you are a member of the Church. Those who are in and out of the Church will have an opportunity to learn by your example.* (It was all happening so quickly, but I thought maybe this meant I was supposed to serve a mission, which I had no interest in doing.) *You have the ability to communicate. Develop that talent.* (Yes! God and I were on the same page about my writing apparently. I *could* communicate. It was, like, my thing.) But then: *When opportunities are given to you to spread the gospel you will have the knowledge and the spiritual ability and the language to communicate so that people will understand. They will feel of your spirit. You will be able to convert.* (That damn mission thing again.) *I bless you with the desire to serve your Father in Heaven* (Yeah, yeah, I got it. I was supposed to Bible thump my way to the Celestial Kingdom).

Is now the right time to mention the Mormon church denounces divination? Their official statement is that such practices "are frequently condemned in scripture." But in *Early Mormonism and the Magic World View*, historian D. Michael Quinn highlights the folk magic and superstitions that influenced early Mormon leaders. Joseph Smith made no secret about the fact that he practiced scrying; God gave him seer stones to translate the ancient language of the golden plates into what became the Book of Mormon. His contemporaries are quoted as saying Smith buried his face into a tall hat with supernatural stones in the bottom that revealed scripture. Witnesses also spoke of Joseph carrying on his father's tradition of using divining rods to find water sources for well digging.

The two most important pieces of my patriarchal blessing were there. The pieces all girls were told to hope for, that the Lord was indeed going to provide me with a husband and also bless me with children. These promises arrived as the only glimpse into the spectacular future I imagined for myself, and when tears ran down my cheek and the Patriarch's wife hugged me and said, "I know, it's so special, isn't it?" she had no idea I was grieving that lost spectacular future.

I don't know why I ever expected anything other than what I got.

☾

The year we got married, we solicited frequent tarot readings from Katie's best friend Xing over Facetime.

"Queen of Swords again?" Katie would groan when a flipped card revealed the crowned beauty, adorned in riches and surrounded by sharp sabers and broadswords.

"Fucking brutal," Xing shook her head. Xing was an Ivy-trained anesthesiologist at the top of her field, and she told us that our theme for the year should be "slice, slice."

Katie said, "All I've done this year is *cut what doesn't serve me*. What more does this Queen want from me?" New to tarot, I sat still and listened.

Katie sold her company. We cut ties with friendships that didn't feel reciprocal. Mostly, we stopped thinking so much like women, instead being swift and decisive in our relations with others.

This, it turns out, is the way of *slice, slice.*

In the first chapter of *The Book of Mormon,* God commands the prophet Nephi to kill Laban, who lies in a drunken stupor in the street at Nephi's feet. Nephi removes Laban's sword from his unconscious body and uses it to cut the man's head clean off. Contemporary Mormon treasure hunters still search for the Sword of Laban today, the weapon that proved Nephi's obedience, whose hilt shines of pure gold and whose blade "was of the most precious steel."

God seems pretty pleased by the prophet's obedience. This story was how I learned before the age of five that the severed head of a man God doesn't like, sticky with blood and gripped in the palm of a man God *does* like, was different from the kind of killing forbidden in the Ten Commandments. This story was also how I learned that God had different rules for everybody, and that the rules only applied until he himself changed his mind and asked you to do the opposite. God didn't reward justice, fairness, or morality. God rewarded deference, obedience, and fealty.

If you walk north of the Queen of Swords deeper into Ungulate Woods, in a few miles, you'll hit a tiny body of water Katie and I named Slice Slice Bay. You can sing it to the beat of "Ice Ice Baby" and I am here to testify that it's an absolutely fucking satisfying use of time.

The difference between the prophet Nephi and the Queen of Swords: the queen wouldn't kill anyone just because a powerful figure told her to. Her decisions are ruled by honor and ethics.

She's willing to use her sword when she needs to, but never to curry favors.

☾

I was warned by church leaders my entire childhood against other forms of the woo universe: Ouija was a big no, not because of ghosts but because demons were pretending to speak as ghosts on that board with floating letters. I was kicked out of my dorm lobby at BYU-Hawaii for playing Old Maid with face cards. So many things were forbidden because they were potentially evil, and it only increased their power in my mind.

This was, after all, the same religion that taught children the importance of the handshake test, meant to decipher whether an apparition is an angel or a demon. I knew that I was supposed to confidently offer my palm: if the entity was an angel, it would reach out and shake my hand, having a whole, resurrected body. A demon, though, was fully corporeal. It would reach for my outstretched hand and move to shake it, but I would feel nothing at all. I spent so many years of my life being terrified that I would forget this test the moment my strange visitor arrived, and that would lead to my ultimate downfall.

And in the one form of divination allowed to me, that patriarchal blessing, I was told the story of who I was, what I would become, and what I valued. It was the same narrative I'd been told since I was old enough to cross my arms and listen in church. It was a narrative meant to keep me silent and complacent, to keep me a willing tithe payer, and to ensure I raised children with the same harmful narrative about who they are. Everything in its place.

While I was in college, an article written by Margaret D. Nadauld, a former Young Women's general president, was published in the church magazine *Liahona*. She writes, "Women of God can never be like women of the world. The world has enough women who are tough; we need women who are tender. There are enough women who are coarse; we need women who are kind." How can it possibly be true that the world has enough tough, rugged women? Enough women authentic enough to be considered "coarse"? How can that possibly be true?

Take your time. I'll wait.

If I could wish for anything for my daughters, it would be for them to see *coarse* and *tough* as admirable descriptors for who they might be.

☾

The Queen of Swords, her bark missing in spots and gray in others, wore scars up and down her entire length. Hawk talons, lightning strikes, disease. An austere monument to the passage of time. New life made purchase in her cracks and fissures: climbing vines, bubbly neon fungus, mosses. Her upper barren branches had become nesting spots for bald eagles and spotted owls.

Tough. Coarse.

Once, Marco cowered under the stinging nettle and creek dogwood when a series of long screams rang out from the sky directly above us. Within seconds, three bald eagles tore past on the tail feathers of a large raven. Once the raven had been routed, two of the three eagles perched on the large nest in a nook between two of the Queen of Swords' branches.

It was her stillness, juxtaposed against the dynamic rhythms of the living woods, that set her apart. The Queen of Swords stood as both talisman and vanguard. I wondered who the Queen of Swords was in my own life. Was it Katie?

But I was my own guide. Whenever I lost my direction, there was something inside of me, a compass-shaped lodestone, that brought me back to center.

Fifty years before I first saw the tall, needle-free limbs of the Queen, the Stake Patriarch who had given me my blessing made his fortune in lumber.

When I parked next to his tennis court and walked the perfectly manicured path up to his palatial entryway, he'd already made millions by logging the forests I so loved.

I'd spent my life making careful delineations between mystery, faith, and science, but since moving to the coast and queering my life, I'd been forced to redefine magic. When I stood beside the Queen and measured her heft and size against the weight of those woods, it felt like pure magic to be in her presence on any given day. But for a trick of the light, she would have fallen to the chainsaws, the diesel donkeys, the sawmills. Maybe the only kind of miracle I can bring myself to believe in is the miracle of being in any given place at any given time. The miracle that saved the Queen of Swords from becoming the frame of a house or a lovely coffee table, that saved me from a life that was devouring me whole, and then brought us here, together, on the Minor Arcana Loop in Ungulate Woods.

TEMPE, ARIZONA

(Home of the O'Odham and Piipaash Tribes)

Arizona has ghosts, too. Phoenix borders the territory of the Sonoran pronghorn, an endangered species commonly known as the Desert Ghost (named because of its speed and ability to elude human eyes). It's a small ungulate, especially compared to other pronghorn species, and it holds the title of the fastest land mammal in North America. The Sonoran pronghorn has legs that carry it over sixty miles per hour through creosote scrub bajadas and arroyos. I read about the Desert Ghost during my tenure in Arizona, but I never saw one in the wild. That didn't stop me from searching for them out my car window, hoping for a glimpse of the white chevron stripes on their necks and the curved branches of their keratin-rich antlers.

I was exhausted the day I arrived on campus to meet my cohort and start my T.A. training. (The night before, the desert had welcomed me with my first official panic attack; it started as a heaviness in my chest that spread to both arms, and then I lost the feeling in my hands. Convinced I was dying, I'd pulled myself into the fetal position and sobbed until it passed.) I carried a Big Gulp full of Coke, praying for the caffeine boost, and chose the farthest desk in the circle. Someone buzzed past to drop a name tag and Sharpie on my desk. I'd only been married for two weeks, and it felt wrong to add Matt's last name next to my first, especially using something as permanent as a Sharpie. Still, I wrote it on the tag, slapped it on my shirt, and lifted my eyes.

Against all odds, there were two familiar faces in that room.

I recognized Ginny's long blond curls from a poetry class I took during my year at BYU. She'd left the next term to serve a mission in Brazil, and I thought I'd never see her again. Having Ginny there was a balm for my anxiety. A Mormon! In my cohort! I knew I trust Ginny and that she'd have my back—mostly because that's just who Ginny was, and I saw a good friend in her right away. (From this vantage, I recognize how ingrained the messaging was: all Mormons were trustworthy, and the rest of the world wasn't.) Having another Mormon woman in the program meant I had a bit of a built-in friend. It also meant that I wouldn't be the only weirdo. I knew I was coming in hot, a twenty-year-old with a brand-new husband and funky underwear.

The other familiar face was also from a poetry class, this one at Oregon State University the semester I transferred from BYU. Curtis had been the belle of the proverbial poetry ball in the creative writing department back then, the strongest writer among us. And now here he was, in this graduate student lounge in the Sonoran Desert. Curtis was part of the previous year's cohort, and he was there to help onboard the rest of us.

Three days later, the phone rang as I was unpacking the pots and pans we'd been given as wedding gifts into one of only three cupboards in the kitchen of our minuscule apartment. The sound made me jump, mostly because we were so new to the apartment that we hadn't heard the wall phone ring in that space very much yet. I put down a glass pie dish and wiped my hands on my jeans, hoping to hear my mom's voice on the other end.

"Is this Elissa?" It was a young man's voice.

"Speaking," I said, except I said it like a question.

It was Curtis, calling to say how excited he was to see my name on the list of incoming students. We talked about our scholarships (he was the previous year's recipient of the one I had just been awarded) and briefly talked about our teaching schedules.

"Why don't we meet for lunch this week so I can answer any questions?"

I went rigid.

Only fourteen days after our wedding, I was up against one of the temptations I'd been warned about my whole life. I was a married woman, and I had been invited to dine with a man. Put aside the fact that no part of me thought Curtis's invitation was romantic in nature. He just wanted to help me out, to make my transition into this program as smooth as possible.

I made an excuse for why I couldn't have lunch with him, but I can't remember what it was. By the time I spoke, my heart was pounding and the phone trembled under my jittery hands.

Welcome, Elissa's second panic attack. Pull up a chair.

Every time I saw Curtis in the next two years before he finished his degree,

I was hit with a sneaker wave of shame. I imagined he thought me rude; he'd offered to take me to lunch twice more before he stopped asking. I could almost audibly hear him shrug his shoulders. But I don't think my shame stemmed from that. I think it came from a deeper, darker place that was closer to my heart. I was ashamed that I said no to lunch with a colleague because I had a husband.

No, Elissa. Go deeper.

I was ashamed to be the kind of woman who lived by such strict rules.

I was ashamed of being married at all.

But it was so hard to extricate shame from my life. That would have meant recognizing it. Naming it. My shame was as hard to pull from the shadows as the pronghorn Desert Ghost was to pull from the Sonoran.

☾

Ginny and I became fast friends. It was easy to ignore my complicated dance with shame when I was with another Mormon woman. We spent weekends double-dating with our husbands, swapping recipes, and sharing tattered Wallace Stegner books. She was the only writer in our cohort I invited into my home. Ginny was safe. She understood my life. She wouldn't lead me astray like the non-member writers would.

And dear God, how desperately I wanted to be led astray. I wanted it so ferociously that I took pains to avoid any situation that would tempt me.

Within two months of each other and in the final year of our program, Ginny and I both tested positive on the home pregnancy tests we'd purchased together expired and in bulk from the local grocery outlet. We talked about our babies' nurseries while studying for our comprehensive exams; mused about our future book covers while reading *What to Expect When You're Expecting.*

Just before graduation, Ginny and I showed up to a potluck at our professor's house, a famous essayist whose work was universally revered; MFA students hung on his every word as if he held the secret to the writing life we craved. Ginny had baked a sugar-and-wheat-free peanut butter pie, and I'd made the artichoke dip that every woman in my ward back home had been obsessed with for years. We set our dishes on the buffet in the essayist's dining room and poured ourselves some lemonade. The only thing I liked about being pregnant was that for a few short months, nobody thought it was strange that I wasn't drinking. Our maternity shirts did little to hide our swelling abdomens.

Ginny elbowed me in the side and pointed: the essayist was walking toward us, a wine flute teetering in his left hand. He scooped a good helping of my artichoke dip onto his plate before turning to us. "You are *both* having babies?" he asked, incredulous.

Ginny laughed and then rubbed her belly.

I said, "It appears that way, yes."

"You should know," he said, wiping rogue dip from his chin, "that every baby you have is a book you won't write."

I looked at Ginny. Was this guy for real? The essayist floated into another conversation, leaving us to dissect what he'd just said. We were infuriated. Ginny said she doubted he would say the same to a young male writer. For over twenty years, I heard the essayist's voice in my head as I emptied the diaper pail and taught my classes, dying to prove him wrong.

Arizona found itself in a thirteen-month drought starting in 2001, a climate disaster that decimated the habitat of the Sonoran pronghorn and dried up what little water there once was. The official Desert Ghost population dwindled to just twenty-one individuals. This was a few months after I left Arizona. I'd given birth, defended my thesis, nursed eight-week-old Chloe under my graduation gown, and packed another U-Haul, this one headed north. But it was also before: before I knew that if the church keeps women from interacting with men who aren't their husbands, they'll have a hard time advancing in their careers, which keeps them at home with their children. Before I knew that the essayist was probably right, dammit, but fuck him anyway for saying it out loud to two pregnant women.

Curtis went on to write six books, floating between prestigious universities, eventually becoming the poet laureate of the state where he settled. Ginny moved home to Utah, where she had four daughters and then a son and, according to Google, where she sometimes teaches part time at BYU. And what of the Desert Ghost? Its population has only grown by one-hundred-eighty today. But those two hundred pronghorns don't know that. They still forage for grasses and fords. They still give birth to twin fawns each June. They still lift their white rump hairs erect when they are frightened, a warning to the world.

THUNDERCLAP CASTLE, REPRISE

The evening of our second Christmas together, Katie and I walked along the beach closest to the Castle. The ocean was busy preparing for the arrival of the king tides; it churned and roiled, continually pushing its high tide against the ankles of our boots. I should mention that I, too, roiled with nebulous anger. Katie and I argued as we walked the short sliver of uncovered beach and tossed a ball for Cricket.

"Never turn your tails to the sea!" I called after Cricket and Marco as the water approached. In my hurt, I said nothing to Katie. The angrier she got at my silence, the harder and farther she threw the ball for the dog.

Then, from Katie. "Tails!" A warning. Everyone pivoted until our tails were behind us and we faced the sea. We ran up onto the rocks and hoped we could run far enough to keep us dry.

We'd spent that morning together at the Wetlands, where we enjoyed the background din of teenagers pleased with their gifts and overtired dogs shredding discarded boxes. In the afternoon, we left the kids with their dad and set out for the Castle. We'd planned the custody switch purposefully, so we could be at the coast for the first set of that year's king tides.

The wind had picked up as we drove over the pass; the closer we got to the ocean, the more the car was buffeted from all sides by an invisible force, a forewarning of the wicked storm that would rage for the next twenty-four hours. The first thing we did when we arrived was start a Christmas Day fire, which was out of practicality as much as preciousness.

King tides happen only three or four times a year, the culmination of perfect conditions. A full moon perfectly lined up with the sun and the earth. Pure perigee. Perigee happens the moment in an object's orbit when it is closest to the earth. When the sun is that close to the earth, its gravitational pull increases, and as a result we get the largest tidal range of the entire year. In the Northern Hemisphere, of course, perigee happens in the thick of winter. This must be why the actual scientific name for the king tides is *perigean spring tides.*

We'd argued the whole drive back to the Castle, then while we built the fire and then while we walked on the beach. True to the nature of these things, I can't conjure what we were at odds about. But I *can* conjure the texture of our conflict, because it was so similar to the texture of all our main conflicts. I was an internal processor to her very external one, and my silence sometimes read as indifference. I actively grieved the career trajectory I might have had without the Mormon church, without becoming a mother at twenty-three years old. Katie actively grieved that her intense focus on career success, paired with a chronic illness, had not left room for her to become a biological parent.

The two of us shouting into each other's voids so loudly neither of us could hear the other. What we were saying: *The thing I love the most about you is the thing I feel most vulnerable about myself.*

And then the deeper hurts, the sleights made by others that still felt current in our nervous systems. The sibling who never apologized, the friend who overstepped, the parent who *always wanted something else for you*, the lover who left without explanation, the church leader who asked for more details than necessary. Author and musician Josh Ritter compares a heart to a package, one covered in tangled knots tied by people in our past. We spent hours that Christmas, frantically pulling at other people's knots from the hearts we were so keen to share only with each other.

A fire raged behind the creosote-stained glass of the stove. Dread filled my body, as did the repeated boom of thunderclaps echoing through the Castle's fortified keep. The fire went out while we slept that night; we woke on Boxing Day to a large pile of ash in the woodstove. We pulled on our waterproof shoes and pants to head down to the beach, speaking little to each other.

The winds had become even stronger while we slept. The other thing had intensified, too: we were reticent and short with each other, avoiding eye contact. Still, being the eager storm watchers that we were, we wrestled the dogs into their harnesses and went down to the beach, with hats, gloves, fleece sweatshirts, and windbreakers as our armor against the gusts. Our rewards were the forty-foot swells that bellowed and pummeled the intertidal zone. The waves necessitated a kind of sacred awe, an attention that meant putting our conflict aside. We watched them carefully, looking for clues about which waves would send us running past the beach and into the craggy hillside vegetation. Still, with the tense build-up of each massive wave surge, my own anxiety and frustration grew. I could sense the same was happening with Katie.

By early afternoon, the entire region had lost power, Castle included. Katie started a new fire, and we huddled around it for warmth; we sat in the dark without access to the outside world. We didn't know it at the time, but it would be seventy-two hours before our power came back on. We made small talk about how spectacular the king tides were, the giant swells paired with the waves' long reach, the lines of foam they left behind on the rocks and parking lots to prove just how far they'd gone.

The thing about fire in a storm is that it pulls you closer, begs you to seek relief from cold. Soon, Katie and I were cuddled up with our arms around each other for warmth, listening to the king outside scream and throw rain at the closed windows. And as mysteriously as our conflict began, I felt my body soften against my wife's chest, felt the tension release in her arms as she held me tighter. It had become us against this riled king outside, so we settled into the closest thing our Castle had to a keep. Keeps were the stronghold of any castle, the place its defenders would retreat to when an enemy army advanced. We embraced while the enemy king took shots at our windows and the tall trees outside. Katie recommended we move into the bedroom; although it was away from the heat of the fire, there would be less wind noise. We snuck past the windows, afraid to tip the king off to our movements. That's how we found ourselves with the duvet pulled to our chins, shivering but happy for a moment's quiet.

Turns out make-up sex is more than a solid set-up for a sitcom joke. Relationships are an endless cycle of coming apart and coming together again, not so different from the ocean tides. As the king walloped the side of the house to demand entrance, I turned to my wife. I undressed her, slowly, under the covers with shaky hands. I didn't care if the king was watching. I didn't care if he broke a window in the living room or brought down a tree. The king might have wanted to swallow us whole, but I wanted Katie more.

UNGULATE WOODS, REPRISE

In February a low-pressure trough blew in from the east. I felt it in the patella I'd shattered in college; Katie felt it near the metal pins that have held her shoulder in place since she was fourteen. Forecasters predicted the system would bring a small dusting of snow to the Willamette Valley and brief but steady rain to the north coast. Snow is a relatively rare treat in Portland, so I was disappointed that we'd miss the dusting because we'd be at the Castle all week.

I made kindling with a piece of hemlock and a sledgehammer in the garage, and then Katie used it to get a fire raging in the woodstove. We put our achy bodies to bed, my little spoon nestled inside her big spoon.

We woke ready to start our respective workdays; then I lifted the blinds. The three sea stacks were wearing bright white capes; their faces, if they had faces, were shrouded with veils of ice. The sand on the visible stretch of beach had been replaced with icy crystals and fresh powder. The meteorologists had really gotten this one wrong: that trough, expected to blow over quickly and continue moving west, had stalled over the ocean right off the north coast. For the next twenty-four hours, we watched alongside the Columbian white-tailed deer and Steller's sea lions as nearly a foot of snow fell at the Castle. Flurries of bulky wet flakes billowed and danced from the sky, landing to cover the huckleberry bushes in a thick, shroud of white lace.

☾

The Temple Matron, a woman in her eighties, took one look at my wedding dress and shook her head.

"That's not white enough," she said. She herself was wearing a floor-length white dress with long sleeves and white temple slippers on her feet. My mom and I shifted our weight, both of us in equally white simple dresses. It was my first time at the temple, and I was still recovering from the shock of the ritual I was just involved in. The white veil they made me cover my face with. The promises of obedience signified by Eve's silky green apron of leaves over my white dress.

I'd chosen my wedding dress because of the lack of ridiculous adornment—no lace, no beads, just buttery smooth ivory fabric with an empire waist that cascaded into a full skirt below. The sleeves, to remain modest and be allowed in the temple, covered my shoulders and were finished with small rosettes. That dress was the only thing I was truly excited about on my wedding day, the one choice I made that I felt reflected me.

"How can this be not white enough?" I asked. My mom elbowed me gently in the side.

"She can get married in a white temple dress and change into that one for the pictures and reception." The matron looked right at my mom. "If she's worthy to get married in the temple, her dress should reflect that." She spouted a few more platitudes about purity, without so much as a glance in my direction.

My bishop had determined me worthy of a temple recommend after my "worthiness interview." But if even a slightly off-white dress wasn't pure enough for them, how would I ever be?

☾

Joseph Fielding Smith (not to be confused with the original Joseph Smith, founder of the faith, or his nephew, Joseph F. Smith, who became the church's sixth prophet) made sexual purity one of the cornerstones of his time as the first official Patriarch of the Mormon church, asserting "No more loathsome cancer disfigures the body and soul of society today than the frightful affliction of sexual sin. It vitiates the very fountains of life, and bequeaths its foul effects to the yet unborn as a legacy of death. It lurks in hamlet and city, in the mansion and in the hovel as a ravening beast in wait for prey; and it skulks through the land in blasphemous defiance of the laws of God and of man."

And bequeaths its foul effects to the yet unborn as a legacy of death.

There is but one legacy my sexual sins will leave for my children.

I want them to know there is nothing more pure than wanting. I want them to fall in love with desire.

☾

If white means purity, then Ungulate Woods had become a virgin bride, sexless to her very core. The colossal ferns that usually stood as tall as we did were weighed down with the heavy powder until only the tips of their fronds poked through. Katie pointed out a small patch of trilliums, freshly bloomed, that sat up to their necks in ice.

Both dogs paused at the trailhead. The snow had concealed the trail and its attending footprints the way a key gets tucked into the lining of a coat.

"You've got this, guys," Katie cajoled as we pulled them forward. The four of us stepped into the as-yet-unbroken snow and left a trail of our own footprints behind us, paving the way for anyone who wanted to follow. The low-hanging conifer boughs were so weighted with snow they brushed against our hats as we walked.

Deeper into the woods, the biggest change was the sound. Snow is the ultimate silencer. The snow at our feet and in the trees was nothing more than a mass of six-sided crystals packed tightly together. Each snowflake is porous, riddled with tiny open spaces that absorb sound waves. Hearing the quiet from this blanket of snow meant hearing the quiet of millions upon millions of frozen crystals asking the world to hush. Even the ocean, whose raucous, pounding surf was usually the soundtrack of our hikes, had been muzzled by about seventy percent. The only exceptions were the streams and small falls as we passed them. They were full-to-bursting and louder than usual; waterfalls that were usually just a small trickle flowed as if a hidden high-pressure spigot had been opened.

In my youth, I'd been commanded to be "as pure as the driven snow." After the object lessons about all the ways my purity would be destroyed if I so much as thought about a boy, they'd hit us with the scripture from Isaiah, "though your sins be as scarlet, they shall be as white as snow; though they be red like crimson, they shall be as wool."

We forged ahead past Birthday Point and Marco Point and into Spooky Bog. In the snow, there was nothing spooky about Spooky Bog; the light reflected off the snow to reveal details in the trees surrounding us that we'd never seen. But for the absence of footprints, I would have been convinced someone had come through here just before us and turned on a light switch. The whole forest, really, was lit so differently wearing white. The light bounced off the snow to illuminate pockets of the forest that before lived only in shadows, and the undersides of leafy trees shined with a bright yellow hue. Seeing the underside of the tree canopy cast in sunshine felt akin to donning diving gear to get a glimpse of the dark workings of the deep sea.

None of it spooked Cricket, who sprung from snowy rock to snowy log ahead of us at break-neck pace, the whole wedded world an adventure for the taking. Marco lagged behind, slower and slower, until we realized all four of his fluffy little legs were matted with giant balls of snow that grew bigger with each step. I barely suppressed my laughter when Katie picked him up to shake the snowballs off, but they wouldn't budge. Each ball was stuck so firmly that the only answer was to keep going, get back to the car, and warm his fur up enough to melt that new white pair of knickers off his body.

☾

It's impossible to talk about purity in the LDS church without looking at other connotations of the word "pure" from a Mormon context.

The Book of Mormon, first published during the American rush to discover and claim new land, is essentially a battle cry for white settlers to take up arms against Indigenous people. The entire opening salvo of the scriptural tome tells the story of the Laminates, an ancient Native American tribe that had been cursed "with a skin of blackness." Whereas they were once "white, and exceedingly fair and delightsome," they were cursed by their wickedness with "a skin of blackness." The Book of Mormon prophesied that those who accepted Jesus and the restored gospel of Jesus Christ could reverse such a curse, and they would again become "a white and delightsome people." By the 1840s, so quietly most people didn't know it had happened, the wording in all new printed copies of the Book of Mormon was changed to "*pure* and delightsome." Further scripture in the book remains unchanged and reads thusly: "O then ye unbelieving, turn ye unto the Lord; cry mightily unto the Father in the name of Jesus, that perhaps ye may be found spotless, pure, fair, and white, having been cleansed by the blood of the Lamb, at that great and last day." (Mormon 9:6)

Whiteness and purity are inextricable in Mormon doctrine.

At the end of the nineteenth century, when Brigham Young expressly prohibited Black men from attending the temple and receiving the priesthood at the end of the nineteenth century, he claimed it was instruction directly from

God himself. When I was just learning to walk in 1978, prophet Spencer W. Kimball claimed God told *him* in a direct revelation to extend the priesthood to all men, regardless of race (to this day, there has been no similar revelation about women receiving the priesthood). In both cases, faithful members were told that God was calling the shots and making the decisions, not the prophets.

Holistic sex educator Christina Tesoro writes that "purity culture, to one extent or another, is the water we swim in within a white supremacist, cisheteropatriarchy."

☾

Listen. I'm about to give a revelation.

Joseph Fielding Smith, that chastity-obsessed first Patriarch of the church? He was caught sleeping with his male students at the University of Utah and admitted to gay affairs during his time as Patriarch. In response, he was released from his calling as Patriarch, but the members were told it was because of his ill health. Instead of formal disciplinary action, the prophet sent him to Hawaii with his wife and children, where they continued to be active members of the church. When he died, he was serving as a member of the High Council back in Salt Lake City, land of pure white snow-capped mountains and even purer Saints.

Among the legacy Joseph Fielding Smith left behind was doctrine about the Telestial Kingdom, the lowest level of heaven where the majority of the world's sinners would end up. According to Smith, those sent to the Telestial Kingdom will still experience a full bodily resurrection, but unlike those in the Celestial Kingdom, they would have no genitals.

(Imagine a Ken doll, straight out of the box. Or Barbie's smooth front when you change her dress.)

How much shame must Joseph Fielding Smith have felt.

How much he must have hated himself.

☾

Human footprints weren't the only ones missing when Ungulate Woods was mantled with snow. The labyrinthine series of elk and deer trails that we often used as shortcuts had also disappeared.

Landscape architects call these paths "desire paths." Any unplanned trail, such as those worn by human footfalls in the center of an otherwise grassy field, or those worn by sharp hooves up the side of a steep mountain, qualify as desire paths. The etymology of the phrase is clear: animals, be it people, elk, deer, or bear, won't take a path that doesn't make sense to them, and will go where they please. These paths stand in defiance of planned trails, streets, and sidewalks. Their one unifying characteristic is that once a desire path is formed, it will continue to be used by animals and people as the preferred way to get between two places. Engineer Yujian Tang writes that desire paths "show that although we may not have taken the path given to us, enough of us exist, enough of us took this path enough times, enough of us wanted the same thing that we left a visible trail."

With our well-worn desire paths erased from the snow-covered woods, we had to forge our own way. Sometimes the main trail was obvious, but sometimes we had to guess, climbing over icy rocks and shrubs to form a new sort of trail in the snow.

Is this the purity of snow? The inability to see the paths that others have mapped out for us? Without those paths, we are forced to go inward and find paths of our own. We are forced to say here, yes, this is what I desire.

Reach out. Take it.

Desire is the purest thing of all. I use my lips to trace the desire path I've forged on Katie's soft, willing body, the invisible groove of my wanting. It starts at her collarbone, meanders to her left breast, follows her sternum on the stretch of supple skin down her abdomen, before finally taking a long slow turn towards the fleshy mound above her right hip.

A path I will take again. And again. And again.

OAHU, HAWAII

The first time I reached out for Katie and she lovingly turned me down in exchange for sleep, it shot right through me. I felt what I imagined Matt must have felt, night after night after another endless string of sexless nights. He'd tell me he was lonely, that he needed physical affection and intimacy. We slept next to each other every night and I didn't understand what he meant by lonely, or even intimacy. I didn't want him to hurt, but I couldn't turn toward him when the bedside lamps went off. And I hated my broken shameful self for lying there in the dark, my back to my best friend, unable to will myself to reach for him.

On my fortieth birthday, Matt and I dangled five hundred feet above the Pacific Ocean, our parasail tethered to a boat below. Despite my fear of heights, I was surprised how peaceful it was to float in the sky, the bright yellow parachute above us and the turquoise Hawaiian waters below. The wind picked up and we blew to the right, just as a spray of mist rose like a fountain from the water below us, the tell-tale sign of a humpback whale expelling a held breath in order to take in more. That night, back at our rented condo, I thought he would expect sex, even though we hadn't been intimate for well over a year. I spent all four days of this trip willing myself to have sex with my husband, but at the end of each day we just watched movies until we fell asleep next to each other, not touching.

☾

Matt was not a perfect husband, but by many metrics he was a good one.

1. Despite my ongoing chronic illness, I have never spent a night alone in a hospital room; he always opted to have the grandparents watch the kids so he

could be by my side. Every time I opened my eyes through the night, there he was, sleeping in a chair that often didn't even recline, a flimsy hospital blanket hugging his shoulders. I would watch him while the nurse's station monitors beeped and whirred outside the door.

2. I turned twenty-seven as a mother of a four-year-old and a two-year-old. For my birthday, having sensed my complete burnout, Matt drove me to a nice hotel, handed me a room key, and drove away, promising to be back by noon the next morning to pick me up. Inside the room, he'd left all of my favorite snacks, desserts, drinks, gossip magazines, the novel I was in the middle of, and a suitcase of pre-packed clothes and toiletries. My laptop was on the bed, with a note encouraging me to use some of my solo night to work on my book.

3. The day-to-day, too. The way he left hot tea with cream and sugar on my nightstand just before I woke every single morning. The songs he would write and record for me on a regular basis, some of them silly, all of them sweet. The way he would encourage me, after particularly frustrating days with kids and work, to go to the library and write just to settle my soul.

☾

The whale below our parasail that afternoon in Hawaii wasn't finished. As we watched, it made a complete breach, flinging its massive body fully out of the water and twisting in midair as if competing for gymnastics gold. I knew from one of my kids' recent reports that scientists didn't quite know why whales breach this way. Some would say this whale was breaching to communicate with other whales in its pod; for whales close by, a slap of their flukes or fins on the water would suffice. But when a message must be dispatched from a long distance, the formidable splash created by a breach will carry underwater as far as it needs to. Other scientists, though, say the purpose of a breach is to shake off the barnacles that have collected on the whale's smooth outer skin.

They leap out of the air and twist to lighten their load. To move forward with less baggage from the past.

Matt.

I'm sorry for so many things.

That I couldn't be my best self with you. That you got the version of me that didn't know a happier version of herself was possible. That I couldn't give you a love that included passionate clothes-ripping and the tenderness of falling asleep, still naked and wrapped around each other.

I'm sorry for turning away. Again and again. I'm sorry it took me so long to figure out why.

I'm sorry they sold us a snow job and called it eternity.

Mostly, I'm sorry the things in my secret heart hurt the things in yours.

CAPE KAWANDA
(Tillamook: *Tadalsallo*)

The first time I saw paragliders soaring over the cliffs outside the Castle window, I asked Katie if she'd ever done it herself. Three of them skimmed the thermals near Three Arch Rocks, the striped kites above their gliders puffed large like balloons attached to a parade float. Para*sailing* was one thing, safely attached to the back of a boat. But para*gliding* takes things up a notch. A paraglider must walk to the edge of a cliff or mountain and leap off it, with nothing below them but the wide-open sky and the approaching ground below.

"Nope," she answered as she searched through the junk drawer for a tape measure. I wasn't surprised. Like me, Katie was not a risk taker or an adrenaline junkie.

"But would you ever?" I held my breath. I wanted her to say no more than I wanted her to say yes. I wanted her to say *this is a risk we should take together* and also *are you crazy you have to literally step off the edge of Maxwell Point.*

My new love looked at me from the corner of her eye. "Not a chance," she said. I was (mostly) relieved.

The calculus of risk is achingly complicated. When a risk ends in reward, we praise the risk takers. When it ends with tragedy, we decry them as reckless. Take Lost Boy Cave: if there were indeed a lost boy who drowned in the cave when the tide turned, the takeaway from the story is that he took a risk that didn't pay off. Every one of us who has waited at the end of that rock outcropping, watched the tide go slack, and then run to the cave's entrance has taken a similar risk. But for each boy trapped in the cave by the tide, how many other people reaped the reward—a sweet twenty minutes in an underwater world, the ability to enter a space of magic and come out changed.

I imagine what it must be like to jump off Maxwell Point's two-hundred-foot Miocene-era cliffs, to see, as an eagle might, the pristinely serrated shoreline, the scarred basalt crags made small where they jut from the waves. I imagine absorbing this grandeur from the underbelly of that striped Kevlar fabric, my hands on the rigging. And then to land on a berm on the beach, stopping so quickly that sand fills my shoes.

☾

Mormons have a complicated relationship to risk. The religion was born of risk. Joseph Smith risked ostracism after he told the townsfolk he'd been visited in a forested grove by God and his son, who told Smith not to join any church. What followed were years of torment that became the crux of Mormon lore.

What they said our ancestors wanted us to know:

The world hated us.

We were tarred and feathered.

We were driven from Missouri.

They threw us in jail.

We died pulling handcarts across the plains in search of religious freedom.

All of which translated to:

We risked everything for this religion.

Don't disappoint us.

I mean, sure. I can see how declaring your godly right to take other men's wives as your own, to marry an infinite number of women even at the expense of your first wife who disapproves, can be read as the ultimate risk for faith.

But it can also be read as dangerous. Risk and peril are two different edges of the same blade, but they do cut a bit differently. While both danger and risk make us vulnerable to harm, risk carries the tempting promise that if you can avoid the harm, a reward awaits you. What might have just been a risk for a man wanting four more wives is a danger for the fourteen-year-old girl with no say in the matter. What might just be a risk for a family crossing the plains to get to Utah becomes catastrophic for the nineteen-year-old in a bumpy wagon, feverish and eight months pregnant, with thousands of miles to go before she reaches Zion.

The constant refrain from a Mormon childhood: *we suffered, we suffered, we suffered.* And if you don't heed the faith and avoid risks as the church dictates them? You will suffer even more. It's easy to see that I married Matt at twenty because I was so tired of my constant vigilance about daily risk. I was convinced that I would sin at any minute, that life was one big dodgeball game against a Satan who threw constant temptations at me. Not only would Celestial Marriage procure me a spot in heaven, but maybe it would stop my impure thoughts, my need to touch myself. Maybe it would be a prophylactic against future uncertainty and suffering.

For a young Mormon woman, getting married doesn't feel like a risk. Despite all the messaging in the broader world, to us marriage was not a crapshoot leap of faith to take with another person. Rather, it was a calculated move to mitigate *eternal* risk. After an almost fatal infection spread unchecked in my body when I was barely thirteen, my calculus of risk became quite complicated. Shaking hands with death that young is enough to make anyone stay the course.

☾

I woke weeks after my thirteenth birthday in a tangle of pain, as if someone were driving a red-hot poker through my left eye socket. I pulled myself out of bed and made my way to the bathroom through the pounding heat. I tried to look in the mirror, but I'd lost the crispness on the edges of my vision, and the searing pain with each step made everything I saw take on a psychedelic tint. I did not yet know that my left eye was swollen shut, that when I stumbled into my parents' bedroom, crying out in pain, it was the beginning of an event that would shape my entire childhood, my entire life. My mom rushed to get dressed and my dad helped load me into the car. The pediatrician took one look at me and told my mom to put me back in the car and drive me to the hospital. "Don't make any stops," I like to imagine him saying with a vehemence that conveyed his concern, though in actuality I remember him jokingly calling the hospital the "horse-pistol" as if it were a grand adventure. The serious nature of what was happening to me was saved for my mom, in fervent whispers when I was turned the other way or cradling my head for some semblance of relief.

I spent the next twenty days in a sterile hospital room, though I wasn't conscious for most of them. I had developed stage three orbital cellulitis, the result of a bacterial infection that had leaked unchecked from my torn sinuses into my eye socket. The doctors didn't know I was awake when they told my parents that the infection was moving toward my brain, that this meant I was facing several risks, including meningitis, blindness, permanent brain damage, even death. Months later, after I made an unexpected full recovery, I was told that among the six doctors who had worked on my case the weeks I languished in the hospital, they'd only ever seen a combined three cases of orbital cellulitis, and none of those children had survived.

The week before I got sick, I'd been at our ward's Deacon and Beehive dance (when boys turn thirteen, they become Deacons; when girls reach the same milestone, they are called Beehives). I learned later how unusual it was for local youth leaders to allow (let alone plan and promote) a dance just for the under-fourteen set; we weren't even allowed to date until sixteen. But somehow, we convinced them we needed to *practice* for the age-fourteen-and-up dances in a highly supervised format, so our leaders held a dance for us at one of their homes. The music was mostly slow and all night, I rotated between the arms of two eighth-grade boys I didn't know well because they went to a different school. From where my head perched in my hospital bed, my right eye swelled to the size of a tangerine, I couldn't help thinking I might not live long enough to get that first date. Don Henley's "The End of Innocence" and Bad English's "When I See You Smile" repeated on a loop in my head.

Right before I was wheeled into surgery, my dad and our bishop came into the room to give me a priesthood blessing. Both men rested each of their palms, one atop the other, on my head. My dad opened a vial of consecrated oil and put a dot of it on my scalp. I whispered to my dad, "I don't want to die," and his eyes welled. I wish I could remember exactly what was said in that blessing. Time and pain meds have distorted my father's words in my head, but I remember that he commanded me to get better, and that God revealed through him that I was meant for great things, and this was not the end.

This is how Mormons deal with risk that is out of their control, risks that they are forced to take to avoid something even more perilous. Anoint with oil. Press palms to scalp. Demand the result you want. Attribute all positive outcomes to God, all tragic ones to his will.

When I came out of surgery, a card was waiting for me from Darren, one of the boys I'd rotated between the night of the dance. "Get well soon," he said. "We need you at the dances." I didn't tell him that I'd only danced with him as much as I did because our leaders told the girls it was unkind to say no when a boy asks you to dance or to take you on a date. After all, he'd really put himself out there by asking. That should be rewarded.

We need you at the dances. He didn't say, *Because I couldn't live without you* or even *Let's hang out when you are better.* He needed me at the dances. I was a warm female body he could pull against his while soft pop music played in the dark. I was a still-undeveloped Beehive, but even then, I knew that I posed for Darren the ultimate risk: Eve, sweet apple juice dripping down my chin, the end of innocence.

☾

Most teenagers believe they are impervious to death. Like trendy caped superheroes, they push the envelope and take risks that those with more fully developed frontal lobes would logically avoid. Psychologists call this the "invincibility fable" and note that it stems from a particularly egocentric pattern of thought—common to the teenage years—that risky behaviors can't hurt them. But I never got to enjoy that kind of pre-adulthood. My brush with death had taught me that the wolf was always at my door. From the first weeks back at school, where I walked around campus in an eye patch mostly to shield my peers from the sight of my swollen, black-and-blue eye socket and the surgery scars next to my nose, every step felt like borrowed time. When my father pulled me from the brink of death in the name of God, his oily hands pressed to my scalp, my relationship to risk was forever changed.

The shadow of a scythe stretched over me and knitted with my own. My high school years were marked with additional surgeries and a seemingly endless stream of antibiotics. My body promoted the narrative that I was fragile in a way most of my peers were not. When I developed an unremitting case of kidney stones at sixteen, it was further proof. Every car ride held the possibility of death by fire, every pang in my body the possibility of death by disease. Because the grave felt so sure, so imminent, I clung harder to the promises of religion. From the Book of Moses: "This is my work and my glory—to bring to pass the immortality and eternal life of man." Mormons take it a step further with their additional scriptures, promising not just eternal life, but an eternity with the people you love the most. If you want to get to the Celestial Kingdom, then you must marry a righteous man in the temple. The catch for me, I thought, was finding a righteous man who was also willing to be with a wife who was often too sick to fold the laundry.

During my bout with kidney stones, my mom asked Matt to come sit with me for a few hours while she ran some errands. Here came this sixteen-year-old boy who proceeded to hold the bucket for me while I puked and then washed it out in the sink, only to repeat the cycle until my mom came home to take over. My mom told this story to her church friends on repeat. The end of the story always held the same punchline, delivered by someone who thought she was the first to say it: *Marry that boy, Elissa.* I took it to heart. Tacit in their joking encouragement that I marry Matt was, *Men are callow. Our husbands don't take care of us.* To me, it meant that I would never find a man willing to take on my health problems the way Matt did. To let go in search of anything else was a fool's errand. I needed a man for my salvation, and this one was better than the others.

As it turned out, Katie also had an ex she stayed with for years longer than she should have because her health necessitated it. The moment when I saw her through my car window the first time I pulled up the Castle, Cricket barking in the backseat, had been made possible because of those people in our pasts, because of our common experiences, and because of the ones we didn't have in common, too.

☾

Unlike our pioneer ancestors, modern-day Mormons are incredibly risk averse.

An incomplete list of the things I was told would bring eternal suffering: gambling, alcohol, French kissing, heavy petting, smoking, cannabis, coffee, tea, watching R-rated movies, dating before sixteen, dating outside the faith, peer pressure, masturbation, porn, going to the grocery store on the Sabbath, eating on fast Sunday, reading anti-Mormon literature, feminism, rock music played backward, Ouija boards, playing cards, caffeine, being too intellectual, laughing too loudly, not paying my tithing, wearing skirts that rose above the bottom of my kneecaps.

We were also expected to be proactive in our risk aversion by planning for any potential dangers and mitigating their damage beforehand. The church website advises members to "store foods that are a part of your normal diet in your three-month supply. As you develop a longer-term storage, focus on food staples such as wheat, rice, pasta, oats, beans, and potatoes that can last thirty years or more." This is why I still have two fifty-gallon water barrels and thirty pounds of expired canned grains in the shed behind my house.

But once, on a visit to the Cape Meares lighthouse, Katie and I followed a deer trail into the forest. To the right was a three-hundred-foot drop straight off the cape; shore pines grew sideways out of the cliff underneath us, stretching horizontally in the direction of the sea. Above us were western hemlock and alders, their branches knitted together. We stepped carefully under them and over the wild thorny berries through which the deer had carved this path. The view expanded and our hearts beat faster with each push forward. The trail ended abruptly ten feet ahead of us at another cliff's edge. Through the brush at this height we could almost make out the entirety of Lost Boy Beach and the cave's entrance, roiling with salty water.

An inner voice said, *A bit more. See that flat ledge? Don't you wonder what is directly beneath this side of the cape? Do you want to be the one human who has seen it and lived to tell? Can you imagine how epic the photograph would be, there, where the bottom falls out underneath the manzanita and red-flowering currants?*

I inched forward, but Katie grabbed my gloved hand.

Enough.

Enough risks for the day, when simply being in love was maybe the biggest risk of all.

☾

The first time Katie and I took the half hour drive south to Pacific City, where vehicles are allowed on the beach, I was in the passenger side of her Subaru Outback. Katie followed the signs and then drove right onto the sand, bouncing over small dunes, the car rocking and twisting like a boat on choppy water.

I'd like to say I was exhilarated. But that would be a lie. Risk and its attendant fear had me convinced we'd end up stuck in deep sand or flipped like a new turtle hatchling on its way to the surf. ATVs zipped not far from us. I gasped at every turn with my hands over my eyes.

"*You're* freaking *me* out," Katie said as she stopped the car in the middle of the beach and opened her door. "It's your turn to drive." My heart dropped. An old park pass swung from the rearview mirror as I climbed over the console and then behind the wheel. Katie buckled in next to me and I hit the gas. I found bravery that can only exist when my hand is on the wheel, when I am in control. I drove right up to the shoreline and made a sharp turn before we hit the waves. Katie's face registered fear, but she laughed and nodded at me to keep going. A man and his son stood next to their four-wheelers, helmets under their arms, and stared at the middle-aged lesbians joyriding at low tide.

I wondered if this was why God saved me as a thirteen-year-old. So I could do beach doughnuts in a Subaru with the woman I loved, forever codifying on the sand that I no longer believed in him.

☾

In loving Katie, I risked so much daily. What was once transgression became the most veracious expression of myself in my animal body—this body once conceived from other sweaty bodies and that will someday become earth. Late at night, while the sky fell in graupel pellets on the Castle's roof, I learned that leaning into risk begets more pleasure. I put my tongue on my lover and felt a jolt of electricity; I was the conduit, she the fitting. This was the apple, right? Right there in my mouth? The fruit that Eve was told never to pluck and taste but oh thank fucking god she did.

I once chickened out of paragliding. Less than a year after I fell in love with The Poet and admitted to myself that I was gay, I spent two weeks at an academic seminar in Rio de Janeiro. A group of women in my cohort planned to paraglide at Praia do Sossego on our off day later in the week, and they wanted me to join them. Halfway around the world from my husband and young kids, I could squint just enough to make myself believe that my life was utterly different than it was, that I was allowed to tap into joy. That I was the kind of woman who could walk right off the edge of a mountain and ride the South American updrafts until I landed on Piratininga Beach.

The night before we were supposed to launch, I lay awake in my roach-ridden hotel room and thought about my fear. The way it consumed me. The way it sat in my body, a constant buzz in my ribcage too deep to touch, a hot knot I would excise if I could only reach it. I thought about my young kids, about them having to explain their whole lives that their mother went to Brazil, jumped off a mountain, and never came home.

I didn't show up with the others at the launch site. Instead, I sat on a sandy hotel towel on Ipanema Beach and tried to focus on the novel in my hand. Four topless women in thongs plunged repeatedly into the waves in front of me, and I was frozen by their lack of fear. I tugged my nine-inch shorts lower on my thighs. I was desperate to be the kind of woman who ran topless in the surf, who *kissed* women who ran topless in the surf, who walked off mountain cliffs and gave very few fucks.

But then what are my nights with Katie if not a kind of stepping-off from the ground beneath my feet, a run at pleasure that often leaves me breathless with adrenaline and oxytocin? I'd been warned about it my whole life, after all. The LDS pamphlet given to all teens when they turn twelve states firmly that "Homosexual and lesbian behavior is a serious sin. If you find yourself struggling with same-gender attraction or you are being persuaded to participate in inappropriate behavior, seek counsel from your parents and bishop." To top it off, the same pamphlet admonishes, "The prophet Alma taught that sexual sins are more serious than any other sins except murder and denying the Holy Ghost. . . . All sexual relations outside of marriage violate the law of chastity and are physically and spiritually dangerous for those who engage in them."

In some ways, the church isn't wrong. Sex is risky. We risk our hearts, our bodies, our most vulnerable selves to find pleasure in someone else's body, hoping that they will find pleasure in ours. After all, what was Eve doing if not taking the first human risk? She knew there would be consequences to eating the fruit. She also knew it would be delicious, and that she'd be given knowledge. Where Adam wasn't brave enough to take the risk first, Eve was. She leapt off that mountain. And, according to the speaker in Natalie Diaz's poem who compares her lover to Christianity's first lady of fruit, "she bites the apple and there is music—/ a branch breaking, a ship undone by the shore, / a knife making love to a wound, the sweet scrape / of a match lighting the lamp of her mouth."

☾

During our first year together, just after hibernation season, Katie and I stepped out of the car in front of the desolate road that led to Ungulate Woods. We turned just as a black bear sashayed across our path in that sultry way only bears have, about twenty-five feet in front of us. The bear looked behind her, still swaying, as if trying to usher unseen cubs to safety. We hadn't yet unloaded the dogs from the car, which was a small miracle. Katie opened her car door to jump back in while I took a small step toward mama bear.

"Where are you going?" Katie whispered as she caught my sleeve.

"I'm just going to get a slightly closer look."

"Absolutely not," she told me, the fabric of my coat still bunched tightly in her fist. "I just got you and don't need to lose you to a bear." I performed the risk analysis: was smelling the musky earth on that bear's long black fur and looking her dead in the eyes worth the risk of her turning on me with all five hundred of her pounds and her mighty claws? I knew Katie was right. But the pull toward that apex predator was so strong, I sometimes still see her behind my eyelids when I try to sleep, swaying as she steps with her five-toed paws. I have spent so much of my life afraid, but she reminds me that sometimes you must choose between unknowns, to hold each outcome in one of your soft palms.

What are the risks of stepping away from a religion and an entire community? Of dissolving the marriage that was supposed to be your salvation?

And what are the risks of *not* stepping away? Of nodding your head and saying yes, yes, I am who you want me to be, when in your deepest cells you know it isn't true?

And what of the risks of meeting a bear just after hibernation, an intimacy with the wild.

ST. GEORGE, UTAH

(Paiute: *Kaib-Whit*)

I followed Katie through a crack in the red cliffs. We had entered a narrow slot canyon where it was possible to stretch my meager wingspan and touch rock formations with the fingers of both hands. From under our boots, red dust rose in puffs, remnants from the oxidized iron rocks on either side. When we tilted our heads back, we could see hollows and small tunnels that had been forged into the rock whole epochs ago by water and time.

Southern Utah was the most otherworldly place I had ever been. Katie and I were there to help Elias get settled into his first apartment; he'd unexpectedly been offered a marketing position in St. George, and there wasn't much I could do but laugh. I'd spent most of his life trying to shield him from Mormonism, and now here he was, twenty years old, stepping aboard the mothership.

While Elias was at work, Katie and I explored, which is how we discovered the slot canyon in which we stood. I hoisted myself up into one of the canyon's crimson walls and found the perfect nest for my body etched into the soft red stone. A haunting noise tore through the canyon, amplified by the way the sound waves bounced back and forth between the cliff walls like a pinball in an old machine. Rock pigeons, who roost in crevices like the one where I currently sat, were calling to each other, their coos amplified until they sounded more like roars. I looked at my wife below me, her face striped with red dust. Bearing witness to such a geologic sleight-of-hand, it felt almost impossible to believe this was anything but the work of God.

Deeper in the state park, we hiked past Joshua trees and through sagebrush. Katie took a picture of thin lines in the red sand, curvy like ribbons, left behind by the bellies of snakes. We arrived at a massive rock face, where we could make out names that had been scrawled on the Navajo Sandstone with wagon oil.

Albert Graf, October 18th, 1894. Jacob Gubler, August 30th, 1897. Harman Gubler, March 4,1881.

Pioneers who had trekked to these very canyons, looking for God. It was easy to see why they thought they'd found him.

But then we stopped at the grocery store on our way back into St. George, our hiking clothes coated in sandstone dust. In the produce section, we found ourselves behind a group of five people walking in a row: a man in the middle, and four women, two on either side of him. Two of the women had their arms hooked into his elbow. He had a long gray beard, an imposing stature, and the limp of a man who had been on this earth for a while. His wives, though—I suspected right away that's what these young girls were, *his wives*—looked like they could be as young as fifteen but no older than twenty-two. Like Katie and me, they weren't wearing any makeup, but unlike us, they didn't lift their chins or meet anyone's eye. They wore baby blue dresses with hems that dragged along the grocery store linoleum and long sleeves that slightly puffed at each shoulder. Their hair was swept into a high up-do in front with the rest of their locks running in long braids down the back of their dresses.

I knew we likely had a common genealogy, that it was possible my great-great-great aunt rode in a wagon company next to their great-great-great grandmother. That the men in the group—the Harman Gublers and Albert Grafs—had not only accepted the red canyons as a gift from a benevolent God, but had accepted their many wives as such, too. Women were treated the same way men treated the landscape: as a commodity, a thing to own and tame and have dominion over.

Under those pale dresses, these girls wore the same white garments, with the same strange symbols, that I had once worn.

The line separating us was gossamer thin.

☾

The mortician led me and my mom to a cold, dark lower level of the funeral parlor and then left us alone, closing the heavy door behind him. My paternal grandmother's lifeless body lay supine on a steel table, covered by a thin sheet. We were here to dress her in full temple clothes, her final ritual act before being consigned to eternity.

She'd died in a hospice facility earlier that week while my mom and I held both her hands. My mom had left the church shortly after my father died, though my grandmother hadn't known. Church policy holds that if the deceased received her temple endowed in life, she should be buried in full garments and temple clothes, and only an endowed family member of the same gender could dress a body. Nowhere in those rules did it say the endowed family member had to still be an active, believing member. Mom and I got in on a technicality.

Dressing a person in full rigor mortis was no easy task. Grandma's body was stiff and unyielding as petrified wood. We followed church rules to the letter, starting with the sacred garments. Grandma had told me a decade earlier that she and my grandfather tried so hard to be righteous that they always put their garments on right-leg-first. To honor that, we started with her right leg, then her left, one of us holding the body up in the center to get the elastic up to the waist. We repeated the same with her garment top, then looked down, sweat beaded on our foreheads and upper lips, at the "sacred symbols" staring up at us from Grandma's underwear: a reverse-L shape on the right breast, a V-shape on the left, and short horizontal lines over her knee and at the level of her navel.

Next were the nude panty hose, which in keeping with church rules had to be put on *over* the knee-length garments, even though it left a woman's thigh a wrinkled, uncomfortable mess. When I said as much to my mom, she quipped, "Grandma is too dead to care if her garments are bunchy," and shrugged her shoulders. Our next layer was the beloved floor-length white temple dress with long sleeves that she had sewn herself many decades before. It took my mom and I all of our collective strength to lift Grandma's arms high enough to pull the dress onto her body. We worked both of her feet into plain white slippers. The top layer of her ensemble had three parts: Eve's green silk apron, hand embroidered with fig leaves, a sheer white veil that both tied under her chin and affixed to her hair with combs, and a pleated shawl that we draped over her right shoulder.

I pulled the veil over Grandma's face, then mom and I stepped back, panting and breathless. When we first walked into this dark room, it was for my Grandma Eyvon. But we'd made her into just another Eve in a long string of Eves. She was every Mormon woman, about to go in the ground faceless, indistinguishable from every other Mormon woman.

She was just that villainess who ate the apple.

☾

After my dad's funeral, we met his body at the pioneer cemetery where we had buried his father ten years before. Only a handful of family and very close friends were invited to the burial. His oldest and dearest friend, Steve, carried a beeping handheld GPS device so he would always know the exact final coordinates of his best friend.

The funeral director opened my dad's casket just for the immediate family: Grandma Eyvon, my aunt Marylue, my mom, my brothers, Matt, and me. We had all chosen a token to leave in the casket with him before they lowered him into the ground next to my grandpa. I put mine in the pocket of his white shirt: a handwritten letter and a membership card to a long gone home improvement store with both our pictures on it. I squeezed his shoulder, then recoiled when I found my palm against what felt like cold stone, not the flesh and blood that had raised me.

My father had become a body that was not my father. In his temple clothes, clothes he rarely wore in life because, he once confided in me, he didn't really have a testimony of the temple and he found it strange, he was just one more Adam in a long line of Adams. One more fig-leaf-clad white man who was promised permanent glory in the stars, where he would rule over his own planet and become a god.

But *this* Adam was not God. This Adam was a man, and he was my father, and he was going to lie eight feet underground and not in the stars. Not even close to the stars.

☾

On our third day in Utah, we set out to see the petrified sand dunes in Snow Canyon, just ten minutes north of St. George. The sun blazed down at close to a hundred degrees, so we waited until the cool of early evening to park at the trailhead. The sun was still above the horizon, the sky washed in violet and champagne. Under that, the brick-red remains of massive sand dunes stretched out in front of us, seemingly endless. Each hardened dune had planar lines across its surface, the remnants of ancient sand ripples.

We followed the trail markers as best we could, a tricky feat because they were only small metal plates painted with arrows and screwed directly into the Navajo sandstone. When we rounded the top of a mound, we learned we weren't the only ones on the trail: off in the distance, we counted four separate brides in full wedding regalia, spaced far apart. Their respective photographers must have rushed to catch the perfect shot of the red rocks reflecting against white satin, the brides backlit by the desert gloaming.

How quickly we were reminded that we were in territory settled by the Mormons.

Katie hiked ahead of me, up the side of one massive dune and down another. We hopped over shallow crevices where yucca and creosote grew freely. As the sun lowered, the air grew thick with bats that emitted the high-pitched clicks and squeaks of echolocation. Against our better judgment, we sat on the tallest dune and watched as the horizon swallowed the sun to the west. To the east, the waxing gibbous moon pierced silver through the indigo sky. I photographed Katie with her arm in the air, as if she were pinching it.

That moon helped us get home. We lost sight of the small trail markers on the rocks, so Katie grabbed my hand, and we wove past desert plants, keenly aware with each step of the threat of rattlesnakes. But the moon grew brighter, as if it had lifted a finger to show us the way. Katie's face flickered with shadows of molten honey, as if lit by Victorian candlelight.

The brides-to-be had long since left. But when we reached our rental car, I turned to look in the direction where they'd been posing, where the men who would become their eternal companions had each held a steady arm around his young bride's sashed waist. In another year or two, each couple would be holding an infant, and in twenty years that infant will be photographed with a fiancé on the petrified dunes in Snow Canyon.

Or she won't. She might get out. She might find a way to love the landscape of her people despite never feeling like one of them. She might quilt a whole beautiful life out of everything the church broke in her. She might be pulled to the ocean, to the rhythm of the tides and the shape-shifting dunes. And when she's older, she'll return to these petrified ones and recognize them as composed of sediment from an ancient sea not so different from her beloved Pacific.

☾

The Temple Matron handed me a three-foot-wide white sheet she called a "shield" and told me to strip naked and then cover myself with it. A round hole had been cut out of the center of the shield, turning it into a sort of poncho. I thought about my mom, waiting for me in the white plush area outside the door. Then I walked into the stall, undressed, and lifted the shield over my head, hugging it tightly to my sides in the hopes I could prevent my bare skin from showing as I left the room. A hospital gown would have provided more coverage.

When it was my turn, the Matron ushered me into the initiatory room, which had been partitioned by veils into four sections. The older woman stood over me holding a small bubbling fountain and told me its water would wash and purify me for the next step in the ritual. She repeatedly dipped her finger in it and then dabbed the liquid onto various parts of my body, reciting rote blessings with each dab. Head. Neck. Heart. Lips. Shoulders. Arms. When she reached under the shield to touch the side of my breast, and then again the inside of my hip just above my groin (my loins, as she called it), I remembered my mom's non-answer when I'd asked her if I'd have to get naked in the temple.

We moved through one of the veils for the anointing part of the ceremony. The old woman touched the same body parts she'd already dabbed with water, but this time she used consecrated olive oil, promising me blessings of vitality and fertile loins. I held my breath and willed it to end.

The "dressing" part of the ritual happened through yet another veil. The Matron held a new pair of garments, still in their packaging, the underwear I was required to wear from this day forward. She reached under the shield and pulled the garments onto me, right leg before left, both of us fumbling awkwardly to avoid her seeing or touching any more of my nude body than was necessary. She pulled the knee-length bottoms up each leg and the cap-sleeve top over my head. The garments were ultra-fine and silky, with pleats that allowed room for fuller breasts. *Sister Minor,* she said with her hands on my head, *under proper authority, the garment placed upon you is to be worn throughout your life. It represents the garment given to Adam and Eve when they were found naked in the Garden of Eden and is called The Garment of the Holy Priesthood.*

I was ushered through the final veil, the Matron's hand on the small of my back. The last step of the initiatory ritual was the naming ceremony. I'd never been told that I'd get a new secret name in the temple, and I didn't know what to make of it. The woman continued her recitations: *With this Garment I give you a New Name, which you should always remember, and which you must keep sacred, and never reveal except at a certain place which will be shown you hereafter.*

The name is Lois. I cracked and then quickly stifled a smile. What kind of holy, sacred name was Lois, after all? All I can find today is that Lois showed up in the New Testament only as Timothy's grandmother.

When it was over, I returned to my stall in the changing room, where the long-sleeved white dress I'd worn on the way in hung from a hook above the bench where my balled-up panties and bra sat. I would never need the panties again, so they went directly into my bag. The bra I was to put on over my garments, which made the silky extra fabric for breasts bunch against my skin. I looked at myself in the mirror. Here I was, prepping in the week before my wedding, and I had never felt less attractive than I did standing in those garments with my bra layered on top.

Garments were supposed to save us. When she dressed me, the Matron incanted, *Inasmuch as you do not defile it, but are true and faithful to your covenants, it will be a shield and a protection to you against the power of the destroyer until you have finished your work here on earth.* How many stories had I heard from the pulpit, the kitchen, the hushed tones of grown-ups in the living room, about faithful men being saved from certain death by their garments? There was the one about the man taking down a large tree with a chainsaw when the chain hit a knot and bounced back, sawing him right in the leg. The saw went right through his work coveralls, jeans, and thermals, miraculously stopping right at his garments to spare his leg. Chairman of the Marriott Hotel chain, Bill Marriott, once famously told Mike Wallace on *Sixty Minutes* that his garments saved him during a boat fire: "My pants were burned right off of me," he said in the interview. "I was not burned above my knee. Where the garment was, I was not burned."

☾

Those garments did not protect my grandmother from losing her husband to lymphoma, then her only son to brain cancer. They didn't stop the neuropathy that plagued her from her thirties onward. Still, she wanted to be wearing them when she was interred next to my grandfather, the shared tombstone above the grass all prepped with her name and birth date and an engraved picture of the Portland temple.

I wanted the world to know that we were burying Eyvon, not Eve. A woman of flesh and blood, not one who only exists in gilded pages of scripture. Such erasure, to dress her like every other woman of her faith stretching back to Eve. My grandma was spectacular in her own right; in her lifetime she did so many things, all of which were greater than biting into a damn apple.

Would Eve have been the first in her family to enroll in college in the early days of the Depression, putting her future husband's eighth grade education to shame? Was Eve committed to domesticity enough to bleach every kitchen towel each week and iron her sheets? Did seventy-year-old Eve ever don a life vest and cling to a raft while the Colorado River took her headlong through the rapids of the Grand Canyon? Did Eve spend thousands upon thousands of hours sewing Barbie clothes for children's charities?

Eve was sweet-talked by a snake, but Eyvon wouldn't have taken that bullshit from any creature. When my grandpa caught a king snake in her zinnia beds, she knew her grandkids would love it as a pet. So she wrapped the snake in a burlap sack, draped it around her neck, covered it with a jacket, and walked undetected through airport security. When we picked her up from the airport a few hours later, she removed her jacket and produced the red-and-black striped creature with an *abracadabra* flourish, a grander magic trick than anything Eve could have mustered.

☾

It was by pure chance that our visit to St. George coincided with the open house of the newly restored St. George temple. The church doesn't allow nonmembers or unendowed members to enter a temple, but when new temples are built or restored, the men in Salt Lake City open the building to the general public for a brief time before it is officially dedicated and becomes off-limits. I wanted to walk through the temple with my wife and son. I wanted them to see the inside of one of the buildings that have haunted me for so many years, and I wanted this tour to take the power out of Mormon temples so they didn't loom so large in my head.

I was in my mid-twenties the last time I set foot in a temple. I blended in back then: white dress, nondescript long hair, plastic smile. They were all part of the mask I wore to hide the real me lurking inside. This time, as we walked up to the entrance, a line of blond heads turned and stared. They smiled as if seeing us was the happiest thing that had happened to them that day, but their smiles did not hide their obvious discomfort. Feeling brave, I took Katie's hand, there in front of a Southern Utah temple.

Her hand did what I knew it would do. It steadied me.

A woman called out to us, "Wow, you look like you just stepped out of a magazine! Welcome!" I thought about what we were wearing: designer sneakers and comfortable Thai fisherman pants. My hair was shaved short on the sides and spiked on the top, and Katie wore the black and orange Adidas that I often stole from her closet. We'd been labeled outsiders, singled out as the only non-Mormon, non-straight folks in the entire crowded parking lot. It hadn't even occurred to any of them that I was once one of them, that I had fallen hook, line, and sinker, and that this wasn't even close to my first time in a temple.

Calm settled over me, the same steady feeling I often had at the surf's edge or at the mouth of a crimson red slot canyon. It anchored me as if to the earth itself. That past version of me, the Mormon girl who wanted so desperately to be perfect and good, felt ossified and far away. Being perceived as an outsider shook something loose in me. Their judgment couldn't touch me. I was holding a shield against their shame.

That shield was Katie's hand. I held it during the entire hour-long tour, up marble stairs and through white rooms with paintings on each wall depicting pioneer hardship. I squeezed her hand tight when we were ushered past the twelve golden oxen holding a baptismal font on their backs. When they showed us the Celestial Room—identical to the one I kneeled in wearing a dress that was not my wedding dress to promise myself to a man for time and all eternity—Katie traced my palm with slow, deliberate circles.

Those who practice palmistry claim they can read a person's future by analyzing the heart-line that runs along that person's palm. Traditional Chinese medical doctors, like Katie, use a close study of the palm to learn about the health of a person's heart. But I learned something wholly different by gripping Katie's palm in the temple: because I don't believe we'll be together for the *time and all eternity* promised by my old faith, it is the brevity of our time together, the fleeting nature of love and its attendant loss, that makes her hand in mine closer to the divine than anything else I've known.

TEMPLE SQUARE, SALT LAKE CITY

(Shoshoni: Soonte-Katieahni)

Mormon leaders launched a rebrand campaign in 2018 when they announced from their headquarters near Temple Square in Salt Lake City that they would no longer refer to the church (or its members) as "Mormon." Only two uses of the name were still deemed acceptable by prophet Russell M. Nelson: in proper names (The Book of Mormon, for example, or the Mormon Tabernacle Choir), or when used as an adjective in historical expressions (think Mormon trail or Mormon pioneers).

"It matters what you call a thing," Solmaz Sharif writes in her poem "Look."

☾

I can often identify a family with Mormon heritage by their surname: Snow, Hatch, Romney, Kimball, Flake, Jensen, Mecham, Allred, Smith, Taylor, Young.

A man with Mormon heritage is sometimes easy to spot by his first name: Hyrum, Heber, Ammon, Nephi, Alma, Brigham, Lehi.

But I can't think of a single name that would expressly identify a woman with the same heritage.

☾

Nelson asked that members instead use the church's full name: "The Church of Jesus Christ of Latter-day Saints," with "The Church" and "The Church of Jesus Christ" being the only acceptable shortened alternatives. "This is the name by which the Lord will call us at the last day," Nelson said. "It is the name by which His Church will be distinguished from all others."

This wasn't the first attempt the church had made to distance itself from the name Mormon. Its leaders made a similar push three previous times: in 1982, in 2001, and then again in 2011.

The change never stuck.

☾

The quickest and most effective way to assert yourself as one of the in-group is to know what to call things. Names and their nuances can tell us who is in charge and who belongs. When we were planning our trip to Southern Utah, it chaffed my ears each time Katie talked about visiting Zion.

Zy-on, she would say.

Zy-uhn, I would correct her.

Listening to the pronunciation of names is the easiest way to spot a tourist anywhere. The town of Hurricane borders St. George and Elias laughed when we asked about a store there.

"Everyone around here says Hurri-kin," he told us.

Try saying Ore-gone while in Portland and see how everyone around you reacts.

We also mark what names we are allowed to use by our identities. Before I came out of the closet, I wouldn't have dared to say the word *dyke.* Now not only does it easily roll off of my tongue, but it makes me part of an in-group of gay women who have reclaimed the word. Sometimes it feels like the best way to describe who I am, even though (because?) it could feel like violence in the mouths of others.

A name can bestow the power to change the way we are seen by the world. I've watched the transformation firsthand when trans friends adopt a name that matches their gender identity. That's how a name becomes holy. To call a person by their dead name is also a kind of violence.

In refusing to change what I call the church that made me feel small, unworthy, and unlovable for so many decades, am I also inflicting a kind of violence? When do we respect a name change as holy as opposed to rejecting it?

It matters what you call a thing.

☾

Poet Assétou Xango writes, "I am through with names that leave me unmoved. / Names that leave the speaker's mouth unscathed."

What does it mean that at the time of the prophet's rebrand announcement, the church was funding an international public relations campaign called "I'm a Mormon?" A person walking in many of the world's major cities could look up to see a billboard or a sign on the side of the bus, one that featured a high-profile member of the faith proudly proclaiming the *I'm a Mormon* catch-phrase. A years-long international campaign of that magnitude might have cost upwards of twenty to thirty million dollars, only for the prophet to pull the plug on the entire campaign after announcing that none of the participants, in fact, is a Mormon.

When I talk about the "Mormon" church, when I refer to its members as "Mormons," when I call myself an ex-"Mormon," I'm placing myself decidedly on the outside of the group. Sometimes I pause when "Mormon" slips from my lips, but then I remember the power of names. A doctor who refers to his patient by her first name while offering only his title and last name creates a distinct power dynamic. It's why I have always told my students I prefer to be called by my first name.

If it matters what you call a thing, it also matters what you don't call it. Names are how we create meaning in the world, how we instill order and attempt to understand the people and places around us. An insanely powerful multi-billion-dollar corporation like the Mormon church can't be deadnamed.

I get to name the thing that hurt me. I get to speak that name out loud.

ANCIENT CHINA

Shame is not really anticipated in traditional Chinese medicine unless you peel back the layers. Take the malady *bei die,* a lesser-known illness from ancient texts that stretch as far back as the Eastern Han Dynasty. A patient with *bei die* presents with an inability to eat or drink and a blockage in the chest. According to the *Practical Dictionary of Chinese Medicine, bei die* should be suspected when a patient presents with "apologies in the heart/centre of the chest, prefers to be in dark rooms, and is afraid to the point of wanting to hide upon seeing others."

Shame.

Many acupuncturists believe feelings of shame or guilt, despite being *apologies of the heart,* arise from the spleen. Shame commonly manifests in the stagnation or sinking of *Qi,* which is also a disorder of the spleen; to fix it, one must tonify and raise the spleen *Qi.* This can be done through herbs (an ancient formula of ten herbs called *Bu Zhong Yi Qi Tang* promises to "lift what has sunken") or by the insertion of a needle into the uppermost point on the human body, *Baihui.*

In English, the point *Baihui* has a few different names. Sometimes it's called Hundred Convergences, where all the energies of the body meet. Or it's referred to as Mountain Top, which seems fitting for the acupuncture point closest to the sun. Others use the moniker Celestial Fullness, home of the "hundred diseases" and "hundred spirits." To find the point, run the pads of your forefinger over the midpoint of the invisible line connecting the tips of both ears. Find a subtle depression, a secret, almost imperceptible vacuity through which a needle can pull shame like *Qi* and release it heavenward.

That's it, right there.

Lift what was sunken.

Shame is what keeps us hidden and silent. It is an inward-facing burden we carry from our ancestors. It is the convergence of who we know ourselves to be and who the world *thinks* we should be. Shame is a hundred different things.

A hundred convergences.

A hundred ghosts.

A hundred apologies of the heart.

THE WETLANDS

(Clackamas: *Waluga*)

Two things happened in the weeks surrounding our Utah trip: we listed the Wetlands for sale, and we adopted a five-month-old puppy. Matt had moved out of the Wetlands during his parenting weeks, and the house was just too expensive for us to keep ourselves in addition to the Castle, especially now that two of the three kids had fledged. And the puppy? I defy anyone who sees a picture of this dog to make a different decision, bad timing be damned.

And the timing was definitely bad. In the first two years after Katie and I fell in love, the world around us continued its steady burn. It wasn't just the unrest in Ukraine and Gaza and the still-circulating pandemic virus. In our extended family alone, we'd lost three breasts, an ovary, and a uterus. When Matt and Clementine brought Covid home from a trip to Southern California, it quickly jumped hosts: Katie tested positive and then spent over a year battling long Covid. Her Crohn's disease flared up, often keeping her bedridden. My own chronic health issue—a lifetime spent grappling with dislocated and subluxated joints thanks to Ehlers Danlos Syndrome—also reared its head, relegating many of my hours to the bed with a heating pad on whichever spot was the sorest. Through it all, through tears and conflict and fear and sorrow, Katie and I clung to each other and tried to focus on the path ahead, despite how dimly it was lit.

☾

Calling an area a wetland is essentially a dressed-up way of identifying it as a swamp; a rebrand, if you will. Any place can be called a wetland if the soil there is flooded with water for at least part of the year. I had watched for fifteen years as the water in the swamp abutting the house rose in the winter and dried up in the summer, the sedges and bulrushes filling in the areas where firs felled by previous storms lay rotting on their backs, nurse logs for the next generation.

Swamps are among the most prolific ecosystems on the planet, as biologically diverse as rainforests and coral reefs. They help moderate global climate conditions and purify water. Ours was a riparian wetland, one of the many rich watershed ecosystems of the Pacific Northwest characterized by the trifecta of loam, hydrology, and frondescence. What we saw from our bedroom window was a marshy glen with the occasional nesting pair of mallards, but our wetlands were so much more. They were the transition zone between land and water. Like the beach we walked daily at the Castle, our wetlands were on a continual cycle of flooding and ebbing, though on a slower scale.

But life in a swamp can be a challenge, even beyond the obvious pests like mosquitos. Pollutants from groundwater often flow into wetlands and accumulate in the sedimentation, making growing food tricky. Invasive species thrive in swampy conditions, as the Himalayan blackberries next to the house could attest, and sometimes alter the composition of the ecosystem itself. And, of course, there's the increased risk of flooding during storms.

Through many wet winters, I watched as the water rose by inches and army-crawled toward the house. I could close my eyes and see it flooding the entire lower level, dragging soggy oak leaves and wet soil the texture of coffee grounds onto the blue velvet couches in the living room. I imagined small waves of swamp water licking at the legs of the baby grand piano until they warped.

I am saying there are so many ways to fear a rising sea.

☾

After dozens of bouts of anaphylaxis related to trace amounts of peppers we couldn't seem to get a handle on, Katie's doctor recommended we get a service dog who could alert us to the presence of fatal allergens. We laughed. This was the worst possible time for us to get a new puppy.

Still, we looked at the website of the breeder who brought Marco into the world seven years earlier. She liked to keep one or two puppies from each litter to ensure those dogs were set up for success as therapy and service dogs. We scrolled through her available older puppies and stopped short on Skyler, a blue merle doodle just like Marco but eight times bigger. Katie and I each dreamed about Skyler that night, and by the next day, we'd talked ourselves into meeting him. Katie reached out to the breeder and made plans to meet the puppy that week. Two hours after we hung up the phone, I got the news alert about what was happening on Maui: a devastating wildfire was sweeping across the island and threatening Lahaina. I thought of that gorgeous old banyan tree where Clementine and I sat for lunch on our Maui trip, when Katie was still a flicker of a dream inside my cell phone.

The breeder lived on a farm south of Portland. She took us through a series of gates and brought in two puppies in quick succession—a girl named Ember with a black fleecy phantom coat, and a boy named Cyrus, who was brown with white patches, both five months old. They licked our faces and seemed happy to see us, but I didn't pay them much mind. I was there for Skyler and no one else.

And then she brought him in. And that dog wouldn't stop bouncing. And barking. And being generally cute but definitely crazy in a way that would not work for a service animal or my nerves. We tried to subdue him so we could get to know him a bit, but he was hell bent on bouncing and zooming. That's when Ember walked over to where I sat cross-legged on the lawn and climbed into my lap. She looked up at me quizzically, as if to say *why are you putting up with this bullshit?* I wrapped my arms around her neck, and she nuzzled into me.

Katie looked over at us. "Uh-oh. You look sprung."

"This dog is the one," I said, and because Katie trusts me, she agreed.

The night before, we'd asked the I Ching whether the house would sell and if it was the right time to put it on the market. After the clanging of coins on the table, we were pointed to hexagram 22, Adornment, a stack of six black lines, some broken, some unbroken, whose translation meant "Fire at the foot of the mountain."

Adornment. Dress it up. Make it pretty. The house would sell, the I Ching seemed to tell us, but we needed to roll up our sleeves and put in the work.

Adornment. The backsides of all four of Ember's legs were a bright fiery red, as if she'd pulled on her best pair of boots for our visit.

☾

Fire at the foot of the mountain.

We could feel it lapping at our feet.

Selling the Wetlands required I enroll in a hypothetical DIY crash course that might well have been called "Lesbians and Their Tools." I used a putty knife alongside my wife to spackle drywall holes. She taught me to replace all the worn and mismatched doorknobs with a drill. Together we excavated a long-buried flagstone path from half a foot of dirt with shovels and trowels and when the path was finished, I pressure washed the siding on the back of the house where it had been splashed with mud. I was weeding the backyard with Sam when the *hori hori* I was using to slice through vines went instead through my finger. The blood was warm where it ran down my arm.

"Do you believe me yet about wearing yard gloves?" Katie asked after she'd cleaned the dirt out of the wound. I nodded, humbled, because she'd been harping on me for months to don gloves when I worked in the yard. Sam was back outside already, raising a machete high above his head and then swinging it downward, a soldier in our ongoing war against the blackberries.

Fire at the foot of the mountain.

Katie doused my finger with hydrogen peroxide; my hand felt as if I had placed it directly into a burning flame. We could hear the fervent whoosh of the machete each time Sam swung it against the base of the berry plants.

Sometimes the best way you can adorn a place is to take out the proverbial trash, the flotsam that clings to a life and prevents it from moving forward. All told, when we were done clearing the strip of land that abuts the marsh, we'd found a whole litany of oddities: fir trees from twelve different Christmases, ten balls of varying sizes and genres, one Converse shoe, a busted skateboard.

But it was nothing compared to what we couldn't see, the things I was ashamed to have dumped over that fence during my first marriage. The compounded remnants of fifteen years of rotting stoop pumpkins. Dog shit, picked up from the yard and chucked into the berry tangle. The bodies of bloodied mice who had fallen victim to one of the family cats.

How deep were those blackberry vines?

Deep enough to hide it all: the woman who wore garments to bed and taught Sunday school. The woman who once told her toddler daughter there was no way God was a woman. The woman with the covers to her chin who couldn't leave bed for weeks, months, years. The woman who could create an impeccably lined red lip, layer a perfect stack of necklaces at her décolletage, and squeeze her feet into the torturous pointy toe of a fashionable boot.

The woman who wanted nothing more than to adorn herself enough for the world to like her.

☾

Ember came home with us that weekend. She melted into me the entire ride home, as if she were a black fleecy weighted blanket. Her eyes were trained on the velvet skin of Katie's hands where they lightly gripped the steering wheel at ten and two. Katie was stunning that day, her brown hair longer than she usually kept it and swept off her forehead with a pair of sunglasses.

We'd been following the tragedy in Maui. Reports had come out that morning of an estimated one hundred people who were killed because they had nowhere to escape. Maui had been the place I fell in love with Katie, the place where Clementine and I expanded our definition of family post-divorce. And here was this puppy, dark and brooding and named after the small glowing bits of wood left in a dying fire. I knew from Katie that for Chinese doctors, the Fire element manifests in the heart and must be kept in check; an excess of Fire can be destructive and must be balanced by Water.

People often use embers as metaphors for things that fade: a dying friendship, a woman's beauty, the final throes of a long marriage. But embers aren't so easily boxed and labeled. An ember can exist after a fire, sure, but also during one and, even sometimes, before the blaze in question ever started. If an ember started my love for Katie, it likely would have been something as simple as the tilt of her sunglasses on top of her head, or the way she puckers her lips slightly when she is thinking. It's always enough to set all the cinders in my body to flame.

But we knew that Ember wouldn't keep her name. We needed to choose her name ourselves in order to induct her into the family. That's the weighty responsibility of naming, and also the joy of it. Late that night, after Ember settled in Marco's puppyhood crate and the other dogs snored from their beds on the floor, Katie turned to me and said, "Her name is Cora."

"Cora," I said, trying it out. She'd said it with the same confidence I'd used to tell her this dog was the one for our family, and I trusted it.

"I've been planning to name a daughter Cora since I was fourteen years old," she told me. I held her closer, because under her words were other words. She'd had an emergency hysterectomy the previous winter, a slash-and-burn on her plans for biological parenthood.

"Cora," I repeated. "Cora." I liked the way it felt on my tongue, and I wasn't sure why, but it seemed to fit that wooly doodle with the fiery red boots who slept in the crate next to our bed.

☾

After we'd covered the old paint colors and replaced chipped molding, after we'd scoured and hammered and cleaned as best we could, we consulted the I Ching again. We'd made the house into something new, something it had never been while I lived there. And now we wanted to know if we'd done enough, if we could sit back and wait for the house to sell. We did the customary six rolls of the coins to arrive at our answer: hexagram 64. The very last entry in the ancient text.

The 64th *gua* is called "Before Completion" and the best translation of the hexagram itself is "Fire over Water." What was it with fire? It was everywhere and I couldn't escape it. What we gleaned from the I Ching: we were experiencing the condition before a great transition, and we needed to be vigilant in the last few yards to succeed. We'd come to the edge of the river, even stuck our toes in it, but we had yet to cross.

"The nature of fire is flaming upwards," Taoist master Alfred Huang writes of hexagram 64. "And the nature of water is flowing downward. Their actions move in opposite directions and dissociate. This movement signifies a difficult situation." I felt that. The fire raging upwards, the water pooling at my ankles. When the water can't reach the flames, the fire burns unchecked.

There were so many embers in that house. So many fires, large and small, that had been extinguished but sometimes still felt prone to bursting. Time is funny like that, the way it bends and queers. I could close my eyes and feel the lapping heat:

The smoldering windowsill next to Elias's sleeping head; he'd fallen asleep on the couch and left our bearded dragon's UV light sitting directly on the molding. I had painted over the six-inch-diameter charred circle on the window casing the week before. It took four coats of Benjamin Moore Chantilly Lace.

The lighter that my brother sparked in front of my thirty-two-year-old face when I told him I was ready to try weed. Each time the pipe came back my direction, I inhaled as the singed embers of ground cannabis roared temporarily to life.

The hanging light fixture in the entryway, the one made to look like a modern candelabra, where little Clementine and her friends threw a blanket just to see if it could reach the light. It could. The popping sound started immediately, followed by the distinct aroma of burning polyester.

The scented candle that Chloe's cat Emma swiped off the desk with her paw, igniting the loose pile of wrinkled US history handouts on her desk.

The gas fireplace that we never used except for the year after I'd asked Matt for a divorce. It was Valentine's Day, and he was anxious to join his girlfriend in Salem despite the heavy snowfall. When the power went out and Matt conceded his snow tires wouldn't get him safely south, we turned on the fireplace and pulled the couches and the kids close. For three days in the dark, that fire kept us happy, alive, and able to see each other's faces, however dimly lit.

☾

Cora is short for *corazon,* the Spanish word for *heart.* It felt like a natural trajectory, a good landing place after the five months she spent as Ember. Michael Ondaatje must have known something of Chinese medicine when he wrote the oft-quoted line, "The heart is an organ of fire."

When my dad died, I'd gotten a grief dog, a sweet four-year-old Australian labradoodle named Heidi whom I fostered for a year before adopting. Heidi was my daily companion until she died at sixteen, months after I left my marriage. I still thought about her every day: her curly apricot locks, the silly way she used to weave between my legs when I got home from a long day of teaching. Once we brought Cora home, though, I stopped missing Heidi so much. I couldn't explain it, but when Cora tilted her head just so and looked at me with her intense brown eyes, it felt like I was looking right at Heidi again.

Katie, too, had lost a dog dear to her heart. I'd heard so many stories about Maya, the legendary seventy-five-pound jet black German shepherd mix who had taught our Marco everything he knew about being a dog. It wasn't long after bringing Cora home that Katie started seeing the ghost of Maya when Cora took a sharp corner or got into a particular kind of mischief.

It felt as if Cora had brought both of our old beloveds back to us. As if Maya and Heidi were thrilled that Katie and I had found each other.

☾

Our realtor booked a photographer to take pictures of the Wetlands for the listing, so Clementine went to her dad's house and Katie and I prepared to retreat to the Castle. We'd cleaned every last bit of dust from the house, trying our best to keep the marsh outside. While Katie waited in the car with the dogs, I did one last sweep of the house, picturing the young families who might show up to the open house the next day looking for a place to raise their children.

I walked from room to room, making sure all lights were blazing at full intensity and putting loose objects in their place. I touched up small spots of dirt on the floors and straightened the bedspread in our bedroom. The last spot on my list was the primary closet, the one I had shared with first one partner and now another. Inside was a tiny door to the attic space, practically painted into the wall below the window.

Did the Wetlands have a secret heart?

I'm not sure, had anyone asked me, that I would have remembered the little closet door existed. I knew that Matt had used it to store luggage over the years, but beyond that, I had no idea what I would find when I bent over and pulled the wooden knob. And I knew I only had a few minutes before all three dogs drove Katie insane.

If this was the house's secret heart, why did it hold mementos from a life that I no longer recognized? There were boxes of pictures that stretched back dozens of years. All the film pictures from the kids' early childhood, in the days when pictures were printed and then saved. Pictures from my high school years, from the two years in college while Matt was on his mission. The box of letters we'd exchanged during those two years. Love letters, yes, but also musings about religion and the future. Was I even a glint in her eye, that young girl who wrote to her missionary, who was hell bent on ignoring her own secret heart because she tried so hard to choose the right, to please God and her parents and be blind to desire?

"People don't just happen," Saeed Jones writes. "We sacrifice former versions of ourselves. We sacrifice the people who dared to raise us. The 'I' it seems doesn't exist until we are able to say, 'I am no longer yours.'" I loaded everything into the back and got into the car with Katie and the pooches. I didn't know whose secret heart I was protecting, Matt's, maybe, or the children's. All I knew was that there were things this house still had to work through, chief among them the ghosts of all my former selves clamoring to be heard.

Because if there were fires in that house, there was also water. The house sat on its namesake, after all, a rich wetland that by its very definition was inundated with water. Wetlands *hold* water, in fact. That's what they do. And without the right amount of rain, wind, and sun, wetlands become places of dangerous stagnation. In a continuous cycle of water-begets-water, the best way to maintain a healthy wetlands ecosystem is to allow the rain to enter at will, swirl it around, and refresh. Let the swamp let go of the old water it had been holding and replace it with the new.

So it was with the house generally. I thought about the fifteen years of pain that had been stagnant within its walls. The memory of my dad's only visit to the house, a week after we bought it and a month before he died. The spot in the primary bedroom where I would park myself, day after day and night after night, my depression its own kind of weighted blanket that at times seemed one breath away from suffocating me. The pain of two adults coming to terms with the trauma and abuse in the system in which they were raised. The fights, the confusion, the *I don't think I am straight.* The shame that lurked in every corner. Holes punched in the walls in anger, a thousand small cuts on Chloe's arms and legs before she knew just how much her life was worth.

It's the kind of pain that asks to be felt before it can leave. It begged me to leave some doors open, to blow the ache of grief out with the stagnant water, to let clear rain push through the filter of the marsh, so the cycle could continue anew. Matt had moved out, and we'd fixed the place up past recognition. It was time to let the clear rain of *now* squeeze the past through the filter of the wetlands, allowing the stagnation of *then* to clear out with the muddy leaf litter of the marsh. I needed to allow the rain to purify the place, but not in the white-dress-purity of my youth.

☾

It's easy (and lazy) to speculate that the land White settlers stole was an untouched wilderness, and that leaving the land free of human interference is the only way for the wetlands and forests to survive. On the contrary, the land they stole from the Tualatin band of the Kalapuya tribe had been meticulously cultivated and tightly managed for over ten thousand years. They created fire ecology regimes whose complexity is unmatched in the modern era, through which they kept the big leaf maple and Douglas fir from growing unchecked to allow diverse ecosystems to flourish for century after century.

Until they didn't.

The forced removal of the Kalapuya people led to the swift end of tribal land management practices that had been honed through thousands of years of trial and error. The regular burns stopped with the move from a subsistence economy to an extractive one, the land grew thick with puffy Douglas firs, packed one against the other, sardine-style, edging out other species. Settlers also changed the face of the tributaries, rivers, floodplains, and wetlands through channelization, causing the irrevocable destruction of riparian habitats. Before they arrived, Oregon's Willamette Valley was composed of large swaths of high-nutrient wetlands. Fifty-seven percent of it has been lost. The shrinkage is still happening, according to some studies, at the rate of five hundred acres per year. The list of endangered flora and fauna is long. Case in point: as many as twenty-four percent of the amphibians who call the wetlands home are designated as imperiled.

Fire.

Water.

It's equally lazy not to interrogate my own tinge of sadness about the destructive fire on Maui. What was I mourning? What was the banyan tree in the center of Lahaina to me other than the backdrop for the perfect Instagram photo? The Indigenous peoples of the Hawaiian Islands revere Lahaina as the past home of the Hawaiian royal family and a sacred burial place for their high-ranking ancestors. Like the Indigenous people in the Pacific Northwest, Indigenous Hawaiians carefully cultivated and shaped the vegetation in lowland communities like Lahaina until the early 1800s, relying on controlled flames to ready land for agriculture. In an interview with historian Rosalyn R. LaPier, chairwoman of the Office of Hawaiian Affairs Carmen Lindsey says that "the fires of today are in part due to the climate crisis, a history of colonialism in our islands, and the loss of our right to steward our *'aina* and *wai'* [land and water]."

This is it, right here, the secret heart I've been writing toward.

I'm here to say I finally understand the difference between the fires we set and the fires that catch us by surprise. Between the flames we control and the flames we don't. Between begging a lover for the crisp pain of an elk hide flogger on our skin and the blows that fall without our consent.

It is the difference between letting the world tell us who we are and telling the world ourselves, loud and clear.

And that difference is the closest thing I know to salvation.

MY CHILDHOOD KITCHEN

Sometimes, late at night when the wind over the sea keeps me awake, I relive the moment in my childhood kitchen decades ago. The moment where my dad warned me that "sex is never worth losing your faith and your family" while we ate a midnight snack in front of my mother's floral window valance.

And I feel it: that sinking fishing-float-turned-sugar-beet in my abdomen. Shame.

I am almost the age my dad was when he died. It's only in my most recent years that I know what I would say to him if I could queer time enough to place him alive, somehow, in front of the woman I am today. I'd pass him the salt, point to the sea stacks visible through the glass behind my head, and tell him that losing a religion is different from losing your faith. I'd tell him that though I feared my queerness would make me a woman without a family, it was actually the catalyst for our biggest growth.

Mostly, I would tell him the truest thing I know: my queerness is not about sex. It never has been. Psychologist Liz Powell, when interviewed for a *Cosmopolitan* article about queer identities, says, "Queerness is about being outside of the normative. . . . Queerness is about swimming upstream. It's about your presence in a culture that is heteronormative, that is cisnormative, that is mononormative."

My queerness is about the quiet interstitial moments that punctuate all the other moments of my life. It's about the floral valance in my mother's kitchen, the desire paths I have yet to discover in Ungulate Woods, about the way my breath catches when I watch Katie deftly cross a creek without getting her feet wet. It's the way I hold her to my chest when she's too sick to eat for days. The way she knows instinctually when I am having a hard day and flits about the house to make life a little bit easier for me.

It's about knowing that what makes sense to me might not make sense to the rest of the world. That even if I never touched that softest skin near Katie's right hip, I'd still dream about the small tufts of breath that trail from her mouth when she sleeps, still count the seconds until we could next traipse through Ungulate Woods together.

KILCHIS RIVER

(Named for Chief Kilches, last leader of the Tillamook tribe)

I was born during a flooding tide. Within two hours of my entrance into the world, the tide at Netarts Bay would have been over ten feet, the sand covered in a blanket of swelling water. Aristotle may have been right when he said that people can only be born during a flooding tide; it was the ocean that pushed me into the world, and I've ridden its tide my whole life. It pushed me out of Netarts Bay, over the wrack line and the seagrass-scattered foredunes, over the mountains of the Coast Range, through the Columbia River gorge and Wallowa-Whitman National Forest, and then deposited me into my parents' arms in a tiny hospital room in Boise, Idaho, in the middle of the Sagebrush Sea.

Wait for it: the tide gone slack, two young parents pausing to take in their daughter, a creature shocked by the reality of being in a body and its demands. They swaddle me in a pink cotton blanket and say my name, the weight of it rolling on their tongues. The tide ebbs and with it a slack tide so fleeting that to blink would be to miss it. I wish I'd heard what lapped like a whisper at the water's unpredictable edge: *There is nothing more pure than desire, nothing more sacred than wanting.*

I wonder if the tide knew it would pull me back, that I would find and finally love myself on the beaches of the north Oregon coast. That I would marry a woman during an August spring tide and watch as the flames from our wedding bonfire rose high above the relentless surf.

Katie had her own trajectory, a full forty years that did not include me. In keeping with Aristotle's theory about births and flooding tides, she was *also* born as the water rose. The Tide Lady had just loosened the line in Netarts Bay, and at the moment an obstetrician ushered Katie out of her mother's womb, the water was at just over two feet and climbing. It carried her over mountain peaks and through long stretches of desert, swaddled in its sacred watery arms, until it reached the waves of golden wheat blowing over the windy Palouse. I like to imagine us this way, as two people born from the same primordial muck in the same bay at different times. Two people connected by an invisible tide line that would pull them back, four decades later, and lower the glass cloche over the Castle to drink from the private magic that is falling in love.

☾

The flowers were the first to arrive at the Castle two days before our wedding, their vibrant petals packed into nondescript boxes and left on our porch. White and orange roses, hydrangeas in both green and blue. Baby's breath, too, plus snap dragons and on-the-nose sea lavender. We left them soaking by their trimmed stems in buckets of sugar water stationed around the living room.

Our people arrived second. My bride and I had already lived without each other for a combined eighty years, which meant we distilled eight decades of loved ones into a fifty-person guest list. The result was a cross section of almost every phase of our respective lives. Katie's best college friend, Michael, pulled up laughing and bushy-tailed, despite a cross-country flight and two-hour drive from the airport. While I held small bridesmaid's bouquets together, Michael covered their stems, first with green floral tape and then with jute, regaling us with stories about a young Katie.

Katie.

She was the real floral artist, creating three gorgeous, full bouquets for each skimpy, floppy one we produced. It was Katie who first saw Jen, my old roommate from BYU who parked her Volvo next to Michael's in the driveway and walked up the stairs to the deck off the kitchen. I opened the sliding glass door and wrapped my arms around her neck. The first thing she said to me: "Remember when we drove to Salt Lake City to see Melissa Etheridge and made jokes about keeping away from each other all night because we *were not lesbians*?" I laughed, mainly because Jen had left her marriage and come out as gay about eight years before me. Her arrival rustled the fabric of spacetime, brushed the soft folds of it against my skin. It brought two closeted eighteen-year-olds face-to-face with the middle-aged dykes they had become.

Jen sat next to Michael and held court the way she always does with stories from her life. I chose a spot on the hard floor next to Katie, cutting the stems of hearty roses for boutonnières while we talked through the schedule of the next two days. The next morning, my dear friend Alyssa was set to arrive from Gig Harbor, and both our families would be in town by noon. Xing, who had been ordained online as a High Priestess to officiate, would arrive just before with the rest of the guests at a hydrangea-farm-turned-rustic-venue on the banks of Kilchis River in Tillamook.

Katie handed me a corsage of white snapdragons, their glossy leaves tall behind popcorn blooms, when my phone chimed. It was a text from Dani, letting me know she was sorry, but she wouldn't be coming after all, because she was married to a bishop who didn't approve and they'd been fighting about it. She'd decided to skip the gay wedding and keep the peace at home.

☾

The Mormons got one thing right: a wedding is holy.

But I am not going to tell you about the rustic arch our children decorated with flowers, or the party outside the barn afterwards surrounded by fields of pumpkins and long rows of still-blooming hydrangeas. I won't tell you that the sound system went out, so our first dance was to the soft notes of Elias' cheap portable Bluetooth speaker, perched in the barn window.

The only thing I will say is that I've never felt more pure than I did the day I put on a strapless gown, white as bleached bone, to marry Katie, who stood before me in a custom suit and blue suede shoes and promised to be my companion.

After all, what is purity if not another way to say ecstasy?

What is worthiness if not another way to say delight?

☾

When someone who has never been in a cult asks me why I took so long to leave, I tell them the story of Nephi from Mormon scripture, how he sliced Laban's head clean off out of duty to God. I tell them that when my mother first went to the temple, and her mother before her, she had to agree to "blood atonement" through a pantomime of the slitting of her own throat, her fate should she ever reveal what happens behind all those marble walls.

There won't be a single day in my remaining years when I am not in awe of the things I've manifested for myself. Because for all the trauma I've inherited from my ancestors, I have also inherited tremendous resilience. This is what it means to come from pioneer stock. When they were promised a better life in the west, in the temples of the Mormons, they left everything behind and went in search of it. And here I am, now, today, tapping into that same resilience as a strength that keeps me doing the hard work of deconstruction and healing, even when it feels like my oxen are stuck in whatever raging river I am crossing, and I dream of turning around.

Isn't it the ultimate irony?

I can do hard things because *they* did hard things.

In *Dream of the Red Chamber*, the most well-known of the Chinese classical novels, Cao Xueqin talks about recovery from illness as like unraveling a silk cocoon, one silken thread at a time. I feel that way about my recovery from high-control religion. I don't know how many silken threads there are, or how long I'll have to pull them. It is my life's work. I may have left the community, but I still want to be loved by them. All of them. They were my people and writing this feels like a betrayal almost every day. In my most secret heart, I still fear the vestigial shame of my forebears will swallow me whole.

The shame of my forebears: it had arrived in a sidecar with Dani's text the day before the wedding, riding along with all the ancestors I was letting down and the entirety of the Mormon church. After I read it, I retreated into the bedroom at the Castle and cried like the wounded teenage lesbian I still was inside. And later, after some months had passed, I opened my secret heart and trusted Dani with its contents for the first time in our thirty-year friendship. I told her about the shame I felt growing up gay in the faith that raised us. I told her about how painful it was to leave the community behind. I told her that when she capitulated to her husband's discomfort, it was the final layer in a stratigraphic column of rejection and shame.

Dani answered with an apology so real and unexpected, it might as well have come over the hills in a covered wagon from Missouri to Utah, then been handed down by generations of Mormon women to land here, from Dani's hands into my own: *I mostly want to tell you I am so sorry. I am sorry about all the thousands of cuts that I was a part of. I am so sorry for the pain I thrust on you right before your most special day. I am so sorry for the cuts you've received from my church. And though the cuts haven't killed you, they've come close, and that's awful.*

I read her letter in the Castle bedroom, the same place I'd cried upon receiving her text before the wedding. It was so powerful it made me challenge what

I knew of Dani, made me proud to call her my oldest friend. If shame is about the fear of disconnection, as Brené Brown asserts, then not talking about my pain all these years with Dani and other members of the church I loved only increased my shame.

The only way to excise shame, it turned out, was to name it.

☾

Shame can be draped over places like invisible clothing, and those places wear shame in much the same way people do (head bent, eyes averted). The difference is the shame worn by a landscape doesn't *belong* to the place. Places wear the disgrace of the people who have been there before, and the evil of the things they did there. Naming, as it turns out, was a way for me to deal with and expel shame not just from myself, but from the places I loved. The nameless are hard to speak about, and I have learned that the harder it is to speak things out loud, the more apt shame will be to find purchase and hold tight.

Place naming, especially, can drive out shame because when we know the name of a place, we have a context for our experiences. And that context makes it easier to talk about the things that happened there. Shame thrives in silent landscapes, the dark corners and unnamed riverbanks. I've spent decades teaching the art of narrative, and I always stress Janet Burroway's assertion that "nothing happens nowhere" to my students. Place is crucial for good storytelling, and storytelling itself is a vital anecdote to shame.

This is the only kind of naming I am interested in. I am not interested in naming as erasure and ownership, the way men give women their last name after marriage, the way crucial parts of the female genitalia are named after the male physicians who first "discovered" them, the way landmarks originally named by Indigenous tribes were rebranded to reflect the names and wishes of colonists. When I name something to wrestle the shame from it, it's an unofficial name, my own way of classifying the world, never meant to replace the names given by those who have gone before.

Places witness our shame. The stacks of Three Arch Rocks had watched me sob when Dani told me she wasn't coming to the wedding, and they were witness, again, to my tears when I read her letter. One of the biggest lessons I've learned living on the north coast is that all human relationships should mirror the tide, the way it ebbs and flows, how drastically circumstances can change right before our eyes. So it is, too, with the relationships humans have with places. There are so many ways to leave a landscape in shame—extracting all the fossil fuels, watching as wildfires tease annihilation, or any of the numberless things we do each day that will have raised the temperature at my beloved north Oregon coast by six degrees in the next thirty years.

☾

A secret: I married Katie three months before our wedding, standing on Future Wife Point in Ungulate Woods, just the two of us, our dogs, and the elk that must have watched through the alders, wishing they could munch the trees in peace. We walked up to the point on parallel desire paths carved into the mountain by the hard keratin of hooves. Under our hiking boots, the forest floor had erupted in soft pink sprigs of glowing pink blossoms, as if the woods had rolled out a carpet strung with white blinking just for us. Every spring thereafter, when those blooms reappear, we would be reminded of the vows we took over the water. She promised to be a safe landing place when I fell, to celebrate my successes when I triumphed. I promised to challenge her, to encourage her to change instead of fearing that she might.

The ocean brought the drama as it lapped at Cape Meares beach below: earlier that morning, a low tide at -2.6 feet had swung back to over seven feet at its height, where it stood covering the beach while we said our vows.

Three months later, we'd hike through Ungulate Woods with our beloveds the morning after we made public vows on the banks of the Kilchis River. Siblings, college friends, parents: we'd march them all up to the edge of Future Wife Point, but keep our earlier clandestine wedding there folded up and tucked in our secret hearts. My eyes would meet Katie's, icy as the bluest sea glass, and an understanding would kindle between us, as subtle as a shifting tide, that salvation was as simple as knowing which flames to fan.

But first: the dogs, the elk, me, and Katie.

My Katie.

I got to know this place in much the same way that I got acquainted with her body. The curvature of the earth as seen from Future Wife Point will always conjure the frank arc of her back the night of our secret wedding, the way I yielded under her palms as if it was the only rapture worth naming.

Desire become invocation. As if wanting was a prayer we spoke in the dark.

EPILOGUE: THREE ARCH ROCKS (REPRISE)

Our third February together, Katie and I followed the dogs as they meandered down the beach at sunset, parallel to the foamy stretch of waves that lapped at our feet and paws. Every few minutes, Cora leapt in the air and twisted her wooly body in anticipation of Katie lifting the Chuck-it above her head to send a tennis ball sailing over the sand.

"Do you see that?" Katie laughed. She pointed to Marco where he sat on the shore, quietly judging the other dogs on the beach.

"What a ridiculous creature," I said. Cora leapt and twisted again, but this time she was backlit by the setting sun.

"No, *that* is a ridiculous creature." We urged the dogs to come closer in the fading light. In front of us, a stretch of boulders the length of a football field had emerged from the sand thanks to the weekend's exuberant king tides. On the other side of the boulders was the sea for miles, and then Three Arch Rocks and our always stalwart guideposts.

Katie took my hand. "What are you thinking about, baby?" she asked. She wore the same hat she had on our first date, low on her head to cover the tops of her ears.

I cleared my throat, but I didn't take my eyes off the arched rocks. "I was thinking that the only thing that devastates me about death anymore is that I won't be around to see how these sea stacks have changed in two hundred years." The fear of death that had plagued my whole life had simply vanished in the years since I fell in love with Katie and tucked myself into our nook above the Pacific. It wasn't even a whisper of a distant memory. I had been afraid to die, and then I was less afraid to die, and then I wasn't afraid at all.

Katie pulled her hat lower over her ears, a gesture that always caught at my heart. Streaks of pink pushed at the edges of the horizon. "Maybe you will,"

Katie conjectured. "Maybe we will find each other again in two hundred years, right here, and we'll see them together." All I could hear was the true fact that someday, we were going to lose each other to death. And an even truer fact, given our middle-age, was that it would happen sooner than it would have if we'd found each other at twenty or even thirty.

I watched Katie throw the ball for Cora and admired her muscled arms and athletic frame. A kind of sadness rose from the boulders hidden under the beach, through the thin layer of sand under our boots, and into my bloodstream. With it came the pure knowledge that someday, the world would pull us apart. It was, in fact, that one thing I knew about our future for certain.

"Ocelot," Katie called, using her name for me. "You look sad."

I was sad because I thought of the continued refrain from my childhood. The one that said if I didn't *do* or *think* or *watch* or *want* anything sinful, then when I got married in the temple, it would be an *eternal marriage*. Standing on that beach with Katie, I understood for the first time why, when the missionaries knocked on a person's door, the promise of never losing the person you love would tempt even the most rational of people into the baptismal font. I was sad because of what I'd lost, despite never realizing while I was Mormon that I wanted it: the promise of eternal companionship.

We stood on our deck later that night with a blanket around our shoulders and listened to the waves clap against the sea stacks below. Katie and I were in love, but the period of the glass cloche had reached its end. We were entering the broader universe now. If the three rocks we loved so much didn't get to hang out together into eternity, why should we? The only sensible thing to do was grab on with both hands and thank the universe for the chance to sit side-by-side in this current moment together.

Two hundred years is roughly the same arc of time that stretches backward between us and when Joseph Smith founded the Mormon church in upstate New York. I can only guess that maybe two hundred years from now, our three arched sea stacks will have begun their erosive decline from the inside out. What started as a sea cave in each rock became an arch, and someday the arches will erode through the rock and divide it into two smaller sea stacks each, until the waters off Maxwell Point are scattered with craggy stacks instead of just the three we know and love. And the ground where the Castle now stands will house two other people who love each other or don't, who found each other or didn't, or no people at all. Maybe it will have returned to the local herd of Roosevelt elk that I hope still roams our forests.

I couldn't tell you. I won't be here to see it.

Or maybe Katie is right, and we'll be living other lives after this one but still find our way to each other on this sacred stretch of the north Oregon coast. I'll recognize the timber remnants of Ungulate Woods as readily as I'll recognize the craggy remains of the Three Arch Rocks offshore. But mostly, I'll recognize the glint in a supposed stranger's eyes as the two-hundred-year-old echo of devotion that started in a castle that was not a castle, with a woman who would become my wife, on a cliff above the still-roiling Pacific.

Maybe what I gained when I lost my faith was the ability to hold two truths, bright and prickly as sea stars, in my tired palms at once. In my left hand, the stark knowledge that I can only trust what I see with my own eyes. And in my right, the certainty that what I can see with my own eyes is only a sliver of the true universe. Each starfish is leathery to the touch, slimy and heavy in my palms. The tiny ocelli under each one's five limbs tickle the arc around the base of my thumb, the line a palmist would trace to divine the length of my life.

Maybe, when we meet again in two hundred years, the person who used to be Katie will chide the person who used to be me for removing a keystone species like starfish from the water. Maybe, she'll hold my palm up to her face (will her eyes still be blue?) and nod her head slowly as she says, "I can see all the people you were and all the people you will become."

And the surprise will be that I see them, too. A long stretch of all the people I have been and could be, not a single one of them just another Eve in a long line of Eves.

I want to hug them all. Every single worthy one of them.

ACKNOWLEDGMENTS

One acknowledgment matters above all others: the beaches and forests that I explore in this book were for untold generations the home of Salish-speaking Nestucca and Tillamook Bay bands of the Tillamook tribe. Oregon's north coast, including the land where I wrote this book, is their home first and foremost.

I owe my reverence for nature to my mother, Nancy Judd Minor, the memory of my father, Warden Morris Minor, and my stepfather, Jerry Kuykendall. It was through their love of birds, Western landscapes, and wildlife that I learned the importance of stillness and awe. Just last month, my mom taught me to look at beak size when determining if the red-tipped bird on the tree outside my window was a hairy or downy woodpecker.

When this book found a home with Oregon State University Press, it felt like striking gold. Thank you to Kim Hogeland for first seeing the potential in this unconventional manuscript, to Micki Reaman for her seamless editorial hand, to Erin Kirk for turning my wife's painting into a beautiful cover, and to Katherine White for her role in marketing.

So many people were willing to read early drafts of the book either in its entirety or as individual chapters, and I want to thank them all: Jamie Cattanach, Erin Ergenbright, Nancy Minor, Xing Fu, Katie Stem, Chloe Friedgen-Minor, Sophie Moshofsky, and Justin Rigamonti. Thank you to Christine McKinley and Lara Messersmith-Glavin for providing publishing resources and advice. And to Blake Hausman for his willingness to engage in conversations about where stories live and who has the right to tell them.

I have immense gratitude for those who walked alongside me for all or part of this story. For my brothers, J. Minor and Quinn Minor, who no doubt have their own versions of most of these stories. For my beautiful and resilient children, Chloe, Elias, and Clementine. For their father and my former husband, referred to in these pages as Matt. For my in-laws, Don and Deta Stem, who showed up with encouragement and unwavering support. And for the friendships that have gotten me through: Alyssa Paquette, Jen Mosinski, Jessica Lee, Julie Bolt, Erin Ergenbright, Calin Anderson, Emily Harrington, Becca Pinon, Janell Cinquini, Elaina Rafn. For the dogs, who don't let us miss a day in the forest. And for Katie Stem and the sexy domesticity we share here at the edge of the continent; she is my first reader and the one whose opinion matters the most.

I am forever indebted to therapist Michelle Adkins-Hepler. I don't know if I would have lived to write this book without her constant but subtle pushing and support. And on the other side of it, therapist Stacey Johnson has been instrumental in helping me sort through the levels of my trauma, process how they made me who I am, and push myself to do better.

But none of this would have been possible without the previous version of myself, the Mormon wife who knew her outsides didn't match her insides. The woman who took a leap into the pitch black, hoping someone would catch her on the other side.

And someone did catch her in that darkness: me. I held that past version of myself and thanked her for being so damn brave, for getting us to this moment. I pointed her in the direction of the sea, and she went.

I owe her everything.